The Great Tompall

"Tompall was significant, not just important, to country music." *Kinky Friedman*, musician, author and politician

"What I remember most about Tompall is the fact that he was 'independent from others'—such as from record companies like RCA." *Cowboy Jack Clement*, record producer and songwriter

"I feel that Tompall is one of the most brilliant characters I have ever met. I've never known anyone like him… Tompall was a one of a kind, unique individual, whose place in music is not recognized the way it ought to be." *Willis David Hoover*, singer, songwriter, reporter and author

"The truth is, Tompall was a remarkably good singer. He had a really cool voice and could do a lot of things with it." *Kyle Lehning*, sound engineer and former president of Asylum Records

""Tompall's greatest contribution to country music, in other words, 'why did he matter,' was the fact that he was a trailblazer. He kicked doors down for others. It should never be overlooked how important Tompall was." *Marty Stuart*, singer, songwriter and performer

"Tompall taught me about country music…I learned so much when I was with Tompall—it was just like going to college for a year and learning about a subject. I feel I would not have been successful in Nashville without first understanding the roots, the soul, of Nashville country music. And that is what Tompall taught me." *Jimmy Bowen*, former president of Elektra Records

"When Tompall was onstage, there was no one better." *Hazel Smith*, publicist, writer and columnist

"If things would have *twisted a bit differently,* Tompall would have been a *huge phenomenon."* *Del Bryant*, BMI President & CEO

"I believe that Tompall Glaser & The Glaser Brothers were the original outlaws in country music. I believe that they inspired Waylon Jennings, Willie Nelson, Kris Kristofferson, and others who made great contributions to the outlaw country movement." *Mike Curb*, songwriter, producer and president/CEO of Curb Records

The Great Tompall:

Forgotten Country Music Outlaw

The Great Tompall:

Forgotten Country Music Outlaw

The Authorized Biography of Tompall Glaser

Kevin L. Glaser

RIGHT SIDE CREATIONS, LLC   OCONOMOWOC, WISCONSIN

Library of Congress Control Number: 2014914931

Disclaimer and Terms of Use Agreement

This book comprises many people's memories, opinions, and personal experiences. As such, time can change how a person recalls events, and no two people will remember or experience them exactly the same. With this in mind, know that great effort was made to research, interview individuals, and to otherwise prepare this book. The author has, to the best of his ability, accurately represented statements that were made to him by each individual who was interviewed, or who has otherwise contributed to this book. Therefore, the content of this book reflects the views and opinions of individuals interviewed and does not reflect the views or opinions of the author. As a result, the author makes no representations or warranties with respect to the accuracy or completeness of the contents of this book.

The information contained in this book is strictly for entertainment and educational purposes. It is sold with the understanding that the author shall not be liable for damages arising from errors

Contents

Appendix

Acknowledgements

This book is the result of contributions from a great many people. Each person noted below gave their precious time to me to share information and their memories about Tompall Glaser and without them this book would not have been possible. Please know that your kindness is appreciated more than you can know. Thank you!

John Glaser
Peggy Motley
Bob Kirsch
Kinky Friedman
Cowboy Joe Babcock
Jimmy Payne
Frances Williams Preston
Clint Miller
Del Bryant
Ken Hatley
Cowboy Jack Clement
Hazel Smith
Stan Laundon
Jimmy Bowen
Bill Littleton
Dave Hickey
Willis David Hoover
Danny Finley (Panama Red)

Mike Curb
Mickey Jones
Peter Thall
Claude Hill
Bill Holmes
Billy Swan
Chuck Feller
Marty Stuart
Mac Wiseman
Jimmy Buffett
Jimmie Rodgers Snow
Marshall Chapman
Kyle Lehning
Gary Vincent
Joe Osborn
Richard H. Frank, Jr.
Red Young
Vicki Mead

Special Thanks: I am especially indebted to three individuals who helped make this book possible in its current form.

First, thanks to Tompall's sister, Eleanor Ryan, for sharing photos of Tompall and his army letters home with me. Without her thoughtfulness, inclusion of these important and insightful letters would not have been possible.

Second, many thanks to Jane Poole for sharing her precious memories and her road diary of Tompall's last major tour of England. In addition, Jane provided moral support from start to finish. Eleanor and Jane's contributions have allowed this book to more fully reflect both challenges and achievements in Tompall's life.

Last, I am grateful to Florence Rosner who spent countless hours proofreading and providing final edit suggestions for my book manuscript. Florence is a truly wonderful person who gave her all to make this book grammatically correct and with whom I've developed a lifelong friendship.

Foreword

The thing that lifted country music out of its perpetual honky-tonk sentimentality was a history-making concept album released in January of 1976. The cover displayed a bullet-riddled wanted poster featuring three rough-hewn desperados and one luscious gun moll. It became the first country album ever to sell more than a million copies. It was titled *Wanted! The Outlaws*, but over time it was referred to as "… that outlaw album with Waylon Jennings, Jessi Colter, Willie Nelson, and what the hell's that other guy's name?"

This book is about that other guy, the forgotten outlaw: The Great Tompall Glaser. He could be loud, obnoxious, overbearing, self-indulgent, argumentative, downright offensive and physically aggressive—all of which aptly describe any self-respecting outlaw. Tompall was also a musically-gifted singer and master songwriter who had a sensitive, playful side that could be charming, brilliant, funny, spontaneous, and wildly creative. He was a roaring, Jack Daniels-swilling nocturnal nomad, with an ever-changing band of merry men that might include Bobby Bare one night and Waylon Jennings or Kinky Friedman the next.

The one constant in this roving menagerie of neon-electric campfire misfits was its focal point: Tompall. Like Jesse James a hundred years before him, Tompall was the undisputed leader of the gang.

Then came *Wanted! The Outlaws*—with the glory, crescendo, cheering crowds, hyperbole, and the inevitable decline and fall of the country outlaw phenomenon. Many members of Tompall's gang went on to become anointed, iconic figures. Waylon and Willie were inducted into the *Country Music Hall of Fame*, along with other musicians like Kris Kristofferson, Merle Haggard, and Johnny Cash who all fit the "country outlaw" brand.

And that other guy? The desperado whose name was hard

to recall? The hombre some of us consider the original country music rogue? The unwanted outlaw? His bright star simply faded.

The author of this book, Kevin Glaser—Tompall's nephew—now sheds light on the whys and wherefores of Tompall's life with some help from friends, family, acquaintances, onlookers, and the enigma himself—the outlaw known as The Great Tompall.

Willis David Hoover

Author's Note

Let me state this right off: Thomas Paul (Tompall) Glaser is my uncle. I am the son of Tompall's older brother, John Glaser. This biography, while it is intended as a tribute and celebration of the life of a man who happens to be related to me, is more importantly a commemoration of the many accomplishments of a professional musician and music businessman.

Few now remember Tompall Glaser, the original "Country Music Outlaw," and even fewer are aware of what he has accomplished. His work in Nashville spanned more than three decades, and his friends and working partners included many great and recognizable country music legends.

What a shame that someone so influential in the country music culture of the 1960s, 70s, and 80s has been all but forgotten. This book tells Tompall's important story and shares why country music would not be where it is today without him.

Much of this book contains information and memories from people who knew Tompall personally and/or had the opportunity to work with him during his career. I have also extensively interviewed Tompall himself. I invite you now to take a historical journey with me to learn about the life of Tompall Glaser, the one man who—perhaps more than any other—defines the oft-used moniker "Country Music Outlaw."

Personal Note: This book is about Tompall Glaser, not Chuck Glaser and not Jim Glaser. These three brothers made up the Tompall & the Glaser Brothers trio, and each has his own unique and important story to share. I leave it up to them to do just that. I want to make it absolutely clear that in no way does my focus on Tompall in this book diminish the many great accomplishments of Chuck and Jim during their lifelong music careers.

Introduction

Tompall Glaser passed from this earth on Monday, August 12, 2013, at 11:46 p.m. He was less than one month shy of his 80th birthday.

From the very start of writing this book my intent was always to get it published and printed while Tompall was still alive so that he could further enjoy people's respect and admiration in the waning years of his life. Alas, it was not meant to be. After a lengthy struggle with health issues, Tompall finally succumbed and has now joined country music legends that have gone before him. This book shows the great void left with his passing and is a tribute to his important and colorful life achievements.

Please note that while this book was not available prior to Tompall's demise, it was completed before he died. Therefore, some of the syntax used refers to present tense rather than past tense.

* * *

Who is Tompall Glaser and why is he important in the annals of country music? Tompall Glaser belongs to a very small group of individuals who shook up the country music industry during the 1970s and 1980s. Together with Waylon Jennings, Willie Nelson, Billy Joe Shaver, Kris Kristofferson, Hank Williams, Jr., Bobby Bare, and a handful of others—Tompall Glaser put the country music establishment on notice that the *status quo* was no longer acceptable.

There are many opinions about what encompasses a country music "outlaw" and a number of different definitions of the term. From my perspective, an outlaw is simply this: a person who is unwilling to do what he is told simply because "that's the way it's always been done in the past." Apply this definition to the 1970s Nashville music industry and you will find that, up until this time, the record companies were clearly in charge, and performing artists had little say in the record production process. Record companies were after a formulaic sound that resulted in many records sounding very similar to one another. This was based on the premise that what worked in the past (i.e., a hit country record) should also work in the future. The Nashville sound of this time was heavily influenced by session (professional studio) musicians. Since session musicians did not travel with the bands for live concerts, it was difficult for performers to reproduce the sound heard on their records during their live concerts.

Tompall helped change this. At his Glaser Sound Studios he encouraged Waylon Jennings, John Hartford, and others to experiment with their sound and to stand up to the Nashville recording industry. He helped pave the way for artistic freedom for singers and songwriters. He "kicked the doors down" (Tompall's words) for others and he paid the price—never becoming a household name as several of his compatriots did.

The Great Tompall

Forgotten Country Music Outlaw

The Authorized Biography of Tompall Glaser

Kevin L. Glaser

1

It's in the Genes

"I want to walk down the street someday and see young people coming here, writing good songs, proud to be here again. When I first came here, a lot of people were proud to be here. It was a good feeling. It gave you pride. You didn't give a shit whether the rest of the world liked you or not. And we were the underdogs of the music business. Our music was the least respected of popular music, but we had our pride among ourselves. It was like a family suddenly going sour, and I want to have that same pride again. The public can sense—an individual can sense—when something is real and when it isn't. The people know.

"When we started, people thought we were going to destroy Nashville. Who wants to destroy Nashville? It's a long way from my mind. But if a guy can't offer a good, decent alternative, he should shut the fuck up. But if he's got a good, decent alternative, all he's got to do is keep *doing it, and pretty soon the whole fucking industry will be doing it because there are too few people in this town who know what the fuck to do. Because they don't love it; they're doing it for the fucking salary."[1]*

Tompall Glaser, 1976

Tompall Glaser changed the world. To get your head around this statement, you must first understand the one crucial question that applies in *all* situations. That question is "Why does *(fill in the blank)* matter?"

There are certain institutions or people who impact our lives to such a great degree that we cannot imagine life without them. For example, think of fast food franchises. Perhaps we can live without Hardees, but what about McDonalds? Is it significant that JC Penney exists or is it more important that Walmart continues to be in business? What about people? If actor Paul Reubens had never acted would we give pause? But what about Robert De Niro?

To me, if something ceases to exist or if someone no longer participates in their chosen profession—singer, actor, business owner, or whatever—the question that one must answer is, "Do I care?" In other words, "Why does *(fill in the blank)* matter?" If we truly give a damn, the follow-up question then is, "Why so?"

Country music has not been the same since 1958, when Tompall Glaser moved to Nashville, Tennessee. He established a music empire that included writing country song standards, recognizing and publishing hit songs that others wrote, encouraging artists to record at his independent studio so their music sounded how *they* thought was best, producing notable albums for many artists, developing a unique harmony arrangement for live performances, and appearing in the *Billboard* Top 100 charts several times during his music career. During my conversation with Kinky Friedman, a noted singer, songwriter, novelist, and Texas politician, he succinctly told me, "Tompall was significant, not just important, to country music. The president

---

[1] *Michael Bane, The Outlaws: Revolution in Country Music (Country Music Magazine Press; 1st edition, 1978), 52.*

is important, as are senators, mayors and other politicians. However, they are not significant, in my opinion. Tompall has had a profound impact and influence on the world around him. Sometimes this was overt, and sometimes not."

Tompall's influence on country music resulted in a seismic chasm in the way things were done in Nashville. New artists could finally record and established artists could finally achieve the sound they desired. The rigidness of the music industry vanished with Tompall's involvement and recording artists could work at their own pace—experimenting until their sound was *perfect* to them.

Tompall brought a unique perspective to Nashville. Part of his outlook developed as he grew up on his Nebraska family farm. Therefore, it's important to start the story of Tompall's life with his heritage and with the nature and nurture that impacted him during his early childhood.

* * *

Glaser is a German surname that is loosely translated as "glassmaker." We are not many generations removed from our Austrian ancestors, yet we are the epitome of the hordes of immigrants who came to the United States to find a better life. Glasers have contributed to our American nation as farmers, scientists, financiers, and in nearly any other occupation imaginable. Of note, the mineral $K_3Na(SO_4)_2$, which is known as Glaserite, was developed by ancestor Christopher Glaser. A great number of Glaser men have fought for America as part of her armed services, and we are proud to call America our home.

Charles and Anna Glaser, Tompall's grandparents, came to the United States from Austria in the late 1800s with other members of the Glaser family. Like so many others during this period, they sought a better life for themselves and their children in America. Some of the Glaser families settled in Oklahoma and others settled in Nebraska. Charles and Anna eventually ended up in the western sand hills of Spalding, Nebraska. The majority of people living in this area make their living by farming—mainly growing corn, and by raising farm animals, mostly feed cattle.

Charles and Anna had nine children: John (Johnny), Cecilia, Joseph (Josie), Carl, Mary, Martin, Madeline, Louis (Louie), and Rochelle (Ricky).

Louis (Louie) Nicholas Glaser (b. 12-6-1901) was the fifth son of Charles and Anna, and he was Tompall's father. He was slight in stature, standing about five feet eight inches in height, and had a slim build, weighing in at around 150 pounds. His brothers, Johnny, Josie, Martin and Carl, each stood nearly six feet tall, but to a person, they knew better than to irritate Louie. Louie decided early in his life not to take crap from anyone. He was *intense* and had a temper like no other. His eyes were a deep, dark brown and he was a man of few words. Of course, all he had to do was look at you to communicate. You always knew you were doing something wrong when he gave you the glare, and you would immediately change your current course of action to the appropriate action he had in mind.

I spent the summers of my 8th, 9th and 10th grades working on Grandpa Louie's farm, mainly cutting noxious weeds, such as musk thistles. During these early teen years, I learned about farm life firsthand, and I was taught how to drive and how to hunt. Grandpa let me drive his 1955 Chevy Cameo ½ ton Series 3100 pickup on country roads and on rural highways. It was an all-white pickup with a 3-speed manual transmission located on the steering column and a starter pedal located on the floorboard. I was fourteen-years-old and unsure of myself, so it took me a long time to get the hang of driving. I killed the engine while letting out the clutch. I ground the manual transmission gears. And I just couldn't keep that pickup on the right side of the centerline of those rural roads and highways. Needless to say, Louie found my slow learning excruciatingly painful.

When Louie Glaser got upset he let loose with a string of expletives, though quite mild compared with today's cussing. His typical recitation was, "well…gol-dam, son-of-a-bitchin' bastard," which would be repeated two, three, or four times. Each time his voice would increase slightly in pitch with further emphasis on each word. Without a doubt, I raised Grandpa's ire several times when I was behind the wheel of that pickup—and on many, many other occasions. Keep in mind that at this point in his life Louie had *mellowed considerably*. Although it is not something Tompall will speak of, one can only imagine how it must have been for Tompall growing up as Louie's son.

As long as I live, I will never forget my first hunting experience. After a full day of weed-cutting one summer evening, Louie and I drove into a field so I could rid the farm of one or more of the bounty of rabbits that had become nuisances. Up to that time, I had merely shot at various targets around the farm trying to become a good enough shot to earn a hunting trip.

Louie handed me his beautiful, shiny Marlin .22 caliber semi-automatic rifle. We loaded it to capacity with long rifle shells, and Grandpa told me to choose a rabbit to shoot. I spotted a good-sized rabbit next to a haystack about 50 feet away, aimed, and shot.

It was a "gut" shot that stopped the rabbit, but it was not a clean "kill" shot. Rather, the rabbit thrashed about next to the haystack, writhing in pain as its life ebbed. I watched the animal, not knowing what to do next. Grandpa was unfazed. He told me to pick up a nearby stick and then bash the bunny's skull to put it out of its misery. I was an impressionable 14-year-old boy at that time, and I had much difficulty easing my queasy stomach enough to crack that rabbit's skull; nevertheless, I eventually found the courage to do as I had been told. My first strike did nothing but cause the rabbit to increase the velocity of its thrashing about. My second and third clubbing did not do much better. Grandpa grabbed the stick from me and with one hellacious swing, killed the rabbit where it lay.

This is who Louie Glaser was: he was frugal, not wanting to waste the few cents an extra bullet would have cost, and he was unimpaired by needless emotions. He was truly the epitome of a "man's man" and unlike anyone else I have ever met. Of course, his demeanor did not mean that he was a bad man—it's just who he was. Like anyone, he was a product of how he was raised and the times in which he lived. Louie was also known for giving the absolute tightest hugs of anyone I have ever met. While he was a man of many different facets, one thing is certain: you always knew where you stood with Louie Glaser.

Louis found a love of music at an early age. He was a self-taught musician and began playing both guitar and fiddle in his family's farm home. But mostly, he played guitar. Louie and his older brother Martin found a niche playing dances in Spalding and in surrounding towns. They performed frequently and became rather well-known in their community during these days. Eventually, Martin and Louie had a falling out over their music. No one knows for certain what caused this rift, but one story that has been handed down is that Martin wanted to travel farther distances to play music, and Louie had no interest in doing so. Louie wanted to spend more time working on his farm rather than "wasting" time on the road.

Louis Glaser married Alice Marie Davis (b 1-1-1902) on April 14, 1925. Alice, known to most as Marie, had relatives who came to Spalding from the South. In fact, it has been said that one of her relatives included Jefferson Davis, the president of the Confederate States during the Civil War. Tompall has often said that he feels he would have enjoyed much more success in Nashville if he had used the surname Davis rather than keeping the name Glaser. Throughout his career people thought he was Jewish, and he felt that Jews were not readily accepted in Nashville's southern culture back when he began making music.

After they were married, Louis and Marie bought the "home place" from Louie's dad, Charles Glaser. The property included a house, approximately 1,200 acres of farmland and pastureland, and some outbuildings. The house was Louis and Marie's pride and joy. It was a beautiful two-story frame home that contained intricate woodwork and sturdy lathe and plaster walls. It had character. Louis and Marie would raise their children in this home.

The home place began its life as part of a now long-forgotten early Nebraska settlement, named Moranville, and the home that sheltered Louis and Marie had served as the town's hotel.

Moranville had included not only the hotel but a one-room schoolhouse and a wheat mill. The nucleus of the town was the wheat mill, and teamsters (wagon drivers) would come from miles around to deliver wheat. The hotel was located a short distance from the wheat mill, and legend has it that visiting teamsters would seek companionship at the hotel from local girls. At times, Charles and Anna would offer visitors a place to stay at their large home, and Anna was known to keep the visitors in line with her thick German accent and a broom that always seemed to be attached to her right hand.

Louis and Marie loved the land that they bought. They set about making it their own by planting fruit trees and sculpting the fields to prevent the chronic erosion problems their land was subject to due to adverse weather. Chickens, pigs, cattle and horses could be found on the farm, and these provided both sustenance and cash for the family.

The union of Louis and Marie produced six children and included a couple of miscarriages, as well. Tompall was born in September of 1933, and he was a middle child. His siblings were Robert "Bob" Glaser (b. 1926), Eleanor Glaser Ryan (b. 1928), John "Jack" Glaser (b. 1929), Charles "Chuck" Glaser (b. 1936), and James "Jim" Glaser (b. 1937).

Having wed in the spring of 1925, life was good for Louis and Marie in those early years after their marriage. They had three children in the first four years of their marriage, but not long after John was born this family's life would change forever.

NEBRASKA

2

The Early Years

By most historical accounts, *The Great Depression* began in 1929. However, its devastation did not immediately strike across the nation in full force. Rather, it hit rural Nebraska in the early 1930s. During this time banks closed and depositors lost everything. According to Eleanor (Glaser) Ryan, one of these bank depositor statistics was her father, Louis Glaser. He lost his entire life's savings and this left an indelible mark on Louis. Not surprisingly, it took many years before he would once again deposit money in any bank.

Thomas Paul Glaser was born on September 3, 1933 at home on the farm like most of the children in rural Nebraska during this time. Tom acted no differently than most other babies during his first year of life, with two interesting exceptions. He began *humming* when he was nine months old, and as he lay on his back in the crib he would move his foot to keep time with music at this same age.

Tompall said, "My mother reminded me several times during my life that I showed musical ability very young, and that I would often hum and keep time with songs, starting at nine months." Louis tested Tompall several times, always with the same outcome—when he played music Tompall would move his foot to the beat, keeping time with each song. Sister, Eleanor Ryan, confirmed this, saying that she clearly remembered Tom's extraordinary abilities.

During Tom's early childhood, he had his share of health issues. He contracted both whooping cough and later, the measles. These two diseases nearly killed him. Health issues plagued him later in life, as well, including a terrible bout with the mumps, which had a devastating effect on his health and ultimately rendered him sterile.

When Tom was four-years-old, he picked up a guitar and showed an interest in playing. So, his father began teaching him some basic guitar chords and bought him his first guitar when he turned six.

Louis recognized Tom's budding talent and spoke with the radio station manager at WJAG radio in Norfolk, Nebraska. The manager agreed to let him perform. So, at age seven, Tom began singing on the radio. "I would often receive fan mail at home after my radio appearances," he remembered. When Tom was ten-years-old, his youngest brother, Jim, began singing with him (Jim was four at the time). Tompall recalled that later, when Jim began playing guitar, "I used to stomp on his feet when it was time to change chords."

When Tom was in his early teens, the Glaser Brothers not only sang on WJAG radio, but also began performing publically at nearby county fairs, school talent shows, and anywhere else that they could. During this time, their brother Chuck who was about twelve then, would "front" Tom and Jim by announcing them and their songs to the audience over the microphone. Four years later, Tom taught Chuck to play guitar, and Chuck began singing and playing with his brothers.

In these early days, the Glaser Brothers' act changed some-what from time to time. When Eleanor was 16-years-old and Tom-pall was 11, she joined Tom and Jim on stage and sang a few songs.

Thomas Paul Glaser in 1946, at age 13. Courtesy of Eleanor Ryan

However, she said that she didn't care to be in the spotlight, so she stopped performing with them after a couple of shows. Also, young neighbor JoAnne Poland sang and played the piano with the group for a while in an attempt to provide some musical variety to their singing act. Shortly after this, another neighbor Deanna Beck appeared on stage with the Glaser Brothers and tap-danced. Both of these acts were short-lived.

Even though Eleanor shied away from performing on stage, she helped her brothers in these early performing years by listening to the radio and writing down the lyrics of popular songs. She gave the lyrics to Tom, and he would figure out the accompanying music so that the brothers could play these songs during their shows.

Tom, Chuck, and Jim never used a music stand during their performances and always memorized their songs. Their father was adamant. Music stands were props and true performers did not use them.

Childhood friend Joe Babcock, who would later join Tompall and Jim in 1959 while Chuck served in the US Army, remembers those early years:

> The first time I met the Glasers was when they played Popcorn Days, which is an annual event in the little town where I grew up in North Loup, Nebraska. We were about the only country music players in all of Nebraska, I think, other than Ed-

die Soseby and the Radio Rangers in Lincoln. My dad owned the movie theater in North Loup, so I got him to hire them for a show at our theater. I remember that Tom, even at the age of 16, stressed the need for a lot of promotion. So we did, and we had a good show. The boys sat on chairs on stage, sang and played, while their dad, Louis, introduced each song from backstage, unseen by the audience. They were good even then, harmony perfect, and they accompanied themselves on guitars.

The three brothers continued to play their music together during their teen years, performing at local school programs and becoming even better recognized in their community. When Tom was about 16, he and his brothers began playing at television station KHAS in Hastings, Nebraska, some 72 miles from their Spalding home. Louis arranged to have his sons perform for 30 minutes each week for thirteen weeks on the television show. Unfortunately, back then, Louis Glaser didn't own a television set, so the family couldn't watch Tompall and his brothers perform.

Tom and his brothers also continued to perform at various talent shows as part of fairs and rodeos. Louis Glaser drove his three sons to and from each performance during those start-up years; he took pride in managing their careers and announcing the group's playlists.

Eleanor remembers that Tom, Chuck, and Jim won every single contest they ever entered, including the Bartlett Rodeo—that she said was a "pretty big deal." The Bartlett Rodeo is an annual, long-standing event, part of the Wheeler County Fair, and it draws people from many miles around. It's a competitive rodeo, part of the Nebraska State Rodeo Association, and it includes entertainment for its fair and rodeo attendees.

Tompall remembered that once he turned sixteen his father would take him to town dances twice a year. Tompall danced with

The Louis and Marie Glaser Family in the 1940s. Front Row, L to R: Chuck, Louis, Marie and Jim. Back Row, L to R: Tom, Bob, John and Eleanor. Courtesy of June Glaser

all the girls and was quite popular with the opposite sex due, in part, to his radio show. He also had "striking good looks" according to women who knew him.

As might be expected, some of the local boys were not too pleased with Tompall's popularity. In fact, one night a boy from a nearby town decided to challenge Tompall by calling him a litany of profane names. Tompall demanded that he "meet me outside to fight." Tompall got in the first few punches and hit the name-caller in his solar plexus, his ear, and smack dab in the middle of his nose. Tom then kicked him in the butt and pushed him down into a near-by ravine. Tompall said that he didn't have problems with any of the other boys in town after that fight.

In spite of the boys' growing musical success, life on the farm was not easy. In addition to the grueling work, Mother Nature was seldom kind to the Glasers. Over the years, blizzards, heavy rains and floods, tornadoes, and drought-like conditions waged war with them and the other Spalding farmers.

In 1947, when Tompall was fourteen, a fire burned the Glaser homestead to the ground. To this day, there is much speculation about the cause of the fire, but no one is absolutely certain of the cause. Regardless of the origin, the fire broke Louis' heart. He had been so proud of the former hotel and had a very difficult time recovering from the impact of its loss.

John ("Jack") Glaser, my father, was the 2nd oldest son born to Louis and Marie. He has led an interesting life and always seemed to be working to support his family of nine. He has worked at *least* two jobs at the same time during his adult life, and he stayed at his primary occupation for more than 50 years. John served in the U.S. Army during the Korean conflict and laid communication cable on the front line. If I had to pick three words to describe John, these words would be intelligent, hard-working, and reliable. Indeed, friends and family have always known that they can count on John.

John clearly remembers the devastation caused by the burning of their home and how life changed for him and the rest of his family. The fire burned throughout the day, and that night he recalls sleeping in an oat grain bin. He can still picture "mice running over my body while I tried to get to sleep."

Tompall, too, remembered those nasty mice and agreed that neither John nor he slept much that night. He also said that he gathered 300 bushels of potatoes from the cellar of their destroyed home after the fire and stored them in a different location.

Tompall also recalled two separate tornadoes striking the Glaser farmstead. The first took place around 1940 when he was 7-years-old. The second occurred in 1955, and this latter one destroyed a garage, a barn, a chicken house, grain bins, a portion of their new house, and a tractor shed. At this time, only Chuck and Jim were living on the farm as Tom was finishing his army service.

Tompall's sister, Eleanor Ryan, was the only daughter born to Louis and Marie Glaser. Eleanor is an upbeat person and has always been enjoyable to be around. She got married at age 22 and left the Glaser family farm at that time. She moved to Greeley after marrying and seldom returned due to her new family commitments.

Life was busy on the Glaser farm, and each person in the family had daily work assignments. Eleanor said she often felt like a surrogate mother to the younger boys because their mom, Marie, was so busy doing her various chores around the farm and leaving the three younger boys behind in the house with Eleanor. While busy, Eleanor remembers that those days of adolescence held many good times, and she also recalls that all of her brothers were good friends growing up.

Tompall did not go to high school, nor did any of his siblings with the exception of Jim. At the time that Jim graduated from grade school, Nebraska had recently passed a law stating that all children must attend high school. Even though Tompall never went to high school, Eleanor said that she nevertheless considers Tompall to be "brilliant."

There are conflicting stories concerning why Louis refused to send his children to high school. One of these is that he needed their help on the farm. Another was that he held some hard feelings against the educators at the local high school. Whatever Louie's reasons, the fact remains that Tom and Chuck, as well as Bob, Eleanor, and John accomplished much in their lifetimes without the benefit of a high school education.

Tompall really did not like to talk in detail about his childhood. Throughout his entire life he had some unresolved emotions relating to those early years on the farm. However, he did share with me that he and his father had frequent, strong, and often loud disagreements.

Eleanor said that both Tom and Louis had terrible tempers. In her opinion, she felt that Louis wanted to control his sons' careers and that Tompall would have none of this.

Tompall's recollection was that Louis did not *argue* with him; rather, Louis made up his mind about something and simply refused to change it—regardless of what Tom would say. As Tom turned 21, he was worried more and more about his future. He said, "I had no formal education, and I didn't even know how to do my own laundry. I knew for certain that I did not want to spend the rest of my life on the farm, so one night I took my brother John's car off the blocks (John was finishing his active army duty in Korea at the time), and I drove over to the enlistment office in the nearby city of Bartlett and signed up for army service."

3

The Special Services

In 1954, after one of his more memorable disagreements with his father, Tompall enlisted in the U.S. Army. The Korean War's active conflict had formally wound down under the auspices of the Korean Armistice Agreement that had been signed in July of 1953, so there was not an active military confrontation taking place when Tompall volunteered. However, the army was still doing what the army has always done: training its soldiers for potential future conflicts.

Family and Morale, Welfare and Recreation Command (FM-WRC) is a little-known branch of the armed services. It is also referred to as the "Army Crafts Program" or "Special Services" by some and as "Special Assignment" by others. This segment of the Army traces its roots back to 1941 when military commanders decided that Armed Services' morale could be boosted by providing positive "free-time" experiences to soldiers, and that some of these free-time experiences should be incorporated into a soldier's daily army life.

The Army Crafts Program included recreation activities such as sports (i.e., basketball and volleyball), libraries, service clubs, and Soldier Shows. The Soldier Shows involved a wide variety of acts, from magicians to comedians and more. The shows also included musical and theatrical acts, and these proved to be some of the most popular Army Crafts programs.

After his enlistment, Tompall attended a 16-week basic training course. His first eight weeks were spent at the U.S. Army Post in Fort Bliss. This post spans 1,700 square miles and is situated in both Texas and New Mexico. His next eight weeks were spent training in Fort Ord, in Monterey, California. This base was closed in 1994, in part due to its prime location by the coast. However, for many years it served as a staging area for units departing for war or for military overseas travel.

During his enlistment, Tompall was a part of General Patton's outfit (in name only, since Patton was deceased by this time). It seems fitting that his uniform bore a patch on the sleeve that reflected his platoon name, "Hell on Wheels."

Each troop had a talent contest and, as was customary at the time, the winner of this contest would become part of the Special Services unit. Tompall won his troop's talent contest, earning him the designation of "most talented" in his platoon. As a result, he was chosen to become part of the music-related Special Services division, and he would spend almost his entire enlistment as part of this music division. Tompall enjoyed his Special Services years and, in general, life was pretty easy. For instance, he recalled that once, while everyone else in his unit dug foxholes, he was in his barracks listening to his platoon sergeant sing "Red Sails in the Sunset." The sergeant wanted to teach Tompall the guitar chords to this song so that Tompall could play the song during an upcoming Special Services performance.

During Tompall's eight weeks at the Fort Ord Army Base in California, he was chosen as "Soldier of the Month" and received a four-day pass. Tompall remembered visiting San Francisco and other nearby locations during those four days.

After Fort Ord, Tompall shipped overseas to Germany. He was initially stationed at the Lee Barracks U.S. Army Base in Mainz, Germany, which was located on the Rhine River near Wiesbaden (this based closed in 1992). After a short stay at the Mainz base, he was stationed in Bremerhaven, Germany, at the Carl Schurz Kaserne Post (which closed in 1993). Bremerhaven is located at the mouth of the River Weser and is an important city for German shipping and trade.

From Bremerhaven, Tompall was sent to the Kaiserslautern Military Community (KMC) in Kaiserslautern, Germany, where he spent the remainder of his nearly two-year army enlistment. KMC is the largest U.S. Military community outside the United States and is still active today.

While stationed in Germany, Tompall was given much freedom. He lived in a hotel, wore civilian clothes, belonged to seven different service clubs, and had unrestricted access to the staff car at his post. Later, he was even allowed to purchase his *own* personal car and to keep it at the base.

Tompall recalled that it was difficult to obtain car tires during this particular time. He said, "Most of the tires that were available had very little tread and were nearly bald. As a result, I kept three spare tires in the trunk of my car at all times in case one of the tires would go flat."

Tompall traveled extensively around Europe during his time in Germany. He visited Holland, France, Italy and several other countries during his allotted leaves. While in Italy, Tompall visited Rome and attended a group audience with Pope Pius XII. The pope appeared at his window overlooking St. Peter's Square, and Tompall vividly remembered the pope's appearance and obtaining the blessing of His Holiness.

While in the Special Services, Tompall would sometimes sing as a solo act and sometimes as part of a musical group. He remembered that there were different kinds of acts that were part of the Special Services unit, including magicians and someone who "chewed on razor blades."

Tompall also hired out for one night each week, performing with his unit's sergeant. He averaged $20 per night for this gig. He noted, "I was the richest private in my unit."

Tompall became good friends with a soldier named Chuck Feller who was from the Midwest. Chuck completed his enlistment approximately six months before Tompall finished his army service. After Chuck left, Tompall was chosen to take over Chuck's job, which was to drive the Special Services bus and truck. Soon, Tompall was in charge of all show logistics, including transportation, for his Services unit.

Chuck Feller currently lives in Hammond, Indiana, and shared some of his memories about Tompall:

> I first met Tom when I went to pick him up at the base where he was stationed. Tom was temporarily assigned to us, or as the military call it TDY [the military acronym for 'Temporary Duty in the Yonder,' or simply 'temporary duty.' Servicemen on TDY are reimbursed for lodging and meals]. Backing up a little, I was in charge of the USO Soldier Show for the Western Area Command. I heard Tom, don't remember where, and was impressed with his voice. I talked to our officer requesting that we see if we could get him assigned to us. OK. Now back to where we started. Tom and I bunked together in the converted hotel where we stayed.
>
> I spent a lot of time with Tom in the auditorium going over songs with him and putting together new shows. There were about 20-24 soldiers all on TDY living in the hotel. We put together a new show every two months. I was amazed that

Tom could sing country, pop, and classical music. We were able to mix this up when we created a new show to go on the road.

Tom and I became very close friends. I tutored him in stage presentation as he was initially rather clumsy on stage. However, things worked out and we received many calls for a show to return to a base, as well as calls for Tom to return solo with a back-up band. We traveled all over Germany and France. Tom and I once went on vacation to Paris and had a blast. Tom crapped in a bidet while we were in Paris, and the maid was really pissed. While there we went to the Moulin Rouge and saw the show, picked up a couple of babes, and had a wild night.

We were based in Kaiserslautern and coming back to work from Paris to start another tour. That was our life: create new shows and tour. Once, during a break, we went to Munich for the Oktoberfest. The Germans are a swinging group of people: if you had too much to drink, they invited you to stay at their homes. The mainstay for the Oktoberfest is brats and beer. Many times when we were returning to our hotel we would stop at a local bar, put on a show and get free drinks and food. In the summer we had a picnic almost every month.

The show group was between 25-40 people, depending on the show and the musicians required. We traveled year round visiting all the military bases. The best base was the Air Force/Naval base in Wiesbaden. The food was usually steak, baked potato, and salad. When winter came, Tom would help me install the chains on the rear tires of the bus we were using. Many times, when we returned, Tom and I would head to the bar across from our hotel and have a beer and a steak sandwich. We would then return to our room, crash, get ready the next day, and start all over again.

Our second vacation was in Garmisch during the winter. The country was beautiful. This was where Hitler used to have his home. Southern Germany with all the castles and cathedrals is a real show place. Tom and I would walk the castle gardens, which were well- manicured. We often talked about returning when we got discharged, but that did not come to pass, just as many other ideas we had.

I got discharged before Tom. I believe he was discharged about six months later. Tom came to our house and purchased a car to use going home. I co-signed for his loan. We sort of lost touch after that even though we still discussed my being his business manager. I had been planning to visit his home in Nebraska, but the timing was not working to our favor.

I did get a call from Tom in the winter of 1961, and he wanted me to come to Goodlettsville, TN. However, we got caught in a snow storm in southern Indiana and never made it. After that I lost touch 'till one day I received a call from Tom in the winter of 1981. Tom called from Canada and sounded pretty plastered. I'm assuming he was on tour at that time. He wanted me to fly to Canada the next day, but he wasn't quite sure where he was.

P.S., Tom had a nickname for me. He called me 'Professor Four Letter.' How that came about I'll never know.

Tompall's German Special Services unit was made up of a colonel, a staff sergeant, and Tompall, who served as a private at this time. Tompall's unit performed at different locations throughout Germany, and on several occasions they performed at the Royal Canadian Air Force Base located in Baden, Germany. This base was officially known as the RCAF Station Baden-Soellingen base. The RCAF base was located close to a large body of water, which resulted in the foggy, wet weather, both at the base and in the nearby vicinity.

One day, Tompall's colonel ordered him to drive a staff vehicle over to the Canadian base to perform a show, so he did as he was told. In order to get all of the performers (musicians and actors), as well as the needed equipment to the Canadian base, it was necessary that a truck, a bus, and a staff vehicle be driven to and from the base. This situation became the *defining moment* of Tompall's short military career, and something that he thought about from that day forward.

On the return trip from the RCAF Station Baden-Soellingen base, Tompall was driving the Special Services truck. The weather was foggy and visibility was very limited. Try as he might, Tompall could not see what was in front of his truck. In what took only seconds, but felt like hours, he lost all control of his truck and became part of a terrible multi-vehicle accident. As a result, the bus carrying the show's performers was severely damaged.

Soon after the accident, Tompall was notified by his Special Services colonel that the military was placing 100% of the blame for the accident on him. According to the military's practice at that time, if a soldier damaged any army equipment that soldier was responsible for paying for all of the resulting damages. Tompall was to be held accountable for the damage to each vehicle that was involved in the accident, and he was told that he owed the Army several thousand dollars.

Aerial view of RCAF Station in Baden-Soellingen near Rheinmunster, Germany in the early 1950s. The Rhine River is evident in the lower portion of the photo and the runway in the upper portion of the photo.

The colonel went on to tell Tompall that he would have to re-enlist in the Special Services unit for an additional three years in order to pay for all the damages.

Tompall strongly protested his colonel's decision. He decided to fight back and sought out an Army Judge Advocate, or JAG (an armed services attorney) to contest what the colonel had told him.

After listening to Tompall's explanation of the accident, the JAG wrote a formal letter to higher-ranking army officials on Tompall's behalf. The army brass reviewed the facts and decided that, in fact, the blame for the accident should be placed upon the colonel—for poor decision-making—rather than upon Tompall. It was determined that the colonel was, or should have been, aware of the treacherous weather conditions that surrounded the Royal Canadian Air Force base. The foggy weather should certainly have come as no surprise to him. In addition, as part of the outcome, the colonel was demoted to a sergeant. As you might guess, this new sergeant was not at all happy with Tompall.

Things in the army were never the same for Tompall after this incident. Soon after the situation was resolved, Tompall was asked to leave the army and was given an honorable discharge. As a result, Tom's entire army enlistment period encompassed a total of approximately twenty-two months.

* * *

Tompall's Army Letters Home:

During Tompall's nearly two years in the U.S. Army, his mother wrote him almost every single day. His brothers Chuck and Jim who were still at home and performing musically on the radio, on television, and for nearby community events, also wrote Tompall frequently. Tompall's father, Louis, wrote only a couple of times.

Tompall's letters home provide a fascinating look into the life of this young man who had dreams of becoming a professional singer and musician. During his two years of army enlistment, from the age of 20 until he was almost 23, Tompall sang, performed on stage in various venues, learned staging and stage lighting skills, was frequently a Master of Ceremonies (MC), thought up ways to earn money by playing music on the side, and created some very successful *European Grand Ole Opry* concerts that resulted in sold-out shows and over-capacity crowds. Some of these shows included venues where the crowds numbered over 800 people. In many of his letters home, Tompall frequently commented to his mother that he was "learning a lot" and applying what he learned.

Tompall's musical abilities evolved during this time, and he experimented with a variety of musical genres before settling on country music, known as "hillbilly" music back then. He also gave acting a try and commented that he really enjoyed it. As he matured during these two years, he made some noteworthy comments. One of these was his statement in reference to Germany, in a letter dated November 10, 1955, where he wrote, "The people here are so very poor, as only war can make them, but they are working like mad, and

I mean from young to old, women and men, and they are building their cities better than before. The silent plan seems to be to someday be strong enough to gain back the rest of Germany." Tompall said this 35 years before German reunification actually took place.

Most of Tompall's letters home were replies to letters he received from his mother, Marie, but the other members of his family were not far from his thoughts. Tompall wrote an average of one letter per week. I have not included all of his letters, and I have edited some of them for the sake of brevity, but what follows gives us tremendous insight into Tompall's life as a young man.

In these letters he gives a running commentary of his military life; he expresses his hopes and his frustrations. He wrestles with what he will do when he gets out, and how that will affect his brothers and his parents, and he draws interesting philosophical conclusions from his experiences. His letters are full of interesting anecdotes accompanied by his thoughtful reactions to them, and they show his progression as a musician during this critical time in his musical development. These letters provide a valuable look into the mind of a young man with a big dream. But what is really important, especially when you consider how young Tompall was when he wrote them, they reveal the thoughtful man Tompall was and they set the stage for Tompall's future contributions to the music industry he was just beginning to learn about.

* * *

December 7, 1954 – Fort Bliss, Texas

Well, here I am at Fort Bliss. The I & E [Installations & Environment] office spent almost an hour with me when I came through, only to tell me it is impossible to get into Special Services, that I'm not "name enough." But that pertains only to this fort. If I go someplace like Fort Ord where they have that sort of thing, I can get assigned to a unit. But here I can only work on my own. I auditioned at the service club, and I can get on there after I'm out of basic. After basic, I can get time off to do shows.

December 8, 1954

When I got to Grand Island (Nebraska), on my way down, it seemed like everyone in the bus station had seen us on TV. They acted like they were glad to see me. Also, some guys on the train had seen us, but it took three of them until Kansas City to figure out where they'd seen me. One guy, who now bunks with me, didn't figure it out 'till we were here at the base for a day or two. It was sort of funny— we were in chow line and he asked me if I was on TV. Then he said, "Well, what do you know, guess I can write home now—I've got something to write about." Dad, I tell you I had to get my hair cut short. I haven't got a hair on my head that's a quarter of an inch long. That's the army.

December 12, 1954

This is Sunday and I'm in my famous hut waiting for church time. Mass is at 9:00 a.m. There are quite a few Catholics here, really a fine bunch of guys. The chaplain gave us a talking to in Class C, the other day; also the captain, on morals and going to church. I played at the service club tonight, again. I guess I made a little ripple with the C.O. and attendees there at that. They invited me back and promised to send for me again later. Everybody seems to remember me singing here and is always stopping me and asking me when I'll be on again, and they do come back too. I bet I sang "Skokiaan" and "I Couldn't Keep From Crying" a million times since I left home. Boy, you know a lot of guys saw that TV show. They come around and look me up and act like I'm a real hero.

December 16, 1954

I'm debating whether or not to go on sick call. I've got a sore knee, a reaction to a smallpox shot, (I hope), and I've got a sore throat. Everybody has them. I'd fall out to the field only it would kill me to do physical training.

December 17, 1954

I got your first letter yesterday and you can't imagine how good it was to hear from home. Funny how I used to cuss it, and I guess I really loved it all the time. I've been restricted to quarters last two days. I had to take three shots and some erythromycin pills. I'm glad I went to sick call; it helped my cough. Well, Mom, I miss you an awful lot, seems funny that you're not fussing over me. Don't worry about me—just be sure to be there when I get home.

December 22, 1954

I really feel good now except that I still have a sore throat, but that's on the mend. The NCO at the service club recognized me last Sunday night at one of the service club dances, and he asked me to play for some orphans on Christmas night and also for some on Sunday night. He seems to want to help me, and I can't think of a better way to spend Christmas here in Fort Bliss. I sure hope my guitar gets here in time, or I'm just out of luck.

December 26, 1954

Well, this is the day after Christmas. I went to mass at St. Michael's Chapel here at Fort Bliss. The organist is really great. He has more feeling than I've ever heard. I met a guy who's really good playing guitar. He plays just like Chet Atkins. He's in basic, too, and we are hoping we can work something out. We all lack guitars. Right here I could give some advice. Jim and Chas, learn to follow sheet music guitar symbols. Learn to do every chord. And mostly learn to understand why. Chas, you should take some off-campus math courses or you'll have a red face like I did; it's no fun believe me. The local talent did a show for the orphans Christmas night. I sang "Jolly Old St. Nicholas," and "O Come All Ye Faithful." I guess they liked it okay.

January 1, 1955

My guitar is here and I'm really happy about it, but of course I worry about it. Everyone knows I got it so that makes it worse. I don't think anything will happen. A lot of guys like to hear me, so I guess they'll help me. I'm writing this in our day room. It has a pool table, two candy machines, milk machine, a TV set, easy chairs, writing tablets, and a lot of dirt that comes from poor structure and mass living. I went to El Paso yesterday and got my Christmas shopping done. They really had some excitement while I was there. Someone set off a tear gas bomb in a nightclub. I was in front of it, and I really got a good shot before I knew what happened. They had to get the fire department to clear it up. Somebody's joke. There sure were a lot of tears shed. It seemed funny to see grown men running around crying like babies. There isn't too much going on, so we got a quartet together. We sing stuff like "Peace in the Valley" and "Just a Closer Walk With Thee."

January 5, 1955

It's really good to hear from home. I don't think a man could get so hard he didn't miss the home folks. The guitar came in fine shape. Today we fired the 3.5 rocket launcher (bazooka). We had to march 12 miles, six both ways. That is, the rest of the guys did. I marched out and fired, then came back at 2:30 pm in a truck to pull guard. I got picked as the sharpest guard, so I don't have to do anything but sit in my hut. I suppose Chas told you I sang with the biggest hillbilly band down in this part of the country. It sure was fun. This week if we pass the inspection we get to go to Juarez, Mexico. I may go one day and see a bullfight and get a real good steak. Last weekend I went to Las Cruces, New Mexico.

January 16, 1955

Now let me tell you, there is an Indian here—his name is Dreadful-Water. He's studied music seven years and sang with a quartet on TV in Oklahoma City for two years while in college. Now this little boy can really sing. Tonight he got a guitar from someplace, and we had a jam session from 5:30 to 9:30 pm. I really enjoyed it. I'm learning about music here, not a whole lot, but I'm learning how to sell myself to a different audience. I'm learning how to live with people, and I'm not the only one that's having trouble. They had another fight here today. I came out of my deal okay; I really had to get rough. So far I've never had a fight. But I may. I find the more you tell them off the better you get along. My guitar is really my buddy. It's gained some respect and of course makes me a lot of friends, or should I say makes people think well of me and feel they know me, and since they don't they can't hate me, so they treat me alright. Of course some guys are jealous.

January 23, 1955

Well, I got to sing with the great Eddie Novac & band, and let me tell you they are good. First I sang my biggest song (down here) "Skokiaan"—it always makes a hit; then I sang "The Golden Rocket." It was too low for me so it didn't sound too good. Then I watched a while, and guess what, some more guys from Nebraska had seen the Glaser Brothers on TV and remembered my ugly face. They told Eddie a lot of guys wanted to hear me sing again. I thought he was just trying to make me feel good, but when I stepped on the stage, I felt like a king. I sang "I Walk Alone" and got it in the right key this time, and they really raised the roof. Made me feel so good.

January 31, 1955 – Fort Bliss, Texas

From here I will go to Fort Ord, California, for advanced infantry combat training. Fort Ord has the greatest Special Services possibilities in the whole U.S., and after I get back from New York, I'll have a real recommendation. It is almost certain I'll be able to get into it. I've had a call from the Special Services department here in Fort Bliss that I haven't been able to answer yet. They want to see me and I can't get any time off to go to their office until Thursday, and this is Monday. Now I'll get to fly from coast-to-coast when I go on TV. It's going to be easier to get out of the infantry than the artillery and get stationed here. There are many different branches of the infantry even if I don't get Special Services. But something has taken care of me so far, and I'm going to trust He continues.

February 21, 1955

Now, about the deal here. From where I sit, I think I can make it. I've seen what they have, you know. I've seen some of the shows they have and I think I can make it. I've got to think I can, because I've got to. They have some good entertainers, but no act just like what I do. My record is good. The recommendation I have really swings weight, but I still have to audition and so far I haven't made an appointment. Then also, my M.O.S. [military occupation specialty] must be high enough to rate a job or position of some kind in some branch here, so I can be pulled. It isn't going to be easy, and I don't suppose I'll get to stay here. But I'll work for the Special Services while I'm here and then when I go overseas, if they have an active unit there, I may be able to continue. Really, I guess what happens to me is up to God.

March 2, 1955

Well, I just got back from the telephone where I called you and broke the sad news about the contest I didn't even place in. Now this has really got me floored; I can't believe I'm not good enough to even make it. I'm not polished enough. I've got to get better somehow. They are going to use me in some of their Sunday night shows here. That will help. Now these guys that won have been stationed here and have made quite a splash already. Now, I'm not disputing the decision of the judges. They made a good choice, and if I could stay here I might win it someday. But I do need some polish. These guys grew up in Hollywood. They really know show business. I'm at the bottom. I'm in the infantry and I know I'll never make Special Services, and I doubt if they will even pull me out of this and put me with another outfit so I can stay. This is the first time I've run up against somebody who does the same thing I do, only better. Someday I may get good enough but tonight I was not. I'm shook I guess. I'm lost. And now I'm sunk.

This place is flowing with gamblers. They just gamble their heads off. They get paid and the crazy fools lose it all before they even feel it in their pockets. One of my buddies has it in his blood, and he really gets excited. In fact, his blood runs wild and he talks to those dice like he was saying his prayers. Another thing that really gets me down is the knife pulling that goes on around here. I swear I'll come as close to killing the first man that pulls a knife on me as I can. It makes me so mad I just shudder. Running around with some of these "Mexes" here, I've seen some of the ugliest scars you can imagine. And they are proud of them. I'll kick the head right off the first one who tries to leave his mark on me.

I hope you don't think I'm a crud for not winning but maybe another time. I can't believe it's all over for me; I'm sure I'll make it someday, but I've got to master what I have.

March 11, 1955

This last weekend I went to San Francisco; it was really an experience. By the way, I play this Sunday and Wednesday nights. I'm still no hero but I may gain on it. If I make a little stir Sunday and get them interested in me, I'm going to try and get transferred into something so I can be stationed here permanently. But there is not too much of a chance. We are to ship overseas someplace. But if I do go, I will still have a good chance to be in Special Services there. I just can't stop trying, although I'm almost certain I don't have what it takes to be a big star. I was the sharpest guard again the other day. The colonel here is real "gung-ho." Even took my picture. I'll send it to you, and you can do what I should have done with it. I never tried to be the hero he made me out, it just had to be somebody so it was me. I was supposed to be the colonel's personal guard, but he didn't need one over the weekend, so I just got a pass, didn't have to walk guard, and this weekend I get a three-day pass.

March 15, 1955

This weekend we get our last pass before we leave. I went to Monterey last Friday and really enjoyed it. There are so many things to do and see here; I know I can't even begin to cover everything. I'd like to come back someday and really look it over. But home is still best—I guess because it's home, and no place will ever seem like home. Wednesday evening I got back from the service club. I was in another post talent contest for the month of March. I won it, but it really doesn't mean too much; I had a combo with me. A real great piano man, the best I've ever seen. He played backroom style behind my songs, "That's All I Want From You," "This Old House," and "Skokiaan." Also there was a bass and drums. But due to the fact we had only a short time to go over our songs, we weren't exactly together. In fact, the last two stank. For winning first prize I get $7.50 worth of credit at the P.X. That's good, I can always use money.

My lucky break will be if I can stay here at Ord and work with special services. Then I can get a job with a local TV station in a town called Salinas close to here and pick up some more money. But I'll probably go overseas and see the world. But the chances are better for Special Services over there so I'm not going to complain yet.

March 18, 1955

My luck really has picked up again. And it's funny because I'm just floating along. This New York deal came as a surprise; my letter must have done some good. The deal is that I am to leave the

SPALDING SOLDIER—Pvt. Thomas P. Glaser, son of Mr. and Mrs. Louis N. Glaser of Spalding, was selected as Colonel's Orderly for the 20th Infantry Regiment at Fort Ord, Calif. Chosen for his outstanding appearance and knowledge of the Army, the 21-year-old soldier was given a letter of recommendation from Col. Franklin R. Sibert, commanding officer of the 20th Inf. Regt., shown above congratulating Pvt. Glaser. He was also given a special pass for his efforts, the former Spalding rancher and entertainer is undergoing basic infantry training there. (US Army Photo.)

Used with permission of The Grand Island Independent Newspaper

28th of March unless I'm notified different between now and then. I'm hoping my M.O.S. will be changed and that I can work with Special Services. I should have a good chance. And also Wednesday night, I entered a post talent contest and won first place and will get to make a recording of my voice someday soon. Big deal. Also they took my picture, and it will be in panorama. All in all, I'm getting to be pretty well-known here at Ord. This Colonel's Orderly [award] turned out to be quite an honor. They put my picture in the paper, although I haven't seen the paper, but the commanding officer gave me my personally autographed picture and letter in front of the whole company. And last but not least my big deal of the moment is the song I wrote. One fine day the first sergeant called a formation and told us the colonel wanted a regimental song, and said if there were any songwriters in the crowd, they could win either some money or a leave. We were permitted to use either our own tune or any other tune as long as the lyrics were original. So I whipped one real gung-ho ditty together and turned it in. If the competition isn't too great, I may win a leave. As far as I'm concerned personally now, I'm situated and am getting along fine. I've gotten to know these people and learned to get along with them. I've never been called down or put on detail since I've been here. My guitar is my best friend. I'll always get along fine. So just relax as far as I'm concerned.

March 24, 1955

I don't go to New York now until I finish basic. That is really a break. This basic is something I have to do before I can get any kind of an assignment. I'm really lucky to get a vacation after basic. The rest of my company will get right on a boat and ship out. They don't even get a weekend pass. They're afraid there would be too many AWOLs and they are right.

April 6, 1955

Last night we took a shower 'neath the moon. The water was mountain water that had been pumped into tanks about 20 feet in the air. Of course it was ice cold, but it really felt good to be clean. Being chilled out here doesn't seem to bother much. We got our orders yesterday; not the individual orders but everyone who is Europe bound receives a series of shots. I'm very happy to say I'm Europe bound. It's going to be a great experience. Lt. Runner said my chances for Special Services there were very good. I won't have to go to the field there if I can get out of it here. But there I will be officially assigned to Special Services.

April 24, 1955 – Aboard *The Butner,* Somewhere in the Atlantic Ocean

Thursday morning we left Camp Kilmer at 8:30 a.m. and left for the New York harbor, boarded the gigantic *Butner*, and at 2:00 pm we sailed for Europe.

[**Note:** The U.S.S. *General H. W. Butner* had regular voyages from Brooklyn, New York, to Southampton, England, and finally to Bremerhaven, Germany, supporting American military commitments in Europe until decommissioned on 1-28-60.]

Watching the New York harbor and the massive skyline surround the Statue of Liberty and then fade into the horizon is a sensation that will remain for some time to come. New York itself is a masterpiece of human ingenuity. Nothing has ever made me feel less important, for it seems that some person, somehow, has thought of just about everything. Never have you seen so much concrete piled in one place and so high, too.

Aboard the *Butner* is not at all what I expected. In the first place, I'm not at all sick. The truth is I was far more airsick than seasick. Maybe it's because we haven't hit any rough weather yet. So far, I'm enjoying it very much. There are a lot of air force personnel aboard. Those boys spend three years over there; it's only 19 months for me. There are 3,500 military personnel on the ship besides the crew and officers. Some are trying to put on a stage show. I'm going to be in it, not because it's such a big deal, but because I can get released from detail to practice. Some of the officers' wives are going to participate. Two of them are crazy about hillbilly music. Not my style but the real whiny kind. One southern gal from South Carolina is going to sing "One by One" with me and she sounds like Kitty Wells. Pretty cute, too. To me, she had this to say, "Where y'all from?" "Nebraska," I said. "Oh, you're a damn Yankee," she said. "WHAT???" I said. "Listen, she said, "I was 21-years-old before I knew damn Yankee was two words." I about died laughing, but to her it was no joke.

I'm in good with all of the sailors who like my kind of music, and they take care of me. They go to the PX for me and let me drink coffee and write letters in their quarters and that really helps. It's so crowded here it drives you crazy. I got split from most of my buddies when we left California, but I've made some new ones that are better than I've ever had before. So goes the army.

We've got U.S. Army, Navy, and Air Force here and they get along famous. All we need to spoil it is some swell-headed Marine to show up. Those guys shoot sharp pains through the portion on which I am now sitting. All they have that the army doesn't have is a better publicity staff.

You know, it's hard for me to remain a Nebraskan! Every time I play, some cool kid wants to know where I'm from; when I tell him he gives me that faraway look and says, "It just don't figure!" Sometimes one of my buddies would even say I'm from his state. Of course I always correct them because I'm proud of my home state. I asked this one kid last night why he insisted on saying I was from California. He said, "Well, kid, let's face it broadly! Your biography is all fouled up. You've just got to be from California or Tennessee." That really shook me up. Some people sure live by the book. I have a great time though. I'm not the greatest musician who ever lived, or singer, or entertainer, but I might be able to make a fair living at

The U.S.S. General H.W. Butner, U.S. Navy photo courtesy of www.navsource.org

it. I'm sure of one thing: I've never seen a trio like ours and probably never will. I'm sure together we can make quite a stir. Entertaining people is a very sensitive business. The most important thing to be really great is to be really good at what you feature. Now, with us it's singing. Next, back it with the best that's possible.

May 2, 1955 - Zwingenberg (Baden), Germany

April 30, we left the U.S.S. *General Butner* at Bremerhaven, Germany, boarded a train and 18 hours later arrived here in Zwingenberg. The trip on the Butner lasted 11 days. The show we did aboard ship was a big success. The sailors all said it was the best they ever had aboard that ship since they'd been with her. Some had been in five years. We put it on twice—once for 2,500 troops and once for the officers. Never in my life did I get as much applause as I did when we put that show on the deck. I could feel it in the air. It almost knocked me down, if I may say so without any hint of conceit. I'm sure these sailors in a foreign land are going to eat that right up. Anything that is symbolic of the American way. My advantage is that both country and popular fans seem to find equal interest in the work I've done so far. You know my IQ is very low. I'll not get far in this world on my brains. Sometimes I feel very shallow. You can have an average IQ and still have good sense. I'm hoping I do.

May 7, 1955 – Mainz, Germany

Well I finally got assigned to a unit in the company. Here in the armored infantry battalion, Company "C" 42nd Division is where I'm going to spend my next 18 months. I suppose you already know that Germany became a sovereignty as of May 5th, and we are no longer occupation troops but guests of the German people. So they are using us mostly for show. The 42nd, or should I say the 2nd Armed Division was originated by Gen. Patton. They are really proud of it, too. We wear all the decorations they can hang on us.

Last night was the first night I've spent here, and it so happens they had a show at the service club, so I went down and sang with them. This gal, who is supposed to be quite a wheel with Special Services, loves country music and sings it also. She told me I was "just perfect." Well that suits me because it is through this place I get my break if I get one. I have a very good chance, I think; they don't have much here.

May 20, 1955 – Mainz, Germany

I auditioned for TDY [temporary duty] last night. I put the talent together they had here along with my own and got the whole bunch in. They've been here and auditioned before and never made it. Made me feel good. And won me a little respect from them. Now the big stinker is getting released from the company. That is pretty rough. If I have enough pull I may make it. If I don't get out of this infantry, I'll go nuts. If I do make TDY, I'll have it made. My life will almost be my own.

May 28, 1955 – Mainz, Germany

The service club is the only place anything like home on the whole post. The barracks in which we live are huge things made of stone, and they have so many doors and windows it's like living outside. It's usually colder inside than out. This service club is really nice; they really work in the interest of the soldiers. They have pool and ping-pong, a music room, writing room, photo room, crafts room, and a kitchen where they have coffee. And every Friday night one of the guys—any guy—can go in and cook something. Then they serve ice cream. I come in here often and just sit in the big easy chairs and read or sleep.

I ran into the Davids Brothers last night again. They are really good Joes. They are from Iowa and have worked with Earnest Tubb and Web Pierce. They are good, but not as good as the Glaser Brothers you can be sure. Maybe I'm just conceited, but I think we have it. I know it takes time and you've got to be in the right places.

June 3, 1955 – Kaiserslautern, Germany

Well I made TDY finally and now I'm stationed here at Special Services headquarters in Kaiserslautern, Germany [about 80 miles southwest of Frankfurt and 295 miles northeast of Paris, France]. I really like it here. It's as close to civilian life as you can come in the army. We have no inspections, no reveille, and no formations of any kind. We have a show about every night of the week and travel all over Germany. Hold your breath, but I have the best deal the army can offer right now. Few guys get it. It's luck,believe me.

June 5, 1955 – Kaiserslautern, Germany

You know, Dad, you always talk about my rhythm being off; well, I really found that out. But Cal Neumann, our fiddle player, has taught me to play rhythm. And I've really found out about my ignorance. But I'm learning slowly and it will really be an accomplishment. You know people think anybody can play hillbilly, but really you have to learn and study it. I don't know if I'll ever be great, but I'm sure in love with music. And I'm hillbilly from the word go. The more I learn about it the more I like.

June 7, 1955

We had GI parties all afternoon and all night. You know what a GI party is, don't you? Well it's just this: you take a brush in one hand, soap in the other, and away you go. Some deal. Our beds have to be tight, shoes shined, equipment clean, brass shined, and clothes clean. We are to be in Class A uniform, well shaven, and of course the hut must be scrubbed from ceiling to floor. The army is a crazy place, but you sure can't fight it.

June 20, 1955

Garsh, Mom! I wonder if you and dad will ever get out of the rut. You've really had a long hard pull, but I find there just isn't too much in life. If you've got a home and a few things of your own, you're doing okay. I sure hope I can make a place for me as well someday. I know now it's a long hard pull. I'm sure I'll be happy in a home of my own if I ever get one. But I doubt if I will ever have any more than a hotel room. And you know? I hate them already. I still don't know what I'll do when I get out. It will be in December 1956. If it's okay with all concerned, we could get our TV show back, and I could do odd jobs until it got going. We could push personal appearances and make good money if things go right. If not, I can give the Big Southland a try. But I'm not sure just how things will be when I get out. Of course I'd want to push the music for all it's worth, and dad is still a farmer and the kids are his and yours. It will be up to you and them. That's why I thought a winter would be a good time to give it a try. The big boys in country music, Ernest Tubbs, etc., of the *Grand Ole Opry* think like dad, that the Middle West is a good country. But you'd have to hit it with a good outfit. Well, we've got lots of time so I won't worry about it now.

June 25, 1955

I got a letter from home today, in fact two of them, but this *one* sort of shook me up. You sounded like I was trying to shut you out of my life. Well, nothing could be further from the truth. The truth is, life isn't so great here as you think. The only decision I have to make is whether I want to stay TDY or go back to my company. The shows we do stink compared to what I've done in the States. The instruments are worse than any I've ever had before, and our guitar man doesn't play my style at all, so I've had to conform to his. I sing all fast songs or sing with the banjo, which by this time drives me crazy. This is still the army and it's still rotten. I got here because I used some pull. Two service club girls who like my singing and maybe me too, I can't know, just wouldn't give up until I got an audition. Then it just so happened they were organizing a hillbilly band,and the one I had in Mainz wasn't too bad. Then the big stroke of luck came when the Davids boys auditioned me. They were good friends of mine, too. That is, I'd met them once before and they liked my style. So they pulled for me and that's how I got here so quick. Also my guitar player who is strictly jazz. The songs I sing are "Skokiaan," "The Train With A Rhumba Beat," "That's Alright," "Blue Moon of Kentucky," "Davy Crockett," "Yellow Roses," "Hello Sunshine," "Hello My Baby," "Don't Forget," "Chicken Song," "Be Sure There's No Mistake," and so on. Mostly junky arrangements.

I got the tape the other day, and I was so glad to get it. It was good to hear you all again, only it was so short. I'm sure you guys could make it without me. Let's face it, you're good. But so many problems arise. What to do when I get out. Now I'm not going to come barnstorming back home and try to steal all your help with big talk of how good showbiz can be. I've been around long enough to know how bad it can be. If it is satisfactory with everyone, I wouldn't mind trying our old TV spot for a while or one similar and see what kind of a commercial show we could work up, or see if it will work out at all. You see, I get out in December, and if the weather is decent maybe we could at least visit for a month or two. If it just won't work, if it causes too much disturbance, and if my manpower won't give us some spare time evenings, I suppose I'll give the big time a try for a while.

Joe Babcock is in Chicago now and is getting a pretty good band together, so I understand. Joe has asked me to join him if anything happens to the trio. He understands modern country music, and let's face it, *country music isn't three chords any more*. But I guess you should know that I still feel the same about music. Also, that I'm still a country boy and hope someday to be a good country singer.

July 10, 1955

So I decided for sure now, I want you to send my Martin [guitar] as soon as you can. I know it will have to be crated and sent by parcel post. Of course I want you to insure it for all it's worth and then some. Also, see how much it will cost and if it's in the neighborhood of $10, get it on the road right away. Now if you are busy and don't have time to box it, to build the crate, have Semper or Louie build it. I'm sure it wouldn't cost too much, and of course I will pay you as soon as I find out just how much it comes to. I'm really serious, and I've been hesitant for so long because I knew you would have to go to a lot of trouble; this is a busy season, but let's see—July 10th should be sort of the slack season if there is such a thing on a farm. But I do need it, and I'd appreciate it if it could be sent as soon as possible because it will take a couple of months to get here.

Did I tell you I saw Billy Graham? He was in Vogelsberg, not too far from here. Vogelsberg [Rhein-Main Air Base] is the largest American city in Germany. It's where all the officers and their families live.

July 15, 1955

Did I tell you they are making a theatre here for plays and vaudeville, and if I can just get a few more details worked out, I'll be putting a little *Grand Ole Opry* on in it. Of course I've got to exert my skill with a hammer and saw so I can have a part in it but it will be worth it. If we make it work, AFN, the radio station here in Kaiserslautern, will broadcast a half hour of it. It's a good deal and will keep me on TDY. Also, I may be able to move into a hotel and out of this barracks.

July 16, 1955

Some good reports came back to Special Services officers about a certain Tom Glaser who got four encores at a service club. A few near occurrences so I got re-auditioned and now they are getting me and my banjo man some new suits to wear—wait a minute; they are "gay '90s suits." I sing "Hello Sunshine," "Five Foot Two," "Hello My Honey," "Please Don't Talk About Me," and many more with a tenor banjo, ragtime piano, and guitar. Also, I sing "I Walk Alone" with Cal Newman, Mac Weissman's fiddle player to back it. They are going to let us play for money now, they didn't before.

July 22, 1955

Did you know Kaiserslautern is headquarters here in Germany? The general in command of W.A.C.O.M. [Western Area Command] has an office about 100 feet from my barracks. Also, just 6 km from here is Vogelsberg, the largest American city in Europe. All of the officer and civilian personnel working for the government live there. Also some NCOs [non-commissioned officers] and NATO [North Atlantic Treaty Organization] officers live there. It's the closest thing to Stateside we have. I'm pretty lucky, not just because I'm in Special Services, but two of my buddies are drivers and have cars (government issued) checked out to them at all times. So of course I get in some extra travel time. I'm not fooling when I say I know southern Germany better than most Germans. I really like Frankfurt, I'm going back Monday; it reminds me of San Francisco, only of course it's much older.

You know, one thing the army does do is to take the average and below average guy who probably would never get out of his home state on his own, and puts him in some foreign country and makes him live there, and you can't help but learn. It makes everyone love the States more. And also helps us to understand these people with whom we have our international differences. I know it's taught me a great many things.

August 2, 1955

Today is the day we leave on our 10-day tour. Our show would go over much better if we had some women in it, but so far they can't find any good enough. I'm going to Paris for three days when I get back from this tour. There are about six of us from Special Services going. They have special tours for the servicemen that let you see everything and do everything for a cut rate. Three days in Paris will cost $25.00. That includes travel and meals and guided tours. I've been meaning to tell you how the Swiss live here. From 16 to 60 all the men are in the army. They go to training so many times a year and keep their full equipment in their homes. I'll sure go crazy if that's what I'm in for. On our way back from one of our shows, we stopped at a German Gasthaus and really got a reception. Since then, we have gone back, played and sang with them and they always call in all their relations to join the party.

August 5, 1955

Well, I'm going to be glad to get back to the good old U.S.A. and see if I can make enough bread to get a home of my own. I love to travel and I probably always will be on the road, but I've got to have a home where I can do what I please and be my own boss. Sounds to me as if the Glaser Brothers are doing alright; be sure to write and tell me the news.

How good is the girl you're singing with? Must be O.K. You know I've learned a lot about country music from Cal Newman. He's a real hillbilly and has no time for anybody who is on the fence. He loves Faron Young and good bluegrass music. I just can't seem to find myself. To tell the truth, the crowds don't seem to dig my hillbilly voice as good as some of the things I've done. I'm sure I wouldn't have won my trip to New York, but on the TV show I sang "Live Fast, Live Hard, Die Young." They may not even show it. I'm really lost, I'm not even sure I can sing. The real Eddy Arnold type ballads don't go big for some reason.

August 12, 1955

Did I tell you that Special Services started booking us in NCO clubs on our free nights, and they pay us $6.00 a night and $1.50 overtime (per hour). It isn't big money, but it doesn't take big money to get by in the army. It helps. So far we've only played three deals, but there are more on the way. At first when they booked us, they demanded the Davids Brothers and now, believe it or not, they ask for me. It makes me feel pretty good. The cats really dig our swinging band. I may find my style if I keep trying. But I'm not saying for sure what my style will be. They are having a new play here called "Barbara Allen" and I'm supposed to star in it. Of course I'd be a folk song singer like Burl Ives. Most of the guys think my voice is more suited to that kind of singing. I'm going to give it a try; I've always wanted to act and this is my chance. It's a real sad story about a witch boy who becomes human and marries Barbara Allen, but in a year he turns into a witch boy again. I play the witch boy. Jack Palance played it in New York. Really, I'm all worked up about it. The script hasn't gotten here yet, so I haven't started on my lines yet. If I make good in this, it will really be a feather in my cap.

August 15, 1955

Well, I got back from Paris last night, had a big pile of letters waiting for me, and it was really good. Finally got a letter from dad, but I imagine you've been so busy you don't know what's happening. Sounds like times are pretty rough back there. I'm sorry about that. Seems like you've always got a problem. When will you ever get a vacation? Vacations don't come to you. You have to use your right as a free person with a free mind and take one. But I know how it always was and probably always will be. And so far I'm not in a position to compare ways of life. With my personality I know I need a vacation once in a while. Some people are just that way. I'm a fool to travel, I love it. I guess it's a good thing because my career is going to demand a lot of it.

Boy, everybody is getting married. I'm not sure what I'm going to do. For many reasons, which I view with a more mature mind, marriage is not for me right away. Maybe in eight or ten years when I get on my feet. Show business is so uncertain. Joan is a good kid and for many reasons would be a good wife for me, but it will be two years that I haven't seen her so my mind will be completely made up then.

August 18, 1955

If being in the army does nothing else for me, it will make me appreciate what we have in the States. The people here just have to learn to live without what we use every day. The Germans don't hate us too bad; they hate war worse and what it has done to their country. It's really nice here in our new hotel. I don't know how long it will last, but we have no inspections, no harassments of any kind. It's as close to being a civilian as you can come in the army.

August 24, 1955

Jean Smith, our field entertainment director came to a show Monday night and I got four encores. In fact, I was the only one who got any encores at all. I've been singing Faron Young songs and bluegrass songs since I met Cal Newman, and I never got an encore. And every time I sing "Skokiaan," or "Chime Bells," or "The Train

With A Rumba Beat," or "Ghost Riders," it brings down the house. So I guess that is my style.

I met some little English girls, in fact they stay in the same hotel we do. When I say little, I mean 4' 7 ½" and 4' 8" and 4' 9" tall. They weigh 85-90-95 lbs and are 21-22-23 yrs old. They are professional dancers and pretty good. But I bring them to your attention only for the novelty; you see, they must have tea or they cannot exist. They carry it in a thermos, and of course they talk in that weird way. They are really something to see and hear. They look and sound like elves. I've sure met some strange people since I've been in the army. If I could stay on TDY it would be two years put to a very good advantage because I'm learning a lot.

September 1, 1955

Today was payday and I got my usual little $73.00. This army is too much, and I only live for the day I get out. You know I can get out of the army this month easily if I go to school. So if I go back to my Company, I'm going to finish my high school and apply for a college release, and who wouldn't rather spend these months in college than in the army?

I got a letter from Joanie today, and she sounded pretty disgusted with her new life. I guess we all like easy lives. But I'm not sure I'm going to have one. You know every girl I meet seems to think I'm a free ride to fortune and fame. Well, I'm not too bright or too good and I'm mixed up besides, so I think I'll stay single. You know, until a guy has life all figured out, he's going to be very unhappy.

September 2, 1955

Tomorrow I'm going to be 22-years-old and I can't quite see where the time has gone, and what I have done in so much time. I guess that's why most people finally wake up and realize the most important things in life are free, and that a little love is worth more than any type of money. Here in this man's army I see the same things happening every day. Each boy receives more letters from his mother than anyone else. She is trying to keep her boy, and he is trying to break away. Then finally, he finally wakes from his crazy dream of life and finds his true perspective. Just a little happiness is all there is in this life, and the sooner we stop living for mere pleasure and start planning reality, the sooner we get a sample of that happiness. The army is full of men and women of all ranks who make it their life's occupation with the lusts and habits of animals. They value nothing because they actually own nothing; they don't have to worry about anything but their own neck and flesh. And believe me, they live on it. On this post are stationed many WACs [Women's Army Corps]. I know one WAC sergeant who is as sweet and nice as a person can be. The rest are like men. They live, talk, and love like the R.A. [regular army enlisted personnel] men who make the army their career. I'm not a saint by far and I'm not judging them but when my two years of service are through, I'm going to get me a job I really like, and if I only have enough to eat, I'm going to die doing it! So much for that.

September 8, 1955 - El Rhino Hotel, Kaiserslautern, Germany

Our show has changed considerably since we ran *The Little Show*. It's called Entertainment Encore now and is entirely different. I come out alone, and the combo backs me with drums and bass and bongos to things like "Unchained Melody," etc. Last night I got three encores and I was the only one who got one. My Martin [guitar] is sure a dream and I love it very much. It really makes my number big. But my problem is strings—I need them bad. If you ever get to Omaha, please, *please*, get me about *10* boxes of Gibson Bronze Guitar Strings with plain 2nd. Then I will send you the money. It should come to around $18.00 for that many sets. I'm making extra money now at the NCO clubs. This week I made $16.00. That's good money in the army. I really need those strings, though.

Now for the big news: I got promoted to the office. I book all the soldier shows in Western Area Command. Sgt. Barrett, my boss, told me today if I do a good job I would be sure of getting a transfer from 2nd Armed into Special Services. And the booking job is a snap. I really like the job. I work from 8:30 am to 5:00 pm and book shows like mad. I got the job through my good friend, Chuck Feller, who is a good friend of Sgt. Barrett. If I get permanently assigned here, my primary MOs [military orders] will be changed, and I will be out of the infantry and 2nd Armed. I can change my patch from HELL ON WHEELS to a FLAMING SWORD. If I ever get that done, it will be a perfect example of picking yourself up by your boot straps. But I'll keep my fingers crossed.

September 11, 1955

Today is Sunday and we had rehearsal most of the day and night. We are opening with a new show on Sept. 13th and have invited all our company commanders and W.A. Command's Gen. Reeder, along with all the Special Services officers. The show is put on with a narrator, not an MC, and we take an imaginary trip around the world and feature an act from each part of the world. I take care of the tropics with "The Train With A Rhumba Beat." The combo backs me with bongos and tambourines, and Curly plays rhythm. I'm still working in the office, and I do mean work. The booking and telephone invitations of all the officers was up to me for this premier. I sure hope it turns out good, because if I prove to be a good man in the office, I will get transferred from the 2nd Armed Division.

Bill Haney asked me today if I would play with him. He says I have a style all my own and that I should really go when I get out of the army. But talk is cheap. I'm wondering how our trio will sound. Be sure to work on your rhythm guys. Get jazz records and learn a lot of chords and how to play rhythm. I have more trouble with rhythm than anything. Learn to play the songs with the chords written for them, and the time comes out better. *You've just got to know something about music to survive.* Don't think I know it all, or that I'm a big success here. The only reason I'm here is because I had a gimmick. And after I got here I sold myself. If I stay it will be luck because I'm the dumbest guy in the world, and I find it out more every day.

September 14, 1955

We had our command performance last night and although all the officers invited did not attend, it was a huge success. All of our Special Services officers were there and said it was the best show to ever come from W.A. Command. I'm really proud to be a part of it. *Artistry in Autumn* is its name, and with the lighting and sets we have, it's very colorful. I have to make three changes, but I'm not complaining; it's loads of fun. This Thursday, a big write-up comes out about us in the W.A. Com Currier. I'm going to send it to you. And if it is good enough I want you to put it in any paper you can, even the Spalding Enterprise. Also give them my change of address, and if you put the write-up in the paper be sure to say how long I've been here so they will know I haven't been in the infantry. Also, you can say something about my job as booker for Soldier's Shows, but I'll tell you more about that later.

September 17, 1955

Last night, believe it or not, I got *seven encores!* They wouldn't let me stop. First I sang with Matt and his banjo "Hello Sunshine"; I had to do "Five Foot Two" and took two bows on it. I get a kick singing Dixieland. I do a little dance and even rattle some bones. Matt and I dress up in gay ninety suits as you can see in the picture I'm sending. Then I came out with the hillbillies and sang "If You 'Aint Lovin' Then That's Alright," "Live Fast Love Hard," "Chime Bells," "The Train With A Rhumba Beat," and "When the Saints Go Marching In" with the combo. But I still can't keep rhythm and everybody says its showmanship that sells me, not voice. So to put it mildly, I'm a *cheap* vaudeville entertainer. I'm really at my best with

Bill Haney's band. I could make $50 a week if I joined his band. But to keep my deal here, I must play it cool.

No matter how smart we think we are, the only real friends we have are our own family, and when they need each other they should be there. You really don't need anything when things are smooth. But everyday I'm learning the importance of friendship. You can't buy it and you sure need it. A big question to me anymore is "just what is important?"

October 3, 1955

I guess you probably know by now I made out okay with the commanding general and the chiefs of staff. We really played for a lot of wheels that night and we did O.K. I even got two extra encores so when Capt. Ruddick asked them to transfer me they said, "Sure, take him." My company commander back in the 2nd Armed who disapproved my transfer the first time is going to think he was hit by a truck when he hears from all that brass. It sure makes me feel good because now I'm in Special Services all the way.

October 6, 1955

To tell you the truth, nothing I do here seems to be important. I'm playing all the time, but I really can't get good because I can't find good enough musicians. Cal Newman was the last. But right now I fly high with ballads like "Unchained Melody," etc. I like to sing all kinds of music, but it's hard to get good backing and also find a good microphone. Sometimes, when I'm in my best mood I pull a bum mic and it ruins everything. I'd sure like to be with you guys on a TV show down there again. I'll bet we could really wow them now. I've learned a lot since I've had to play for these soldier crowds. It's really hard for another GI to bring the house down when you have a GI crowd.

It's hard to live on $71 a month. We have to buy our own meals when we're on the road sometimes, and with laundry and personal articles the money just flies. Wish I could get another stripe or two.

October 11, 1955

You know life sure is funny. Sometimes I think I'm well on my way and then I feel like low man. I'll make out, but I hate suspense. I like to know what I'm going to do. But who really does, I guess.

They are having a big country music contest here, and it's to find the best country artists in Europe. Of course, I'm going to enter but don't count on my winning. Europe is big and there are a lot of GIs here. You know, it is the same here as in Spalding—everybody is trying to cut everybody's throat. You have to fight all the time it seems. People always work for themselves and if you're in the way, it's too bad. I'm learning a lot anyway and I'm still not sunk. But it's hard to smile when somebody cuts your throat and just as hard when you cut somebody else's. But that's the modern world, and if you're going to survive you've got to play their game.

November 2, 1955

I've got a good deal if I can keep it. I've got many angles, but I can only hope they work. First off, I'm to take over our theatre ballroom in February, and if that goes through I will be Supply NCO of our billets [living quarters], also bus and car driver. The big thing right now is the Country & Western singing contest. It's the all-Europe contest. I'm sure hoping I win. But this army is so crooked it stinks. If it should be that I lose this contest, I'm going to really feel bad. But I guess I see no real reason I should. I'm sort of an on the fence type of singer, and I don't know if I'll be accepted although I sing with guitar and piano accompaniment.

November 8, 1955

I won the W.A.C. finals as country singer and also with Curly Walston's Western Swing Band. I won two 7-jewel alarm clocks, travel models with my name engraved on them and also how I won them. I won the contest by 100 points, the largest margin of the whole contest. Now on to the Nov. 19th all-Europe finals. If I win this, I'll be chosen as the best country singer in Europe. Big Deal.

You know I really did like the climate here until now. *Anymore, it's so foggy it makes driving almost impossible. Last night it took me 4 ½ hours to drive 80 miles.* These roads are so narrow and the towns come so often it's easy to get lost. I'm getting to know the country pretty good, so I make out ok.

Money is my big problem; there are so many things to do and see here, and I probably won't ever have another chance to come to this country. I'd like to see Italy, Arabia, India, England, Scotland, Australia and Africa, too, if I could.

November 10, 1955

The big thing right now is the contest to be held in Nuremberg on Nov. 19th. I am to be assistant bus driver for the trip. Nuremberg is about 150 miles from Kaiserslautern. I'm not sure just what two songs I will use, but "Alone and Forsaken" will be one of them. I have my own arrangement of it, and I do a very lonesome yodel three times during the course of the song. "Jealousy" and "Granada" are also possibilities. You see you have to do something pretty outstanding here as a soloist to make much of an impression. I would really appreciate it if you could send me the words to "Girl in the Woods." Also, if you know of any of these types of songs, could you write and tell me? I'm running out.

You know, when I first came over here, I thought all the Germans hated us, and I looked for every sign that would verify my beliefs. But now I find they are very friendly and very broadminded. On trains or in their cities, when you get lost you can always find friendly people who will give you friendly assistance. The people here are so very poor, as only war can make them, but they are working like mad, and I mean from young to old, women and men, and they are building their cities better than before. But the silent plan seems to be to someday be strong enough to gain back the rest of Germany.

Have I told you about German money? We get half our pay check changed to marks usually. One Deutsche Mark equals twenty-five cents. One Johenning equals 1/100 of a quarter. I haven't seen American money since I left the States; they pay us in what is called script. It comes in only ones, fives and tens. Also, 5¢, 10¢, 25¢, 50¢, all paper money.

November 20, 1955

Guess what, my luck really held out. I'm in the U.S. Army Hospital with laryngitis and of all things, the *mumps!!!!!* To start my sad story I came to Neuremberg on Wednesday. I felt fine until Thursday—I had to miss rehearsals, but I stayed in bed until Saturday, the day of the contest. Up to that time I had only the sore throat and although I couldn't talk I could sing a little. I went through with the contest although it couldn't have sounded too good. I should have known better. They froze me out when I sang "Unchained Melody" and I came in third. Eddie Novack, a kid whom I had already met (and beat) at Ft. Bliss, Texas, took second place as country music soloist. And some kid who sang some of Hank Snow's songs took first place. I got picked to go on tour of France and Germany, and this morning I woke up with the mumps. So I stay here in Neuremberg for a week. I'm in a contagious ward here at the hospital, and that means I can't leave and no one can see me.

I'd rather have lost altogether than come in third. I doubt if I will ever go on with a singing career. I'm not even the best country style singer in Europe where all they have to draw from are GIs. I'm not going to say I would have won it if I hadn't had the cold, but if I had any brains at all I would have gone all out country style. But I will never know for sure now, and I guess it doesn't matter anyway.

I've suspected for some time now, I just didn't have that something that it takes to make a great singer or a great man. But what couldn't be helped must be endured. Isn't that what you always said, Mom?

November 25, 1955

Today it is snowing here in old "Deutschland." Among the first that they've had. Snow is very beautiful here for it is moist and clings to all the trees and funny houses. The little traditions of the people seem to be the same all over Europe, although the dialect may change. Traditions such as the handshake and speaking to those you know or the curtsying of children are the same as when Grandma was a little girl here. You never see a man without a coat in the summertime here, no matter how hot it gets. No matter how poor he may be, he will maintain that self-respect. In cafes, restaurants and *gasthauses*, the people barely speak above a whisper. These people have an elegance that only their proud ancestry can give. My first impression still remains; they are truly the mother nation, and we are the wild, crazy, mixed-up kids. My mumps have practically vanished, and within a few days I will be back in good old Kaiserslautern.

December 11, 1955

I am now what they call a key man here in Special Services since I'm in command of all Soldier Shows happening in Western Area Command. Right now, I am assistant field entertainment director. I'm right under Bill Drawait in the office. But above all, I'm learning so much. All the guys here on TDY are college men, and Bill had a TV show in New York.

I am the MC in our Christmas show, and the combos back me while I sing two songs, "Sing Ting a Ling a Jingle" and "Christmas." First, I come out as Santa Claus dressed and stuffed with pillows. I come through a chimney, a phony prop, I pull some gags and then introduce the combo and they play. I change and come back in a tux to MC the show. I pull gags and bits all the way through with different guys, and we end up singing Christmas carols. It's a lot of fun and I'm really learning show biz. My good friend Chuck Feller really helps me a lot.

December 16, 1955

Seems my job gets bigger all the time. The MC job really keeps me hopping, but I'm going to stick with it until I get it down pat. I don't know if I've told you just what I do. First, I come out as Santa Claus and of course that kills me. Then I have to go out and pull gags and bits besides my own songs. Then at the end I sing "May the Good Lord Bless and Keep You." All in all it's a big farce, but it keeps me TDY and I'm learning all the time.

December 20, 1955

I sure worry about Patt [Tompall's older brother Bob's wife]. Bob is in real trouble now. If only they can keep on a few years. But I guess those are the problems of life that everyone has, and if you are going to get married you might as well expect to face the worst. A man can be a coward and run from it forever. I admire Bob for the job he's doing. Guess he's a true Glaser the way he sticks with it.

You know, one night we can be in a swanky officer's club and the next night in the field or some mess hall. But I love it. Everyone says the show is great; it makes me feel so good since the load is on me. It seems I have to set the mood for the whole cast. But it is making a showman of me.

December 27, 1955

My transfer was disapproved as you know for the second time. Now once it had been approved and there were no vacancies down here. So Bill really went to work, and got my battalion and company commander to agree to an approval. The main reason he works so hard for me is because I work for him. So it's really fair play. But still, I'm not sure I can get transferred until it's in my hands.

January 7, 1956

Right now we are having a big talent search to find talent for February's show. So I've been busy sending publicity and arranging for auditions. Also I'm getting February's bookings ready, which is quite a hassle. Will play 32 shows in 25 nights plus some hospital ward shows. So I see only work. But I love it. After that comes the third all-army talent contest, which will last for two good months. I'm hoping I can make it to the U.S.A.R.E.U.R. finals at least. But I don't know. If by some stroke of luck I should win I'll get to come to the States. But don't count on anything. I'm not as good as I thought. I've found when you meet really big people, or strangers, it's not so much social as intellectual equals who are compatible. Good to hear from you Chas. You should be a pretty good man by now. Responsibility makes a good man of you. Keeps you thinking and your mind alert for quick decisions.

January 11, 1956 – Kaiserslautern, Germany

Bob Hope is going to Vogelbach, Germany, on February 11 and 12. Last night, Jack Hope, his brother and manager, arrived from London with Capt. Ruddick, the W.A.C. captain. Two step cars [trucks driven on airport tarmac with ladders for ascending and descending an airplane] met them at the airbase and I drove one. Jack looks beat and you'd never think he was Bob's brother. He has a very pretty secretary who travels with him all the time. I spent my nights in rehearsal. I'm going to give the folk songs a try. Songs on the order of Harry Belafonte and Burl Ives. They work much better for a single. I don't seem to be a hillbilly singer, ballads seem to fit me much better. I see Eddy Arnold has a new album of folk songs out now. These songs are accepted by everyone. I nearly was in charge of supply, but this was changed. I don't dig the idea of signing for and being responsible for a lot of property. *If I drive for these people that's risk enough. If I goof up once, I could spend the rest of my time in the army paying for some vehicle I will never see again.*

January 17, 1956

Today it happened, my transfer came through, and I've been accepted here at headquarters. This means the world to me, for now I'm out of the infantry and in the Adjutant General's Corps. My M.O.S. will be changed now from "rifleman" to an entertainer's M.O.S. I can take off my 2nd Armored patch and sew on a USA-REUR Flaming Sword patch. It means for the rest of my stay in the army I'm in Special Services; only three of us hold such positions in this command. It is a wonderful opportunity for me. My first project is one I'm sure will be a big success. Bill Diamant says it's all my baby since it's my idea, so I'm in charge of everything. It's going to be called *The European Grand Ole Opry*. Since the U.S. AREUR Country Western music contest, I'm in contact with just about all of the hillbillies here in Europe. I've already got a place to collect them as my first Sergeant loves my singing and country music. So if I can get the guys here on a weekend pass, put them up for one night, and put the show on a Saturday night, they can stay here until Sunday and catch a train back.

I'm going to make it open to the German public so I'm sure of a good crowd. I figure with a little luck and Special Services behind me, it should be a big success. This last week I did two similar shows and they went great. The show I did was called *Country Caravan* and lasted 2 ½ hours.

I don't know if I ever told you about that article about me in the paper. Special Services is going to send you a write-up about me soon, so you'll know just what I'm doing and have done. I'm really not smart or an exceptional singer, but I've been pretty lucky. And I'm thankful for that.

January 22, 1956

Please don't take offense if I don't write often. I just can't think of anything to write about. The things I do and the people I know, you've never seen, so actually small talk is of no value. I tell you all the big things I do or know, or at least what seems big to me. I'm biding my time until next October or November. Since I'm in Special Services I can fly home when I go, so I'll probably stay over here another month and get my discharge as soon as I arrive in the States. That way I won't have to lie around some dirty re-up camp in the States. Kaiserslautern is really on the BOOM. It's just about built back since the war. They really work, but then it's the only way they will ever get back to normal. I'm not picking up German too good, I guess I should buy a book and study it some, but most of the Germans speak English, so why bother. But I'm kind of sorry sometimes that I can't speak it.

Say, could you get me the words to "Scarlett Ribbons?" Harry Belafonte has a recording of it. It's really great. I'd sure like to see the Opry on TV. I don't know if what I've learned will help us in the hillbilly field. I haven't met many hillbillies.

February 2, 1956

It is down to 15 degrees below zero here tonight. It's supposed to be the coldest it's gotten in 60 years. I'm not going to be in the new February Soldier's Show this month. It's a straight pop show and besides this Opry show is going to take a lot of time. Also, I'm working with lights and driving and, too, on the nights Chuck drives I'm working with professional entertainment in various NCO and EM clubs. I have been to the service clubs so many times they think I'm the only talent they have in Special Services. I'm still accepted well and to date my Dixieland songs went over the best of anything in Soldier's Shows.

February 12, 1956

This month I'm not with Soldier Shows but work some with professional entertainment. I sure like it. These German combos are great. I wish I could speak their language better. Last night I played an officer's club in Pirmasens army base, and they made me sing for an hour straight. They just wouldn't stop. The weather here is really cold. The stories you've been hearing, Mom, are true, but we have no storms compared to the States. The roads are slick because they don't push the snow off, but they won't release our bus from the motor pool for places that the highway patrol declares hazardous.

Sorry to hear of the financial status, but things are getting bad all over. Maybe I should take my discharge over here and make some tax-free money playing on this foreign sand. I like the country here, and I've been offered jobs by some German combos. Still, I make most of my money playing hillbilly. As a pop singer I can make only six dollars a night. As a hillbilly, it's $15.00, and I still get more paying jobs as a pop singer than the pop singers. And more jobs as a hillbilly than both of them put together.

February 20, 1956

I suppose you are still wondering how my *Grand Ole Opry* turned out. Well, not too many musicians turned out, but we had a very big and good audience. The theater seats 750 and well over 800 showed, so it was packed to standing room. I used Bill Haney's band and had about 20 acts besides that. Bill Diamant, my boss from New York, was a little amazed at the way it went over.

Chuck Feller is going home in seven more days, and so I will be in charge of all these men here as well as the lighting technician, driving and administrative NCO in the office. How do you like that I'm acting in the capacity of two NCO's and I'm only a private; it's because I've been on TDY so long. Chuck is from Indiana and is the best friend I have had outside the family. He is a good guy, really wise in the ways of the world. He's helped me in a lot of ways and for what reason I will never know.

March 5, 1956

We got moved out of our hotel and back to headquarters, Company 7812, A.U., so I'm going to have to soldier a little again. It seems the new Special Services officer doesn't like me, so he really gave us the shaft. I don't know why, he just doesn't like my face. I'm really learning a lot. Every time I just get going good, I get set back on my ear. Eight more months to go and I'm a free man. There are too many gods here in the army. It's no place for me.

March 22, 1956

Tonight I'm on my first company duty since I've been in the army. It is assistant C.Q. [Charge of Quarters]. Last night was the W.A. Command finals of the third All Army Talent Contest. I was in charge of the lighting. Everyone said I did a wonderful job. I get sort of a kick out of operating a spot. I choose colors for the stage lights and also the color combinations for the spots. It's very interesting work, and I'm learning theater from start to finish. I had my *Grand Ole Opry* again Saturday night. Once again, we had about 800 people in a 750 capacity theater, and the sergeant who sells tickets says they turned away about 200 people. I had a cast of almost 50 this time.

I'll never understand why no one ever did this before. But it's really a success here, and actually the hottest Soldier Show we have. My boss, Bill Diamant, from New York, is just plain bewildered, but backs me 100% because it goes on his record, and the thing is already Europe-wide.

My latest project is with an organist and violinist. They took first and second place at the All-Army contest. We are going to tour as a trio. My bit is to sing folk songs with their music. Did I tell you we are cutting some sides for King Records? I sure hope they are released.

Maybe now would be a good time to tell you about Amsterdam. I have never seen a country or a people so clean. Germany is a pigpen compared to this fabulous little country. The people are so nice and friendly, and most of them speak fair English. They like Americans and treat us like kings. The women, of course, are the most beautiful in the world, I think, mostly because they are so clean. As I told you, three of us went together and rented a German car and drove it down. It costs us about $25 apiece. We put on about 1295 Km (850 miles), and these are some of the cities we went through: Trier, Germany; Luxembourg, Brussels, and Antwerp, Belgium; Rotterdam, Utrecht, Amsterdam, and Den-Haag, Holland. You should see Holland, Dad. It's all like that bottom by the old orchard—good black soil and all the land is tiled so it can drain. They still use windmills to pump off the surplus water, and they have more dikes than you can shake a stick at. And, Mom, you would love the tulips.

I've got 30 days leave time coming up, so I'm going to Italy, Rome, and Venice. I can hardly wait. Also, Switzerland. The army wants you to travel, so they help you all they can.

The weather here is fine, and I am fine. I'm still right-hand man in Special Services and still trying to learn. Thanks a lot for writing so often, Mom, you too, Chuck and Jim. It's really good to hear from you. When I get home and get my summer stock theater going, The Glaser Bros. will have a TV spot on it. Wait and see. If I can make a success of this *Opry*, I'll do it again in civilian life, and I've got three of the best partners you'd ever find. Can't wait to sing with you guys again.

March 28, 1956

Sunday, we cut our tape for King Records. I used one of my songs and one that a friend of Davids Bros. wrote. His name is Jack Redman; the song is "Sentimental Heart." My song is called "Crazy." Starting about April 15th I'm going to take a 15-day leave to Italy. It is pretty expensive but it should be much fun and interesting. What a fascinating country this is over here. Seven more months and I'm on my way home. What a great day that will be. This army is such a drag. By the way, I'm going to send you some facts from my articles here in Special Services, and I want you to put it in the Grand Island papers.

My *Grand Ole Opry* show was over AFN [American Forces Network] and created a lot of talk. The US ARGUR Special Services officer complemented me on it. But still it isn't the kind of show that would be a success in the States.

May 7, 1956

I have been on leave and it wasn't much of a vacation. When I got back and found all the Santa letters from you, I realized how long it had been since I had written. I rushed down to the telephone office and tried to call you, but to make things worse I got a bad connection, so I really done no good. I waited two hours for them to put the call through again, but then the office closed and I had to leave. I hope the telegram straightened things out.

May 10, 1956

I'm going to Italy April 15th. Boy, am I going to live it up. I'm going to try to fly through Rome, and then work my way back. Venice is high on my parade. I'm really excited about it. This country is so fascinating. I'm going to try to go to Monaco if I can. Maybe I can see Grace Kelly (and maybe I can get a drink at her wedding). I can buy a very good, in fact the best, tape recorder here for $250. It's a Grundig, with every convenience and perfection gadget you can imagine. I'm going to buy it.

May 18, 1956

Right now I'm in the midst of putting on another *Grand Ole Opry*. This time I'm doing it in an E.M. club, make some money myself, and also pay the performers. All in all, it's going to be a

Tompall in 1955 (age 22). Photo from the front of a postcard sent from Kaiserslautern during his army enlistment. Courtesy of June Glaser

big show with the square dance team and all. You know it's funny, it's all my show and when the big write-up came out, Red Jones took all the credit himself. But I don't mind, it's good experience for me.

I'm not sure what I'm going to do yet. I do know one thing, I'm not near the man I thought I was, and I am not gaining on it much. I've got to get out of this army or I'll go crazy. I'm lucky, my first sergeant likes me, and the motor sergeant also. They come to all the shows I do with Haney. My first sergeant helps me no end or I'd probably be in the stockade by now. It's a lot of work to put on this *Opry* show. I'm gone all the time. I got my license back again and Tuesday I went to Mainz and Monday to Baumholder. Everyone is excited about the show, sure hope it's good.

I want to tell you about a friend of mine who was MC for our last show. His name is Ron Pitts, but I guess that's not too important. He comes from Oklahoma City, Oklahoma. He is 24 and a dramatic major in college. He was married once to a fashion designer and college teacher, and his parents did not approve of her. One fine day she went to Chicago to a fashion show and never came back. She wrote at first and then wrote and told him not to try to find her—that she would come to him. Well, the poor guy was very much in love with her and just couldn't quite shake it. He is a fairly pleasant guy who likes to wear cowboy boots and thick-rimmed glasses and is tall, dark haired, and pretty good looking at that. Well, when he took his physical to get discharged from the army they found he had cancer of the throat and that it had already spread into his shoulder and arm. If they try to cut out the tumors his right side will be paralyzed, his head will lean on his right shoulder, and of course they must take out his vocal chords. If they don't operate he has less than a year. He doesn't want them to operate because he wants to be an actor, and it's going to be hard with one side paralyzed. But they are going ahead. I'm going down to see him tomorrow. It's a sad situation and I sure hate to see anyone in such a sad condition, but it just goes to show you can't count on anything, so why try. As near as I can gather he doesn't have much of a chance.

May 31, 1956

I am no longer in Special Services *because of the bus accident I was involved in* so don't address my letters to that section anymore. I just couldn't get along with most of the people there. Right now, the colonel has me under discipline and I have ration breakdown. That means I work in the mess hall. I got along fine with the old group, but this set of officers was just too much for me.

My *Grand Ole Opry* show was a big success and I'm going to be doing it as often as I can find time. I paid out $250 and still made a little for myself. Just to show you how Red Jones fits into the picture, I paid him $20 for services rendered. Six more months in this army and I'll be home and out. I just can't stand for anyone to have a finger in my life. Don't feel put out about the Special Services deal, it's best this way. I still play with Haney, and I still have the Opry show. I may get a show over ATN Network soon.

July 10, 1956

Eddy Nowack has written a song he wants me to record. It made me really happy that he would even consider me. It's called, "A New Coat of Lipstick." It's a Floyd Tillman type of song and is very good. Did I tell you that I don't have to pay for the bus? My appeal was approved and I'm released of all responsibility!!!

July 25, 1956

I really had a good weekend, the band was down to Haney's for dinner and then over to Jim Evans for supper. I don't know if you knew or not that a sergeant can bring his family over here and live on government orders, which are pretty nice in most cases. I know quite a few families over here and therefore get invited to a few Sunday dinners. They are nothing like yours, Mom, but they are much better than army chow. I like German food very much, and Italian food is the greatest.

Now comes some advice for any of my brothers who get the urge to join the army. Don't do it. There are many things to do besides coming to this rat race. It's a big world, still there's no place like the United States, which is home. I doubt if I will ever come to Europe again, two years is enough for me. I'm an American and I'm going to live there until I die from this life.

I'm really proud of the reports I hear about you kids and your shows. Now I don't get any letters from anyone outside the family, but those reports are good enough for me. Keep it up. You may get along better as a duo than a trio. I'd like to take this band back to Nebraska. It's as good as any band from the *Grand Ole Opry* the same size. Those people would lose their senses if they ever heard the one Bill Haney and I have planned. I've got to send you a tape of some of our shows. Also, you should hear some of our jam sessions. They play some nice western swing.

July 30, 1956

Me again, I seem to be the unbusiest man in the world these days. I have no job in particular so I'm just bugging out of everything that I can. There is no harassment to speak of, so I just put in my time here quietly and play with Bill's band at night.

The thing I won't be able to get used to is the hard times you speak of. But I imagine I'll starve many a day before I get on my way. One of the first things I'm going to do is go to the *Louisiana*

Hayride. If I can get with them, I may be able to make $100 a week. Once I get on my feet, the trio could give it a try on the big show. I just don't see how we all could go at the same time and starve. If we had a good song, just one appearance would put us on the way on the Hayride. You want to try Channel 10 with Joe. That sounds like a good deal to me. Never pass up a chance or a bigger deal when you have to work for somebody else. Joe's band sounds great to me; never underestimate the musicianship of that boy. Not a one of us has his knowledge of music. A knowledge of music, no matter where you learned it, is the greatest asset you can have if you're going to be in this business.

Right now I'm considered a short-timer, for I have less than 100 days. Still, the harvest will be completed by the time I get back to Nebraska. I'm not sure, but I think I have to go to Fort Bliss, Texas, to be discharged. But my chances to fly home are very good, for I know people in the right places. One way on a boat is enough for me. Chuck Feller still wants to manage me, but I don't know if there will be anything to manage. Our band has an offer to go to Tripoli to do a TV show sometime in August. I sure hope we can get off.

August 7, 1956

The *European Grand Ole Opry* is just about dead. With hundreds of people anxiously waiting to see the next performance, military procedure and routine have prevented what little talent is left from participating. Old short-timer Tom Glaser just don't give a darn any more since my big feud with the colonel. I don't want to give this army anything. Also, I'd sure hate to see Chuck or Jim come into this hole. I'm getting real jumpy anymore; I can't even see a movie without wanting to get back to the good old USA. But someday I'll probably want to come back as a civilian. There is some pretty country here.

As you probably know I have practically no job whatsoever anymore; I'm not really too good for much, but there are some other sections that I can work in, but the first sergeant won't let me go. He wants me here in case something comes out crossways. So I do practically nothing but play my shows on off-duty time. But I'm so short anymore that I couldn't care less. I guess my attitude is all wrong. I don't want to do anything but sing. When Special Services tried to make a janitor of me or office boy, I went in reverse. I never even tried to get along with Col. Scott. But that's the way I am I guess. I'm going to get what I want, and if I can't do that I don't want to do anything.

September 17, 1956

I took a short leave and went to Denmark and Sweden. Copenhagen was wonderful. Also, I stopped in Hamburg on the way back. Boy, these big German cities fascinate me no end. How they can be so old and so modern I'll never know. Dixieland jazz is going great there and it drives me wild to see them play it. Everything was a copy of America. Even the stage was set up like a huge showboat. I'm going to be discharged from Ft. Sheridan, Illinois, but I have no idea when. I'm a real short-timer now.

October 13, 1956

This is probably the last letter I'll write you from over here, so I'm going to try to tell you all the things you should know. First of all, these boxes I'm going to send you must be opened in the presence of the postmaster. They are packed by the stores here, and to be truthful, I'm not really sure what the items are inside.

Item number two: I'm to leave Germany by slow boat on 30 October. That means I should be in New York before the 13th. From there, I go to Ft. Sheridan, Illinois. No later than the 20th of November, I will be out of the army and on my way to Nebraska.

I'd appreciate it very much if no one knows I'm coming, as I'm not going to stay too long, and I don't even want to see any of those Spalding people. I have some connections at [radio station] KWKH *Louisiana Hayride*, but I must be there in January. It looks good for me; it will be twice as good for the trio. But in these two years I've learned much about that kind of life. I'm not going to be the one who drags the rest of the family into it. If they want to come, OK. I know it will be fun, but it may take a few years without money. I'm putting this right on the table to the whole family. No private letters, Dad, and no scheming. But you've always known what I want to do, and I'm going to try to do it. I'm almost too old now, though.

4

Arthur Godfrey's Talent Scouts

Louis had plans for Tompall and his brothers as soon as Tompall returned home in October of 1956. He encouraged them to enter the *Arthur Godfrey's Talent Scouts* competition. This was a nationally syndicated television and radio show that was on CBS from 1946 to 1958; it was the precursor to television shows such as The Ed Sullivan Show and today's American Idol and X-Factor. Entertainers who performed on the show over the years have included such diverse acts as Lenny Bruce, Patsy Cline, Tony Bennett, Pat Boone, Don Adams, Marilyn Horne, and Roy Clark, to name just a few. The competition to get on the show was tough, and few made it through. In fact, both Buddy Holly and Elvis Presley auditioned for the show, but neither was chosen to perform.

The show was based in New York City, but Arthur Godfrey had talent scouts who would travel across the United States seeking contestants for their national television show. Acts would audition, and the talent scouts would select that week's performers. Mr. Godfrey also traveled throughout the country and would sometimes record his shows on location. Each week three acts performed, and one was chosen the winner based upon a meter that judged the audience's applause. The winner of the *Talent Scouts* television show received a $1,000 cash prize, as well as the opportunity to tape a daily radio program with Arthur Godfrey for one full week.

When the show's talent scouts were looking for acts in Omaha, Nebraska, Tom, Chuck, and Jim were there. Out of the hundreds of musical acts auditioning, the Glaser Brothers and two other acts—a classical pianist and an opera singer—were chosen to perform on the weekly show. The show was taped before a live audience. Louis Glaser introduced his sons and they performed the song "Honeycomb." When they had finished playing, the applause was so loud and went on so long, the show's host, Arthur Godfrey, was unable to announce the week's winner.

As winners of the weekly talent show, Tom, Chuck, and Jim had the opportunity to sing a couple of songs each day for a full week on Arthur Godfrey's morning radio show. A little known fact is that these daily Nebraska on-location radio recordings took place deep within Offutt Air Force Base, at the Strategic Air Command (SAC) base located in Bellevue, Nebraska, about eight miles south of Omaha.

According to Tompall, Arthur Godfrey was a "good guy." He liked country music and he liked The Glaser Brothers. Tompall recalled that early one morning, prior to the taping of the radio show, it was discovered that Jim Glaser's guitar cable was not working. So, at 5:00 a.m., Arthur Godfrey pulled some strings, contacted a nearby music store and had them open early so that a replacement cable could be obtained.

Not long after winning the *Arthur Godfrey's Talent Scouts* competition, Tom heard that well-known country music recording artist Marty Robbins would be performing in Grand Island, Nebraska. Tom and his brothers were excited. They hatched a quick plan, jumped into a car with their father, Louis, and drove 70 miles to the location where Marty was performing. Their plan was to have Louis seek out Marty Robbins and try to get Marty to agree to a

Tompall Glaser in 1957 (age 24) at the start of his professional music career, Courtesy of June Glaser

brief live audition. After some convincing salesmanship by Louis, they were led to Marty's dressing room, where Marty listened attentively while Tom, Chuck, and Jim sang a short medley. Tompall remembered that Marty's band members were also in the dressing room, and that Marty's bass guitar player was especially impressed with The Glaser Brothers' tight vocals. In fact, he was so impressed that he convinced Marty to hire the trio to perform as background singers at an upcoming concert in Phoenix, Arizona.

So, Tom, Chuck, and Jim piled into Tom's old Pontiac and made the 1,300 mile, twenty-some hour trip to Phoenix and began their professional music careers in 1957. Tompall remembered that for this performance, Marty wore a white sports coat, which fit the theme of his recently released song, "A White Sport Coat (And A Pink Carnation)."

Later in 1957, Tompall became the first of the three Glaser brothers to move to Tennessee. He first moved to Memphis and shortly thereafter married hometown sweetheart, Rose Marie (Rosie) Glassmaker. Rosie was from a well-known local Nebraska family—her father was the local dentist in Spalding. Tom and Rosie lived in Memphis for eight months. Then, in 1958, Tom was hired by Marty Robbins to join him in Nashville as part of the *Marty Robins Roadshow*, and Chuck and Jim joined Tom in Nashville soon thereafter. At this point, Tom was 24-years-old, Chuck was 21, and Jim was a mere 19.

According to Tom's brother John, their father was not keen on his sons moving from rural Nebraska to the big city of Nashville, Tennessee. Louis was fine with his sons performing in nearby communities, but he was vehemently opposed to them becoming full-time professional musicians. He not only lost his farmhand help, but was also quite concerned about the potential negative impact that Nashville might have on his sons, especially on young Chuck and Jim. Also, keep in mind that in those days country music, or "hillbilly music" as it was known then, was generally not well regarded in any part of the United States, but especially so in rural communities such as Spalding, Nebraska. Although Louis expressed his concerns, he was all but ignored by his three musician sons.

It was during this period, when first spending time with Marty Robbins, that Tom began using the name "Tompall," which is a combination of his first name, Thomas, and his middle name, Paul. The idea for the name spelling of "Tompall" came quickly to him, and was <u>not</u> the result of taking part of his name from the popular "Pall Mall" brand of cigarettes, which is the legend I had been told when I was growing up.

Tompall wanted to differentiate himself from a fairly well-known folk singer by the name of Tom Glazer who was active in the music business when Tompall moved to Nashville. Glazer was a music book author, radio show host, performer and songwriter. He was perhaps best remembered for writing the children's song "On Top of Spaghetti."

Tompall had decided that in Tennessee he would emphasize the "a" in Glaser as a "long a" sound and the "s" as a "z"—similar to how it is pronounced in the word "laser." As such, it was too confusing to have a Tom Glazer and a Tom Glaser (pronounced the same way) in the public eye.

This new pronunciation of Glaser did not sit well with Louis Glaser. Until the day he died Louis continued to pronounce his name the old "correct" way, emphasizing his German heritage, with the "a" as a "short a" (as in "glass") and the "s" as a *soft* "z" to make the sound "gla-zer." In fact, to this day, most of our Nebraska relatives still refer to themselves using the German-based Glaser pronunciation.

The trio's name "Tompall & The Glaser Brothers" came about because Marty Robbins had begun promoting the three Glaser brothers and had signed them to his record label, Robbins Records. Marty did not feel that a group could become as successful in country music as a solo artist, so Marty initially only wanted to sign Tompall. However, Tompall suggested that his name be accentuated and then add his brothers. Marty was okay with that approach.

Tompall, Chuck, and Jim spent about two and a half years touring with Marty Robbins. Initially, the three brothers and Rosie lived together in a small one-room apartment located above a house garage. One of Rosie's college friends also lived there. During this time, Chuck and Jim found their new freedom exhilarating and would frequently spend their evenings out of the apartment. They'd go bowling and would stay out very late. In the morning when Tompall and Rosie got up, and Rosie's friend left for college classes in the morning, Chuck and Jim would come home to go to bed.

Money was tight in the early Nashville years. Typically, they were paid $100 a day when they worked, but they did not work every day. And this $100 was split among the three of them. To help make ends meet, Tompall, Chuck, and Jim recorded songs as session (musician for hire) musicians. The use of session artists was widespread in Nashville at the time. The brothers would use aliases such as "The Jim Glaser Singers" for these sessions so that they didn't break their contractual obligations to Marty Robbins. Some of their session recordings were released under names that the brothers were not even aware of. For example, a folk album using their voices was released under the name "Newcastle Singers."

Tompall also earned some money from songwriting during this time. Under his Robbins Records music label, Marty Robbins paid Tompall an additional $100 per week to write songs. He was paid by Marty's publishing company, but any royalties he earned as a result of his songwriting were first paid to the publishing company to reimburse them for his salary. Tompall shared his royalty earnings during these early Nashville years with his brothers Chuck and Jim.

Tompall remembered that Marty Robbins recorded two songs that Tompall wrote, and that he earned $10,000 in song royalties for these, quite a bonus after earning so little for so long. One of these songs, "Running Gun" was co-written by Tompall and his brother Jim.

There are three major song licensing organizations: ASCAP, BMI, and SESAC. Publishers register songs with one of these organizations, which then keeps track of where and how often the publisher's songs are played and collects the royalty payments. After subtracting their operating expenses, the licensing organization pays out the remainder of monies to the appropriate publisher. Individual songwriters typically sell their rights to a song for a set amount, and the publishing company pays the songwriter for the song rights. Or, the songwriter and publishing company may agree to split any proceeds on a percentage basis, typically 50/50. In a separate transaction, performance artists are paid by their record companies whenever a song they have recorded is purchased.

While working as backup singers for Marty Robbins, The Glaser Brothers were allowed to record their own songs. Their first single "Five Penny Nickel" written by Chuck Glaser was released by Robbins Records. Soon after its release, Marty Robbins was signed to appear on the November 19, 1957, *American Bandstand* television show. Marty asked that Tompall, Chuck, and Jim be allowed to perform their new single, and the show's producers agreed.

Tompall said that he and his brothers *lip-synched* their record, just like everyone else on the show had done before them. According to Tompall, the main reason it is so rare for a song to be sung live is because it's in everyone's best interest to avoid any number of potentially embarrassing surprises that may otherwise occur in a live show.

Tompall remembered that after their *American Bandstand* performance, the brothers were told that Dick Clark wanted to speak with them. When they met with Dick, he asked them to endorse the check they had just been given for their Bandstand performance back to him. So, while they received some television exposure, they made absolutely no money from this appearance. Recently, more information about how things worked during this era has come to light. An informative film in this regard is Wage$ of $in.

Typically, all three of the Glaser brothers provided background vocals for Marty Robbins during the two and a half years they were with Robbins. However, on perhaps Marty's best-known song "El Paso" taken from the album *Gunfighter Ballads and Trail Songs*, only Jim Glaser sang in the background.

During these early years of singing in Nashville, Tompall & The Glaser Brothers provided background vocals for many recording artists due to their reputation for providing quality harmonies. Here is an abbreviated list:

- **Marty Robbins** – various recordings from 1957-1959

- **Johnny Cash** – various recordings from 1959-1961, and into the 1970s
- **Chuck Mayfield** – "Who's the Biggest Fool," 1959
- **Claude King** – "The Commancheros," November, 1961, #71 on *Billboard Chart*
- **Roy Orbison** – "Leah," 1962, #25 on *Billboard Chart*
- **Hank Snow** – various recordings
- **Patsy Cline** – various recordings
- **Jimmy Driftwood** – various recordings
- **George Jones** – various recordings

In 1959, Chuck Glaser was drafted into the U.S. Army. Tompall called childhood friend Joe Babcock to take his place until Chuck's military service was ended, some two years later. Babcock said that Tompall's call changed his life forever. He was living in his car in California at the time that he received Tompall's call, basically "starving" while waiting to catch a break as a singer.

Babcock actually began making a living from playing music in Nashville after joining Tompall and Jim. He became a session artist, wrote songs, and later joined the cast of the *Hee-Haw* television show. He remained with Hee-Haw for the entire time the series aired on TV—from 1969 to 1997.

Joe Babcock shared some of his memories about Tompall:

I kept in touch some during my college years. I worked on farms and ranches during the summers to pay my way through college; many times I'd finish up the day of putting up hay, drive over to the Glasers, and play music till late in the evening. Then I'd drive back to where I was working, get up at 6 in the morning, and go back at it. I remember part of that time Tom was in the army. Then I went to California to take a year in Theater Arts at UCLA. After that I decided to try to make a go of it in music or starve, which I almost did. I had a few paying jobs, worked the San Gabriel Valley Barn Dance for nothing, and played at a restaurant called the Horn Restaurant with my friend Jackie Lee Cochran on Friday and Saturday nights for all we could eat. I put out a record that did nothing, and I was really poor, living out of my car part of the time, getting by on a few jobs like playing for supermarket openings from the back of a truck for $5 apiece for 3 hours.

In December of 1958, I was broke, out of work, had no income, and had no money even for Christmas presents. I had become a Christian a year earlier, so I said a prayer to the Lord promising that if he helped me get into music somehow, I would not abuse it. As I recall, it was only a short time later that Tompall called, said he had traced me through my mother, and told me how Chuck was going to the army. He said that they were trying to think of someone who could take his place and that my name kept coming to their minds: 'I wonder what Joe is doing.'

Tompall said, 'Joe, I know you're really tearing them up in California (he heard this from my mother, I guess) but could you possibly take off for a couple of years and come out and sing with us on the *Grand Ole Opry* and tour with Marty Robbins?' Well, everything I owned, which wasn't much—a guitar, an amp, and a few clothes,was in my car so all I had to do was go get in it and drive. However, as I was broke, I had to sell my car, and Jackie Lee drove me out to Nashville in his old Cadillac.

I got there with $60 and Tom said, 'We're on the *Friday Night Frolics* this Friday and we have to get you a suit.' So we went down to Levi›s and bought me a suit. It cost $60 so I was broke again, but Friday and Saturday we played the Opry and I was on top of the world, playing and singing with the Glasers and Marty Robbins. I have been very blessed in the music business and have thanked Tom, Jim, and Chuck many times for changing my life. I met my beautiful wife Carol here, have five wonderful children and have been in the music business professionally now for 52 years.

In 1959, Marty Robbins told Tompall that he wanted to break up the three-brother Glaser group. He wanted Tompall to go off on his own, wanted Chuck to get involved in the business end of music, and wanted Jim to continue to sing backup for Marty. So Tompall, Chuck, and Jim decided it was time to leave Marty Robbins and strike out on their own. Marty sold their recording contract to Decca Records, and the three brothers began recording and performing as a main act.

It seems that Marty was not pleased with the Glaser brothers' decision. Tompall said that Marty would taunt them. For instance, when both Marty and Tompall & The Glaser Brothers performed at the *Grand Ole Opry*, Marty would be backstage making loud comments and annoying noises while Tompall and his brothers were performing. Before long, Tompall had more than enough of Marty's high jinks, and he confronted Marty. His problems with Marty stopped then and there and never recurred.

5

Mr. Johnny Cash

As luck would have it, Johnny Cash's manager was looking for a vocal group to work regularly with Johnny Cash as a supporting act. This included local performances as well as performances across the country. Initially, Johnny's manager wanted to hire the Jordanaires. However, the Jordanaires said that they were committed to working with Elvis Presley and wouldn't have enough time to also perform with Johnny. Gordon Stoker of the Jordanaires suggested that they talk to Tompall. The manager went to see Tompall, Chuck, and Jim perform—and he liked what he saw. He offered to hire the group at a rate of $100 per day *for all three of them*. While it wasn't much money, it offered steady pay so they accepted his offer. Tompall remembered that he and his brothers were responsible for paying their own expenses, including hotel charges, and that these expenses alone amounted to $40 or more per day. When they played with Johnny, the three of them traveled together from gig to gig in their own cars.

Eventually, Johnny Cash started paying for the three brothers' hotel bills, and he also gave them a raise.

Tompall fondly remembered the days of performing with Johnny Cash, and said these times were among the best in his music career. Tompall said that Johnny Cash treated everyone in his band fairly, partly because Johnny remembered "where he came from." Johnny had grown up poor, and he never forgot that fact. Tompall considered Johnny Cash one of his heroes.

During their time with Johnny Cash, Tompall, Chuck, and Jim played in a wide variety of venues, including the Steel Pier in Atlantic City; a six-week run at the Showboat Casino in Las Vegas, in 1960; and a 1962 performance in Carnegie Hall in New York City. Tompall said that Johnny had laryngitis the night of the Carnegie Hall concert and apologized to the audience for losing his voice. However, he told them that he was still planning to perform and that he would "whisper the words" to his songs, if need be. That's exactly what he did when his band played "I Walk The Line." Tompall still choked up when thinking about that performance.

Johnny Cash wrote many successful songs and one night Tompall asked him his secret to writing a hit song. Johnny shared that he had a fondness for listening to old "Leadbelly" (Huddie William Ledbetter) songs and "changing them up."

Luther Monroe Perkins was a member of the *Tennessee Three*, which was the backup band for Johnny Cash. Tompall recalled that Luther was quite a character. To make his point, Tompall shared the following story: "Luther would travel from show to show in an old camping trailer. One night, Johnny and I were standing outside the Starlight Hotel in Las Vegas by the swimming pool. Suddenly, all of the lights in the area flickered, and then everything went dark. Johnny turned to me and said, 'Luther's here.' Apparently, Luther's camper had an electrical short, and every time he connected his wiring at a campsite the same end result took place."

Johnny Cash recorded several songs written by Tompall, Chuck, and Jim over the years, and Tompall & The Glaser Brothers sang background vocals on many Johnny Cash recordings during the 1960s and 1970s.

According to Tompall, Johnny Cash and Marty Robbins were as different as night and day. He respected both men for what they had accomplished, but Johnny Cash will always hold a special place in Tompall's heart.

In 1965, talent agent Don Light introduced the Glaser brothers to producer and songwriter Jack Clement while they were touring with Johnny Cash. Clement (known by many as "Cowboy Jack") liked what he heard and brought the Glaser Brothers to MGM Records that signed the group in 1966. Sadly, Clement passed away on August 8, 2013, as a result of liver cancer.

Jack Clement was a Nashville stalwart and was inducted into the Country Music Association's *Country Music Hall of Fame* shortly before his death. He was a well-known and much respected Nashville singer, songwriter, producer, engineer, and song publisher. He worked with many of the great Nashville artists such as Johnny Cash, Waylon Jennings, and Jerry Lee Lewis. Clement was a music icon. In fact, the Irish rock band U2 stopped to visit with him when they were in Nashville. For more information about him, refer to his website at www.cowboyjackclement.com.

I had the privilege of speaking briefly with Clement but, unfortunately, connected with him shortly after a major fire had destroyed his recording studio. While he wasn't in a very talkative mood, he did have this to say about Tompall:

> I produced a lot of music for Tompall. By producing, I mean that I found songs, sometimes wrote songs, came up with musical arrangements, etc. I also helped get Tompall recording contracts.
>
> What I remember most about Tompall is the fact that he was 'independent from others'—such as from record companies like RCA. I also recall that Tompall wasn't afraid to try different musical genres, including rock 'n roll, as evidenced by

the hit 'California Girl and the Tennessee Square,' which I just happened to write.

I feel that among Tompall's greatest contributions to country music were his ability to find songs and his singing with his brothers. The Tompall and the Glaser Brothers trio was different from others in Nashville and they were well-received by the public.

6

Tompall & The Glaser Brothers As A Main Act

The 1960s represented a time of tremendous social changes across the entire United States, and Nashville was not immune. Segregation still existed but "sit ins" were being staged to bring attention to race inequality. John F. Kennedy was elected president, and movies were still being filmed in Technicolor. By 1969, young men were being drafted to fight in the Vietnam War.

The City of Nashville was influenced greatly by its Davidson County Sheriff back in the decades of the 1960s and 70s, some going so far as to say the sheriff ran the city back then; it was not uncommon to hear racist remarks while having lunch in a city diner. The city's population was still relatively small, approximately 170,000 people in 1960, compared with its population of 610,000 today. Eighth Avenue was rife with "health spas" (whore houses) in the 60s and 70s, and the influence of schools like Vanderbilt and Belmont was only beginning to be felt. Clearly, it was a different time and Nashville was a much different city than it is today.

Within this atmosphere, the general business establishment in Nashville was unyielding and remained firmly entrenched, cling-

Photo courtesy of Lekogm

ing to its old ways even during this time of upheaval. The music business in Nashville was no different. Compared to places like Los Angeles, where the music industry thrived during this time, Nashville was much more conservative, stodgy, and slow to change.

If you are a Southerner you understand the history and culture of the South—you've lived it. But if you haven't lived in the southern states, it may come as a surprise that a caste system thrived in Nashville and, for the most part, people were born into their situation in life. Nashville is in the heart of the Bible Belt and has more churches per capita than any other U.S. city. White Protestants controlled the vast majority of the positions of power, and they often did not look kindly on people of different races and religions, including Jews and Catholics.

If you were born with money, you were treated one way (the "best" way). If you made money later in life, you were treated another way (a "good" way). Those who didn't have much money were treated yet a different way (at best, an "okay" way), and those who were considered poor were treated worst of all.

Tompall found himself at the bottom of this caste system. A white, Catholic, farm lad from Nebraska—a man who many thought was a Jew because of his last name and the way he looked.

Dave Hickey is an art critic and writer. He has written for magazines such as Rolling Stone, Art News, Harper's Magazine, and Vanity Fair. He is currently a university English professor. Hickey knew Tompall when he lived in Nashville. In those days, Dave was trying to break into the Nashville music scene, writing songs and trying to get them published. According to Dave:

> In some ways, Nashville is a terrible town. One reason is that it is not a city where someone can socially move up. Everyone in Nashville believes they're going to die at the level they were born at. In contrast, in the West—and in Texas—people always feel like they will make it and move up in life. But there's a

strong culture in Nashville that makes it feel that it is impossible to move up. For example, one night Tompall and I were trying to find a place to eat, and I told Tompall that he should just join the Belle Meade Country Club. Later, I discovered that Belle Meade wouldn't allow country music people in their country club. So there was a real class distinction there that had nothing to do with money, just 'Old Nashville' trying to keep their status quo.

Tompall recalled similar observations about those days in Nashville. However, the discrimination that he experienced first-hand has become even clearer as time has passed. When you are in the moment, when you live through current experiences, there is no choice but to either give up or to press on. Tompall was no quitter. He was determined that *nothing* would stop him, certainly not the existing Nashville music establishment.

Soon after leaving Marty Robbins and striking out on their own, Tompall & The Glaser Brothers travelled the world. In 1963, their booking agent arranged a tour of army bases; they were well received by the soldiers. The Glasers performed in foreign locations such as Japan and Taiwan. During the time they were in Taipei, typhoon *Gloria* struck. Gloria was the sixth largest typhoon to ever hit Taiwan and had winds in excess of 100 mph and rainfall of more than 49 inches.

The typhoon effectively shut down Taipei. Unfortunately, Jim Glaser's foot became infected while they were in Taiwan, and he became deathly ill. Tompall frantically searched the city to get Jim a penicillin shot and eventually found an army nurse to give him that shot. Luckily, Jim regained his health quickly, and the Glasers were able to complete their tour.

While the brothers were in Taipei, Tompall received an urgent call from Anita Carter. Anita was one of Momma Maybelle Carter's daughters, and the sister of June Carter Cash. Anita was a strikingly beautiful woman, and some say that she even caught the eye of Elvis Presley. She was a frequent performer on the *Grand Ole Opry* with other members of the musical Carter Family.

Anita had called Tompall to tell him that she was pregnant with his child. "She was in love with me and wanted me to marry her," Tompall said.

But Tompall was sterile due to his bout with the mumps when he was 22-years-old. He told Anita that since he was unable to have children, there was no possible way that the child could be his. Nevertheless, Tompall was told that his name would be put on the child's 1964 birth certificate. As a result, his relationship with Anita ended soon thereafter.

Tompall did not otherwise speak about his romantic dalliances over the years when he was active in the Nashville music scene, other than to say, "I did all right with women."

Tompall mentioned that he has a soft place in his heart for children, and that he had briefly considered adopting a couple of Japanese girls when he was married to Rosie Glaser. However, he never moved forward with this.

For most concerts in these early years, Tompall and his brothers charged between $1,000 and $1,500 per performance for their trio. From this gross amount, they had to pay travel expenses, the band, and other expenses. Therefore, their typical gross was much less than $500 apiece. According to Glaser Studio sound engineer Kyle Lehning, the Glasers often were on the road from Thursday morning until Monday afternoon, performing across the country.

While Tompall, Chuck, and Jim regularly practiced together when they were living in Nebraska, they found it was unnecessary to rehearse as often once they began playing in Nashville. Band members that backed them up while they were on the road would listen to their records beforehand and were then ready to jump right in and play at the Glaser Brothers concerts.

Many times, payment for performances was made to Tompall in cash. He carried the money in his boot so he would not get robbed. I remember Tompall's brother John Glaser saying that he visited Tompall after one of his concerts in Omaha, Nebraska, during the 1970s and that Tompall pulled a wad of $10,000 in cash out of his boot. Tompall said that in all of his years of performing he never experienced a robbery attempt.

Sometimes it was difficult to get paid. At a concert in Oslo, Norway, he remembered that a promoter had an incredibly awesome sound system that allowed not only the audience to hear concerts, but also anyone else remotely near the performance stage, even though they were outside the paying seats. As you might guess, hundreds of people stayed outside the open auditorium and did not pay for tickets. As a result, the promoter lost thousands of dollars. He quickly understood the error of his ways and the fact that it was too late to do anything about it. So he proceeded to drink…and drink…and drink…until he got wasted. After the show was over, he protested making full payment to Tompall; however, in the end he did pay what he had agreed to.

Tompall spoke fondly about country music legend Hank Snow and said that Hank performed at several Wembley Festival concerts. Hank was a well-known country music artist, who was perhaps best known for two of his hit records, "I've Been Everywhere" and "I'm Movin' On." Tompall said that the Glaser Brothers can be heard singing backup vocals on Hank's recording of "I've Been Everywhere" as well as on several other recordings throughout the 1960s.

According to Tompall, "Hank was a lovable—at times, a bit strange—little man." Once Hank asked Tompall to watch his guitar and suitcase at an airport, and then he left for several hours. Since he was gone for so long, Tompall eventually just left the items right there on the tarmac. To this day, Tompall does not know if Hank ever got his things back. Tompall also remembered that once Hank asked each of the Nashville-based Wembley performers to stay up all night for a group photo—and they did.

Jimmie Rodgers Snow is the son of Hank Snow and an accomplished musical performer in his own right. Jimmie has spent the majority of his professional career as a preacher with a ministry that included 30 years as pastor of Nashville's Evangel Temple. The Nashville church became a familiar place of worship for many country stars. Pastor Snow was also the host of *Grand Ole Gospel Time* at the *Grand Ole Opry*; it began in 1972. Each Friday night Pastor Snow would invite a country music guest to sing on his show. Tompall & The Glaser Brothers performed on his *Grand Ole Gospel Time* show in the mid-1970s.

Jimmie remembers that Tompall was often at his home when Jimmie was growing up, hanging out with his father, Hank. Tompall and Hank Snow frequently drank alcohol during these visits. More likely than not, when the two of these men got together there would be some resulting "craziness," according to Jimmie. He remembers Tompall and Hank playing Cowboys and Indians with loaded guns.

Sometimes, Tompall and Hank would gather in Hank's small, in-home recording studio to experiment. Since Tompall & The Glaser Brothers sang backup on several of Hank's recordings, this gave Tompall and Hank the opportunity to perfect upcoming studio sessions.

Jimmie said that his father, Hank, had many acquaintances but very few friends. Hank could count his circle of true friends without using all the fingers of one hand. And Hank considered Tompall to be one of his few friends.

Tompall thought so much of Hank Snow that he and his brothers reunited in 1990 at Hank's request to perform at his tribute show. This was the last public performance of Tompall & The Glaser Brothers. Tompall attended Hank Snow's funeral in 1999 and was quoted by a newspaper as saying, "he's around more *Grand Ole Opry* stars now than he would be if he were still here."

Tompall, like his father, didn't take crap from anyone. One night he attended a BMI party, and a drunken person came in and started calling him all sorts of insulting names. Tompall told this guy to meet him in the Professional Club bar. Once there, they began to fight—and Tompall kicked his ass.

A club manager ran behind the bar, grabbed a loaded shotgun and chased the two of them out of the establishment. Later, in a strange turn of events, this same person booked time at the Glaser Sound Studios on several occasions. Tompall felt this was his way of apologizing to Tompall for being a jerk. Whatever the reason, Tompall always made this guy pay for his studio time in advance.

Sometime around 1966, as Tompall & The Glaser Brothers' popularity rose, a fan club was started in the USA. Peggy Motley, one of the secretaries at Glaser Publications, answered fan mail for Tompall, Chuck, and Jim. Later, Tompall would have his own fan club, known as the *Tompall Glaser Appreciation Society*, based out of London, England, and run by ardent fan, Jane Glover (now Jane Poole). More about Jane later.

During this time frame, Peggy Motley took a temporary leave of absence from WSM Radio to work for the Glasers. She provided assistance at Glaser Publishing, helping track royalty payments and doing other office jobs. However, for the most part, she ran the Glaser Brothers Fan Club from her home. Peggy was charged with creating brochures and cards that contained updated information about each of the three Glaser brothers and mailing these items to The Glaser Brothers' fan base. Without email in those days, this was a very labor intensive project.

Peggy said that she can't recall the exact number of fan club members but said it was "somewhere over 100 and less than 1,000." One of the things that Peggy liked best about heading up the Glaser Brothers fan club was that several fans sent her nice gifts as personal thanks for her work as head of the club. Peggy said that, to this day, she remains a big fan of Tompall & The Glaser Brothers and that she really loves their music and their beautiful harmonies.

In these early years of entertaining as a trio, Tompall, Chuck, and Jim used to travel to all of their music shows by car. At first, Tompall and Chuck drove Buicks, and Jim drove a Mercury Comet. Sometimes they leased their cars and other times they bought them outright. After thousands upon thousands of road miles were put on these vehicles, the brothers each bought a station wagon. When driving their station wagons, an air mattress was put in the back so two of the brothers could sleep while one drove. Later, each of the brothers purchased Lincoln Continental Mark IVs that they leased over an 18-month time period.

As the years passed, the brothers began renting large buses when they travelled. Band members rode along with the three brothers, but Tompall said that there was not much interaction among himself, Chuck, and Jim while they were on the road going from performance to performance in these huge buses.

Tompall & The Glaser Brothers toured mainly across the United States. However, they also performed internationally. Generally, they played in smaller venues such as clubs, bars, concert halls, auditoriums, and outdoor stages. However, they also performed at several amphitheatres and at some of the larger county fairs.

It is important to realize that country music audiences back in the 1960s and 1970s were completely different from today's. There were no country artists putting on "mega-concerts" at this time, and attendance by 500 people or so was considered a decent turnout. In fact, even after *Wanted! The Outlaws* was released in 1976, Waylon Jennings was still playing the small venues. For instance, in 1980 he performed at the Mississippi River Festival in Edwardsville, IL.

Those days were akin to the early years in professional sports. The players worked just as hard back then but received only a pittance in compensation for their efforts compared to today's professional athletes.

Tompall & The Glaser Brothers toured mainly across the United States. Tompall mentioned that the Carolinas were a good venue for Tompall & The Glaser Brothers. "We went back there several times, although we never quite achieved 'superstar' status there."

Hubert Long was the initial talent/booking agent for Tompall & The Glaser Brothers. He was an influential talent promoter and booking agent during the 1950s to 1960s, and he worked with clients such as country music artists Bill Anderson, Faron Young, and Webb Pierce. Long earned a 15% commission for booking the Glasers across the USA and internationally. Later, the brothers began booking themselves, which allowed them to forego paying someone to do it for them. The money they saved allowed them more flexibility in the price they charged people who wanted to hire them.

Tompall & The Glaser Brothers became well known for "singing over" one another. Picture this: Tompall would stand at the microphone by himself, or with Chuck, and he would begin singing a song that required progressively higher and higher notes on the musical scale. When he reached a note that he could no longer easily sing, Jim jumped to the microphone and began singing these higher notes. Then, as Jim began moving back down the musical scale singing lower and lower notes, Tompall would gently (and sometimes not so gently) nudge Jim out of the way and would start singing once again. This took place as one seamless effort. If you closed your eyes, it would sound like just one person with a tremendous range was singing the given song.

There are other music acts today that mimic this performance routine, but Tompall & The Glaser Brothers did it first, and many say, did it best. Tompall said that he first came up with this idea when Tompall & The Glaser Brothers were playing at a bar in Toronto, Canada. This particular location had just changed from a rock 'n roll format to country music. The crowd was not responding to their country music, so Tom suggested the "singing over one another" approach to his brothers. It took only moments for the crowd to respond enthusiastically to the brothers' on-the-spot act change. From that point on, this technique became standard in their live performances; they kept it in their singing routine for the remainder of their professional careers.

Tompall said that he was the primary marketing person of their group, and that he went to talent agencies, radio stations, and artists' dressing rooms in order to promote Tompall & The Glaser Brothers, as well as songs they had written or published. They also had their own on-staff artist and began giving Nashville DJs hand-painted pictures to set themselves apart from other Nashville performers.

Tompall, Chuck, and Jim began performing at the *Grand Ole Opry* in the early 1960s and became *members* of this venerable institution in 1963. They performed on the *Opry* for 15 years. According to June Glaser, Tompall & The Glaser Brothers received the longest standing ovation ever recorded at the *Grand Ole Opry—nine full minutes.*

What was it like to hear Tompall & The Glaser Brothers perform during this time? An article that appeared in the February 26, 1972 edition of *Billboard Magazine* put it this way:

> *Tompall and the Glaser Brothers were on the [Grand Ole Opry] stage performing and the crowd was giving them a roaring ovation, even after the encore. The Willis brothers were waiting in the wings to go on stage. Realizing that the Glasers were pleasing the crowd so much, they sent word to the Glasers to keep performing and that they (the Willis Brothers) would forfeit their appearance. The Glasers continued for the remainder of the show.*

At times, Tompall would act as the host or MC of the *Grand Ole Opry* show for the entire evening. On one such occasion in 1968 Gram Parsons, an early country-rock performing artist who was a member of the band The Byrds, was in Nashville working on a new album. His record label managed to get him a spot on the March 15th *Grand Ole Opry* show. According to Tompall, the audience wasn't very receptive to Parsons or his band. To make matters worse, Tompall announced to the *Opry* crowd that Parsons would be singing a Merle Haggard song "Life in Prison" but instead, Parsons and his band played one of their own tunes. Tompall was livid that Parsons would disrespect him and the *Grand Ole Opry* by playing an unannounced and unapproved song. Ironically, Parsons would later record Tompall's song "The Streets of Baltimore."

Tompall and the Glaser Brothers initially worked with record producer Owen Bradley (the father of Jerry Bradley, who later became the head of Nashville's RCA Records office). Owen produced the first five of their record releases. After this, they began working with record producer Jack Clement. The Glaser Brothers trusted Jack Clement and would let Jack pick the songs that they would record.

One of the songs that Jack Clement picked for Tompall and the Glaser Brothers was "The Moods of Mary." The recording of this song led to a *Grammy* nomination. Tompall had a cold when he recorded it. As a result, he was able to reach some higher than normal notes in the song. Generally, he feels that he had a three-octave voice. Tompall also mentioned that he felt his audience liked his voice best when he sang higher.

Jimmy Payne (www.jimmypayne.org) is a talented singer and songwriter who is a long-standing country music icon. He signed with Epic Records in 1966 and has been actively participating in songwriting, performing, and touring ever since. He was in the U.S. Army with Chuck Glaser, who invited him to come to Nashville after his discharge. Payne and Jim Glaser became friends and got together on a weekly basis to write songs. One of the outcomes of these sessions was the song "Woman, Woman" that was a huge hit for Gary Puckett and the Union Gap. Jimmy still performs to this day and shared these thoughts about Tompall:

I traveled with Tompall and performed as a part of

the same shows that Tompall played at. It was thanks to him that I was initially invited to perform at the Wembley Festival in England. He talked me into buying my first house, and I still live there.

Tompall was the first person who encouraged me to buy stocks. Unfortunately, the very first stock I bought lost its value to the tune of $2,000, and Tompall replaced this $2,000 that I had lost in the market.

When Tompall walked into a room everyone knew he was there.

One memorable experience for me was the time that I talked Tompall into singing "Ugly Women in Pickup Trucks" with me during a concert. It's something that I'll never forget.

One of Tompall's greatest assets was his ability to hear a hit song.

In my opinion, Tompall had one of the most soulful sounds that I have ever heard.

Another Nashville artist with vivid memories of Tompall is Marty Stuart who has been a part of Nashville for decades now. I was fortunate enough to see Marty and his band, The Fabulous Superlatives, comprised of talented musicians Paul Martin, Kenny Vaughan, and Harry Stinson perform live in Hartford, Wisconsin. It was one of the very best country music concerts I have ever attended! Harry has recorded Tompall's song "I Don't Care Anymore" on his recent CD.

I also had an opportunity to speak with Marty Stuart about Tompall on an earlier occasion. Marty is one of the nicest, most genuine and articulate individuals that I had the pleasure of talking to. Marty shared the following:

Tompall performing in 1983. Courtesy of June Glaser

One of my favorite memories is parking out back at Cowboy Jack Clement's studio during the summertime, getting out of my car and noticing that the studio windows were open. I then heard Tompall, Chuck, and Jim singing 'I'm Not That Good At Goodbye.' The sound of that song coming out of the window and knowing that it wasn't a record was overwhelming. I stood there by my car and cried. It was one of the prettiest sounds I had ever heard in my life.

Tompall signing autographs at Wembley in 1983. Courtesy of Jane Poole

Over the years, Tompall performed several times at the International Festival of Country Music that was held at the Wembley Arena in Wembley, England. He appeared both with Chuck and Jim as Tompall & The Glaser Brothers, and also as a solo act. These Wembley performances were among the largest venues that Tom-

97

pall played during his career with crowds of over 30,000 attending each day.

Mervyn Conn, from England, produced these festivals for 23 years, from 1969 to 1991, and the festival started up once again in 2012. Initially, people came to know this country music concert as the Silk Cut Festival due to Conn's sponsorship over the years by a tobacco company of the same name.

Tompall was popular in all of Europe but especially so in England. Tompall said that one time, when his wife June was attending a Wembley concert with him, a crowd tore down his autograph signing booth in order to get access to him. It was an epic crowd rush akin to the infamous "stampede" that occurred during The Who concert several years ago. Both Tompall and June actually feared for their lives. Another time, during a Tompall & The Glaser Brothers' Wembley performance, the crowd demanded an encore performance and was stomping their feet so forcefully that huge chunks of plaster fell from the ceiling while Tompall and his brothers were back in their dressing room! To appease the audience, they returned for another song.

Stan Laundon worked on the BBC radio in England for more than 20 years. He held a variety of positions during these years, including country music DJ and producer of a show called *Country Time*. More information about Stan can be found at http://www.stanlaundon.com.

Stan attended various country music concerts during these years and recalls the first time he heard Tompall & The Glaser Brothers:

> The first time I saw Tompall & The Glaser Brothers was in April 1973, at the Fifth International Festival of Country Music at the Wembley Arena, London, England. It's a show that I will never ever forget. At the time I was employed by BBC local radio in northeast England. I was a country music producer

Tompall performing at Wembley in 1985. Courtesy of June Glaser

and presenter for BBC Radio Teesside and had a two-day pass for the festival. This allowed me access to backstage areas and rehearsal rooms.

One afternoon I was fortunate to see Tompall, Chuck, and Jim rehearsing in readiness for their show that night. Their set was something special because they performed a medley of songs with Tompall, Chuck, and Jim singing a line, or a few words each,

Sherrill "Shaun" Neilsen, Chuck and Tompall performing at Wembley in 1985, Courtesty of Jane Poole

that included 'Release Me,' 'You Win Again,' and 'Bouquet Of Roses.' Their harmonies were truly outstanding. So much so that even stars like Dottie West, Skeeter Davis, Jack Greene and others all stood and applauded when they'd finished. That, as I said, was just the rehearsal, and no members of the public were allowed in this room.

On stage that night it was even better. Their outstanding close harmonies had the audience in awe. I had never in my 21 years as a broadcaster witnessed anything like it. They received a 10-minute standing ovation at the end. After that show it wasn't the easiest thing to get an interview because they were so much in demand. Thankfully, I did manage it and spoke to all three brothers. It was something I will never ever forget and ranks up there in my all time favourite performances.

Tompall said that his mother, Marie Glaser, went to the Wembley International Festival of Country Music once. She was honored with a bouquet of flowers, had a special seat in the balcony with her name on it, and was introduced from the stage by the trio. Tompall also remembered the time that his brother Chuck and wife Beverly took all of their kids to Europe for one of the Glaser Brothers performances. None of the kids had ever seen French bread before. Two of the youngsters grabbed a loaf and began playing a baseball game, using the bread as a bat and hard buns as baseballs.

Tompall vividly remembered traveling to and from England for the Wembley concerts. A huge airplane took off from a big, private, Quonset hut hanger located away from the main Nashville airport, and this plane carried all the CMA performers to Wembley, England. Tompall remembered that they were all herded onto the plane "like a bunch of cattle." He said that it was "a very, very long plane trip over to England."

7

Glaser Publications, Inc.

In 1962, five years after first moving to Tennessee, Tompall, along with his brothers Chuck and Jim, started Glaser Publications, Inc. Tompall recognized the value of publishing right from the start. But this was a daring move, and it was a starting point for Tompall's anti-establishment stance in Nashville. Up to this time, Nashville publishing companies were made up mainly of a handful of long-established publishing houses, such as Acuff-Rose.

    Why did Tompall want to get into publishing in the first place? In a word, money. While not the only factor, money was, of course, necessary to survive. As a trio, the brothers were paid the same as solo performers, but they had to split their earnings three ways.

    Just what does a music publisher do? In essence, a music publisher promotes songs, obtains copyrights on behalf of songwriters, keeps track of where songs are played, and collects royalties. Royalties are split between the publisher and the songwriter depending upon the contract that is in effect. Some music publishers

Photo courtesy of neurovelho

hire staff songwriters and front them a salary, which is then offset by royalties they receive when a song is played. Recall that this is the arrangement that Marty Robbins had with Tompall and Jim when they wrote "Running Gun." And this is how Tompall ran Glaser Publishing.

In addition to their publishing company, the brothers were busy with other aspects of the music business. Chuck did artist management and production, Jim handled promotion and produced music sessions, and Tompall quarterbacked the overall operations. In a November 7, 1970, *Billboard* article, Jim said:

> *We set up our publishing company in 1962, and that was really the second step in the formation of what was to become a complete complex to help artists who might be otherwise victimized. Tompall is the brains behind our growth. He knows so much about organization, contracts and people as anyone in the business. Chuck is doing much of the production, at which he excels. And I handle the promotion and produce some sessions.*

Glaser Publishing had agreements for overseas rights to its publishing company's compositions. Acuff-Rose had a network of companies across the world with active representation overseas, and Glaser Publishing had an agreement in which Acuff-Rose would collect royalties for their songs when they were recorded and/or played overseas.

As a result of his own songwriting, his ability to recognize and publish hits written by others, and the income received from touring as part of Tompall & The Glaser Brothers, Tompall shared that he was a millionaire by age 31, a mere seven years after first moving to Tennessee. This is utterly amazing considering that he was broke when he first arrived in Tennessee and that he didn't know how, or if, that would ever change. It's important to understand, however, that Tompall had always adamantly stated throughout his career that it was never just about the money. "It was always about the music." Tompall's life illustrates the age-old axiom that if people do what they love, the money will follow.

The music publishing portion of the Glaser Brothers music empire was handled mainly by Chuck Glaser, as was the management of the songwriters. John Hartford was the first songwriter hired by Glaser Publications. He was prolific, writing some 2,000 songs over his music career. However, the song that he will always be remembered for was "Gentle On My Mind," which set sales records and became one of the most recorded songs of all time. It was published by Glaser Publications in 1967 (also in 1972 and 1973). It was the top Broadcast Music, Inc. (BMI) song in the *world* for two years in a row, in 1968 and 1969. The first year it was #1 on the country charts. The second year it was #1 on the pop charts. Tompall mentioned that the Glaser Publishing Company royalty check for "Gentle On My Mind" was $90,000 each year for the first two years after it was recorded by Glen Campbell.

John Hartford was a musically talented man who played several instruments, in addition to singing and successful songwriting. Hartford played fiddle, banjo, guitar, and mandolin. He became a television personality, performing on the *Smothers Brothers Comedy Hour* and *The Glen Campbell Goodtime Hour*. Later on he traveled by bus across the USA playing in a wide variety of venues and selling his memorabilia along the way. During these later travels, he started *clogging* on plywood that had been amplified. According to Tompall, he made a "pretty good living" doing that. Of course, the $100,000+ of royalties for "Gentle On My Mind" that he continued to be paid over the years also helped.

According to Tompall, John Hartford was "a good person and a good friend." Hartford had scruples and refused to commercialize his music. He felt it was important to keep his music "pure." In fact, Tompall said that John Hartford once turned down $160,000 because he didn't want his song used in a television commercial.

However, there were times when it made sense for John to

be paid for his creative work. For example, Tompall once had his New York attorney Peter Thall contact Hallmark to discuss copyright infringement. They were using the phrase "gentle on my mind" in one of their greeting cards without permission. Hallmark argued that they were entitled to use the phrase since it was a "title" and titles cannot be copyrighted. Attorney Thall argued that the phrase was not a "title" but, rather, "an intricate (and copyright eligible) part of the song verses." As such, copyright infringement applied. Hallmark soon thereafter backed off from their initial stance, and an agreement was made to put the phrase in *five more* greeting cards and to pay royalties for use of the wording in each of the cards.

In 1968, after working for Glaser Publications for a number of years, John Hartford wanted out of his contract because the Smothers Brothers wanted John to work for them. At the time, Dick and Tommy Smothers had a popular weekly television variety show, known as *The Smothers Brothers Comedy Hour*. It first aired in February of 1967 and lasted until September of 1969. To give the flavor of the culture during this time, other television shows that were popular then included (1968-1973) and (1969-1993).

The Smothers Brothers wanted John Hartford to showcase his musical abilities on their show, which was typically playing fiddle and banjo.

Chuck Glaser didn't want to let John go, but Tompall said if John wanted to leave it would be best to let him go since his heart would no longer be in his job at Glaser Publications. So Tompall suggested that they charge Tommy Smothers $25,000 for John's release, and Tommy paid it.

A *Billboard* article that appeared in the January 6, 1968, edition provides further insight into the internal workings of the Glaser music empire during this period. It was titled, "Glaser Publications Ends Up 1967 on Happy Note":

> *The move on to the charts by Liz Anderson with "Thanks*
> *a Lot For Tryin' Anyways" signaled the climax of a year*

in which Glaser publications tripled its number of re-corded tunes, both in the country and pop fields. The firm, operated by Tompall, Chuck and Jim Glaser, also operates in the field of management and instructional training. Its greatest success of the year has been "Woman, Woman" written by Jim Glaser and Jimmy Payne, which went strong on the country charts first, then in pop with a version by the Union Gap. The brothers also have an ASCAP firm, GB Music. The most recent addition to this stable is a young man named only Hoover, who will be billed for the pop market, and has signed a contract with Monu-ment. One of the first artists taken under complete direction by the Glasers was RCA Victor's John Hartford, who wrote and recorded "Gentle On My Mind." By the end of 1967, there were 15 cuts of the tune. Glaser Productions has signed such artists as Leona Williams, Leon McAu-liff and Buddy Starcher. All artists double as performers and writers. Chuck Glaser also works as an independent producer, working with many firms.

Bill Littleton was another one of the songwriters employed by Glaser Publications. He worked there for seven years and was released just prior to the company's sale. In Bill's opinion, Tompall's greatest lasting impact on country music was his *nerve*—he wasn't afraid to try something new. Bill agreed with others that it was very "nervy" to start a publishing company in Nashville when big publishing houses, such as Acuff-Rose, already existed.

Bill said that Chuck and Jim referred to Tompall as the "quarterback" of the Glaser music business empire, and that Tompall provided their organization with a lot of its innovation and energy. Tompall didn't care whether something had been done before or not, and he was often on the cutting edge. However, Tompall once commented that it is nearly as bad to be *too early* when introducing something new as it is to be *too late*, because the public might not be ready to accept that new something just yet. Bill said he doesn't know why Tompall alone or Tompall and the Glaser Brothers did not become bigger stars. Regardless, he said that, in his opinion, the harmony blend of Tompall and the Glaser Brothers is unsurpassed—*period*.

One story that Bill fondly remembers happened when he once stood behind the *Grand Ole Opry* stage next to Tompall and the stage manager at that time, Bud Wendell. Tompall asked that he be replaced for the 2nd show the following week, because he wanted to stay home to watch the movie *Giant*, since he had never seen it before and *really* wanted to watch it. Bud told Tompall that it would not be a problem, to which Tompall responded, "but I guess it makes me an asshole for asking."

Bill quickly chimed in, saying, "Why change now?" The following week, Bill saw Tompall at Glaser Studios and caught up with him. He told Tompall he wanted to apologize for his comment at last weekend's *Grand Ole Opry*. Tompall said, "Forget it, Bill." To which Bill said, "You really are an asshole, but you are a lovable asshole." Tompall stopped, stared at him, and then said, "Thanks for making my week, Bill!"

Bill has written extensively about his experiences during his time at Glaser Publications. He has graciously allowed me to include an excerpt from one of his last newsletters, which provides a clue as to what it was like back in those days at the publishing company:

> I moved to Nashville in 1965 to write songs and play guitar. Dozens of real-deal people helped me in many ways as I shifted gears a number of times and eventually focused on entertainment journalism. I had met the Wilburn Brothers on the road, so Sure-Fire Music was the first place I went to pitch songs. Leslie Wilburn suggested I come back after the office closed to sing some songs for "the guy who works with me in publishing" without

the telephone ringing. That guy turned out to be Johnny Russell. The next major connection I made was with Luther Perkins, who listened carefully and suggested I go see Chuck Glaser, who was producing Buddy Starcher. Chuck didn't use anything of mine for Buddy, but he did pitch "Yellow" to Billy Edd Wheeler for Leroy Pullens and got it cut! He also offered me an exclusive writer's deal with Glaser Publications.

John Hartford's cut of "Gentle On My Mind" and Jimmy Payne's cut of "Woman, Woman" were already out before I joined the Glaser group, but the Glen Campbell and Union Gap cuts came in the very early period of my affiliation. Wow. In addition to Chuck, Jim, Tompall, and June, I met people I would have never met and I spent HOURS with such bright minds as Hartford and Payne, Bob Eggers, Leona Williams, Jeannie Pruett, Sammi Smith, Bobby Thompson, a teenaged Barbara Fairchild, Dick Feller, Paul Craft, Johnny Russell again (imagine having lunch with Tex Ritter and Johnny Russell), Dennis Glaser, Gamble Rogers, Jim Buchanan, Bill Holmes, James Talley, Hazel Smith, and the proverbial many others. I did some demos with the Glasers' road/studio band and I scouted the studio for a movie shoot. I've never forgotten those seven years. I didn't get a hit as a songwriter, but no university on the planet could match the education I received.

Someone else who worked as a songwriter at Glaser Publishing in the mid-1960s was Willis David Hoover (known then by many people only as "Hoover"). He is a musician, singer, songwriter, book writer, former newspaper columnist, and currently resides in Hawaii. While at Glaser Publications he received an ASCAP award for songwriting for the soundtrack of the 1970 movie that was recorded by Tompall & The Glaser Brothers. Willis David Hoover is a champion storyteller and is someone who can be listened to for hours on end. He spoke about many different aspects of his time at Glaser Publishing. Here are some of his comments:

> I met Tompall when I first came to Nashville in 1966. The Glaser Brothers had a publishing, management and production company. John Hartford, Jimmy Payne, myself, and Leona Williams (who later married Merle Haggard) operated within all three companies.
>
> Shortly after I was hired, Tompall invited me to go to the clubhouse (the Office Lounge). Tompall didn't remember my last name, so he called me 'Tugwell,' which he later shortened down to 'Tug.' Tompall introduced me as Tug to a tall, gangly guy, Harlan Howard, who had a huge, lantern chin and seemed to be amused by everything. Harlan was nothing but fun. Harlan had one of his songwriters over there, and the four of us played a game of pool (8-ball). It got down to the final shot, and Harlan's songwriter had to get by another ball that was located very close to the 8-ball. He made the shot, but it was difficult to see whether or not he had touched the 8-ball. Tompall began yelling, 'Hey, that guy touched the 8-ball on that shot.' Harlan said, 'Let's ask your songwriter because he was standing right there.' I said that it was a good shot and that he did not touch the 8-ball. Tompall immediately began screaming at me that I should have kept my mouth shut and then began cursing at me. Next, he followed me outside, still yelling at me. I finally said, 'leave me alone...I quit.'

I went back to my apartment and packed my bags and was ready to leave town. But first, I stopped at Glaser Publications to tell Chuck that I was leaving. Chuck asked, 'When are you coming back?' I said that I didn't think I would be back and explained what had happened with Tompall. Chuck did a belly laugh and said, 'If everybody left town who'd been in an argument with Tompall, there wouldn't be a songwriter left in Nashville!' He asked that I not take my disagreement with Tompall personally. Sure enough, the next time I saw Tompall, it was like nothing had happened. It was a brand new day. And that was the way it always was with Tompall.

At the beginning, when I first joined the Glaser Brothers organization, it was very much like family. We had company picnics and get-togethers. This faded out a bit over time as the Glaser Brothers became more and more famous, but I became and have remained friends with each of the Glaser Brothers.

The initial building where business was conducted by the Glaser Brothers was located at 801 16th Avenue in Nashville. It was a three-story house, and the Glasers occupied the second floor. There was no studio at that time—it was basically a publishing company. A building at 916 19th Avenue South was purchased in 1968. An elderly gentleman and his wife occupied the building while it was renovated to become Glaser Publishing Company. Chuck's office was at the top of the stairs, Jim's was downstairs on the right-hand side, and Tompall's was in the back of the building on the left side.

The restroom in the building had a shower to make it convenient to spend the night in the building, which was done quite often.

Tompall used two different sets of attorneys during his years in the music business. One was Richard H. "Dick" Frank, Jr., in Nashville. The other was New York entertainment attorney Harold Ornstein. Attorney Peter Thall is a New York attorney who practiced law with the renowned Harold Ornstein at the start of his legal career and had dealings with Tompall.

Peter Thall specializes in copyright law and the many areas that it encompasses, such as music recording and publishing, theatre, live performances, book publishing, internet content, and more. Additional information about him can be found on his website at www.thallentlaw.com. Thall represented GB Music in the early years of Glaser Publishing.

According to many, Mr. Ornstein was a pioneer in the area of entertainment law. Peter Thall said, "I don't know how Tompall found Harold Ornstein, but it was a stroke of genius on his part. Harold was one of the first, and best, music contract attorneys in the United States."

During Tompall's relationship with Harold Ornstein's law firm, Thall had the opportunity to work with Tompall on a few occasions. As mentioned, one such occasion was when Tompall sued Hallmark for copyright infringement for using the words "Gentle On My Mind." However, one of Peter Thall's most vivid memories of Tompall is the time when Tompall came to New York to visit his law firm. Thall said that he, like almost every other professional in New York at that time, occasionally had sessions with a psychiatrist. Thall's psychiatrist happened to be an old Viennese gentleman, and Tompall arrived at the law office just as Thall's session was ending.

Thall had agreed to give his psychiatrist a ride home that evening, so Thall, his psychiatrist, and Tompall were all in the limousine at the same time. Tompall and the psychiatrist began talking and drinking Jack Daniels during the 15-minute ride to the psychiatrist's home, enjoying each other's company. Thall said that his psychiatrist continued to talk about that 15-minute ride with Tompall for years afterwards.

Peter Thall said that he feels Tompall was unique in that Tompall did not see Nashville as the *center of the universe*. Tompall had a more worldwide view that included Europe and the rest of the world. Thall said he was impressed with Tompall's forward thinking back when they worked together.

Tompall met Peter Thall in New York on several occasions. One trip was taken specifically to obtain an agreement for Glaser Publications to represent Simon & Garfunkel's Nashville interests, which he successfully accomplished. Afterwards, Paul Simon, Thall, and Tompall attended an elaborate New York theatrical performance. Tompall recalled that he was somewhat taken aback at how short Paul Simon was.

Richard H. "Dick" Frank, Jr.was one of the original founding members of the CMA (Country Music Association) and was its legal counsel for 43 years. He was also an initial member of the CMA Foundation that chooses *Country Music Hall of Fame* members. He served as Tompall's Nashville-based attorney for many years.

Dick Frank said that Harold Ornstein was "the dean of the entertainment bar" in New York, and was one of Dick's mentors. Frank said that he is the person who got the Nashville Bar Association Entertainment Law Section going; it did not exist before his involvement.

Frank said that Tompall was one of "the most talented people that I knew in the music business." He feels that Glaser Studio was the center of the outlaw movement, and it was Tompall's creation. Dick said, "I recall talking with him as he developed the whole outlaw movement, for which he never got the credit that he deserved." He also said that Tompall was an extremely talented songwriter and a true visionary.

Frank felt that the Glaser Studio was a magnet that attracted some of the greatest geniuses of the time. He remembers John Hartford, the songwriter who was a part of Glaser Publishing. John had one of the most interesting minds that he says he has ever encountered. In fact, Dick said he felt John Hartford had to be "Mensa twice over."

Glaser Studios was also home to some eccentric souls. Frank remembers a certain "Captain Midnight." Midnight lived in one of the rooms in the Glasers' building and used a blanket roll when night came. During the day, he would pop out of his room and throw steel-tipped darts, trying to hit a dartboard that was at the end of the long hallway. When you visited, you were never quite sure whether or not you would be impaled. Dick said that Captain Midnight also threw sharp knives in the parking lot.

According to Dick, "Tompall built a studio with an advanced sound and provided a home for Jimmy Bowen when he came to Nashville penniless." He continued:

> Tompall was one of the most remarkable, talented intellects that I have known. Tragically, he abused himself, which was somewhat destructive to the talent he had been endowed with. This was not only unfair to him, but was unfair to everyone who valued music and creativity. But I suppose the seeds of destruction are in all of us.
>
> The studio eventually became a financial drain for the Glaser brothers and creatively played a part in their decision to go their separate ways. I was involved with the sale of Glaser Publications when it became necessary to sell it.
>
> Tompall was one of the most talented people that I think Nashville has ever produced. He had a tremendous creative imagination that could see beyond the present and create a musical future that did not previously exist.

Tompall contributed a great deal to the Nashville music industry. And he had the potential to be even more of a landmark than he was, which is the great human tragedy of his story. However, Tompall had a genius for stepping on people's toes.

Tompall & The Glaser Brothers were iconic. They created their own sounds. I believe they are in the *Country Music Hall of Fame* and if they are not, they should be. If somehow it hasn't happened, I am going to do some hellacious campaigning for their induction.

Dick Frank said that "Put Another Log On The Fire" was Tompall's last solo hit record. At one point in his career, Tompall had a contract with Mike Curb, who was then president of MGM records. Mike Curb and Frank had agreed to the basics of the contract, but MGM's legal department was notoriously slow. The album was released, statements were rendered, royalties paid, and the term of the contract expired before MGM ever got the draft of the contract to sign. This wasn't uncommon back in those days. A handshake and faith in the other person meant a hell of a lot more than paper.

Glaser Publication songwriters initially worked out of a downtown Nashville building. According to Tompall, this building was jointly owned by Owen Bradley and the Wilburn Brothers. Both CMA and Jerry Bradley were located in the same building. Tompall and his brothers worked on the second floor. In these early years, Tompall didn't go to the office very often. He said that Chuck was frequently at the building, where he used his office to interview potential new songwriters.

As their publishing business grew, Tompall began looking for a place that he and his brothers could call their own. They had finally begun earning a decent living due to royalties income earned from songs they had published, such as "Gentle On My Mind," "Streets Of Baltimore," "A Girl Like You," "Woman

Woman," and "I Don't Care Anymore."

Tompall found a two-story, four-unit apartment building located at 916 19th Avenue South in Downtown Nashville that was to be sold at auction. However, on the day of the auction, Tompall got stuck in traffic and didn't arrive at the auction site until it was over. He then set about finding out who the successful bidder was. Once Tompall identified the winner, he approached him and struck up a conversation. Tompall found out that this man had just paid $27,000 for the apartment—so Tompall offered to buy the building from him on the spot for $1,000 more. The man accepted Tompall's offer.

There were two renters in the apartment building at the time it was purchased. They were allowed to stay as the building renovations began, but eventually left. One of the tenants moved just next door, back into her mother's house.

Tompall stated that each of the brothers decorated their offices the way they wanted. Chuck and Tompall chose solid oak trim for their offices, while Jim decided to use a less expensive veneer.

When the building was initially purchased, the idea was to just use the building for publishing company offices. However, a short time after the building was converted to offices, Chuck wanted a recording studio (4-track tape was state-of-the-art at that time) to do demos. Before too long, other recording artists found out about the small recording studio and began to request permission to stop by to record their music. When this started happening frequently, Tompall came up with the idea of building a larger, state-of-the-art recording studio that could be rented out and would provide one more revenue stream for the Glaser brothers.

The professional recording studio was added via an addition to the building and was located on the second floor. The main floor remained offices. Beyond the actual cost of the addition, another $100,000 was spent on the preliminary recording equipment including a 24-track digital sound board. This would later increase to a value of approximately $300,000 for studio equipment alone.

After the first Tompall & The Glaser Brothers breakup,

ownership in the studio remained evenly split among the three. However, after the second breakup, Tompall bought out Chuck and Jim's studio ownership interests.

Tompall had hired June Johnson (who would later become Tompall's wife) just prior to buying the new location. When she started, she said there was no money to pay her. However, just a few days later a royalty check came in for $9,000, so she was able to pay herself and others on the Glaser payroll.

Willis David Hoover shared additional thoughts about the time that he spent working for Glaser Publications:

> I feel that Tompall is one of the most brilliant characters I have ever met. I've never known anyone like him.
>
> Tompall was a sage when it came to contracts. I will never forget the day I was in his office and June said to Tompall, 'Wesley is here to see you.' She opened the office door and in walked Wesley Rose from Acuff-Rose Publishing. He showed Tompall a contract and asked him to look it over and give him his opinion of the contract. I was thinking that this is an amazing moment. Here is Wesley Rose asking for Tompall's advice on a contract. Tompall proceeded to put on his reading glasses, read over the agreement, and then told Wesley the parts of the contract that he should consider changing. Wesley was paying very close attention to Tompall's words, and I thought, 'Here is a guy with an 8th grade education giving Wesley Rose advice, which Wesley is very interested in.' I don't know how he got to be so good with contracts, but Tompall was well-regarded throughout Nashville for his ability to understand contracts inside and out.

Tompall is a very hard guy to categorize. He had many moods, and I mean a lot of them. I compare it to the Wheel of Fortune because you never knew where his mood would land. He might be laughing, he might be silent, he might be funny. One day I was following Tompall around with a micro-cassette recorder trying to catch him being brilliant. I never could catch him during his bouts of brilliance, but as soon as I would turn the recorder off, he would tear into something off the top of his head and rant about something that would be brilliant.

He could be hard to get along with. He was temperamental. But I will tell you something: he was raw honest.... he was an honest guy, even though he had some difficult aspects.

Tompall was a one of a kind, unique individual, whose place in music is not recognized the way it ought to be. I know that Bobby Bare has said that Tompall & The Glaser Brothers should already be in the Country Music Hall of Fame. It will happen someday, and I'll be glad when it does.

I feel that all three of the Glaser Brothers were extremely talented, and I agree with Don Everly, who said that their harmony was the best western music harmony that he had ever heard... and I totally agree with that.

There was a real hang-out mentality going on in the studio with several people constantly rotating through its doors.

There was a lot of drinking—and other things—going on at this time, which was part of the 'creative process.' At least it was in those days.

Kinky Freidman and I wrote a song called 'I'm The Loneliest Man I Ever Met,' and it was included on Tompall's *Charlie* record album (titled 'Loneliest Man'). This song was actually written about Tompall. Lyrics of the first verse are:

> Last night he had 'em in his hands and kept 'em laughing 'til
> They left him there with nothing 'cept the bottle & the bill
> And though it was the happy hour there wasn't any fun
> 'Cause the party again was just a party of one.

The 'I'll Fly Away' medley was to be included on the *Charlie* album. However, when Tompall went to record it, he had difficulty finishing the song. He would get halfway through; then he would stop, and then he would start over again. This went on and on and on and on for much of the night. It may have been as many as 60 times that he started, stopped, and re-started the song. One of the musicians said that he would leave because he didn't feel that Tompall would be able to finish the song that night. So, rather than charge for time that he wouldn't be playing, he said he would come back for the next session.

One by one, each of the musicians left. Tompall came into the control room and asked me, 'Where the hell is everybody?' I told him that they had all left because they did not think that Tompall would be able to finish the song. Tompall was furious and accused me of turning the musicians against him. I told Tompall that I did not want him to ever

*Tompall perform-
ing in the Villiage of
Gedling in Notting-
hamshire, England
in November, 1987.
Courtesy of June
Glaser*

say another word to me unless he apologized for this
episode. A few days went by and I was playing pinball at the Bump Bump. I felt a tap on my left shoulder, turned and saw it was Tompall. He said that
he wanted to talk to me in the hallway. He walked
over to the furthest corner and whispered, 'okay you
little cock, I apologize.' Then he yelled, 'But I'll be
damned if I'll apologize to those other fuckers.'

8

Glaser Sound Studios, Inc.

The atmosphere at any music studio is special, but Glaser Studios was truly unique. A myriad of Nashville's most talented people could be found at the studio at any given time. Musicians, songwriters, singers, owners, employees, sound engineers, and a variety of visitors defined this one-of-a-kind country music nucleus.

Part of what makes a music studio unique is the fact that people show up and stay for hours (or days, or months, or even years, case in point being Captain Midnight) because time is surreal. Days fly by listening to artists' records, taking in the music being mixed by sound engineers, interacting with others, and sharing camaraderie with fellow music lovers. Once you have been exposed to the sound studio experience, you quickly get "sucked in." You find yourself showing up day after day and spending time at the music studio becomes a way of life. Glaser Sound Studio was *the* place to hang out at, especially during the 1970s in Nashville.

Glaser Sound Studio claimed a veritable "Who's Who" of notable people. Not only country music royalty, but other famous

Photo courtesy of Eric Chassaing

people could also be found there. Some of the people who came through the doors of the studio (some staying longer than others) included:

Waylon Jennings	Captain Midnight (Roger Schutt)
Jessi Colter	Jimmy Buffett
Jim Glaser	John Hartford
Kinky Friedman	Shel Silverstein
Billy Joe Shaver	Hank Snow
Mickey Newbury	Harlan Howard
Billy Swan	Jack Clement ("Cowboy Jack")
Kyle Lehning	Johnny Gimble
Leona Williams	Chuck Glaser
Johnny Cash	Jon Voight
Chet Atkins	Bobby Bare
Bill Monroe	Hank Williams, Jr.
Marty Stuart	Charles Polk
Carlene Carter	Larry Gatlin

Ray Sawyer (and other members of Dr. Hook & The Medicine Show band)

Mark Farner (and other members of Grand Funk Railroad band)

Mel Tillis	Marshall Chapman
Merle Haggard	Chubby Checker
Johnny Darrell	Dave Hickey
David Allan Coe	Johnny Paycheck
Jerry Reed	Ray Stevens
Willie Nelson	Kris Kristofferson
Jimmy Bowen	Kenny Rogers
Doug Kershaw	Mickey Jones
Buck Owens	Roy Clark
Buzz Cason	Willis David Hoover
Mel Brown	Buddy Spicher
Leon McAuliffe	Doyle Gresham

Bill Littleton
Hargus "Pig" Robbins
Hank Snow
Claude Hill
Mac Wiseman
Billy Joel
Red Young
Deborah Allen
Ben Keith
Wesley Rose
Paul Craft
James Gordon
Linda Small
Hazel Smith
Lea Jane Berinati
Chet Filippo
Gary Vincent
Bobby Emmons
Joe Osborn
Gene Chrisman
Allen Reynolds
Larry London
Bill Holmes
Davis Causey
Rick Maness
Kenny Malong
Pete Drake
Russ Hicks
Moi Harris
Andy McMahon
Bobby Thompson
John Hancock
Billy Joe Shaver
And many, many, many more!

Ken Mansfield
Buddy Emmons
Ron Treat
Leon McAuliff
Paul McCartney
Glen Sherley
Eddie Rabbit
Ted Reynolds
Gamble Rogers
Dick Feller
Fred Newell
Mac Johnson
Pebble Daniel
Marcia Routh
Bob Kirsch
Michael Martin Murphey
Buddy Starcher
James Talley
Gene Chrisman
Bobby Wood
Reggie Young
Bobby Thompson
David Humphreys
Billy Ray Reynolds
Willie Rainsford
Norman Blake
Chuck Cochran
Larry Londin
Duke Goff
Troy Seals
Greg "Fingers" Taylor
Willie Fong
Jimmy Payne

Glaser Sound Studios, Inc. was established in 1968 but was not made available to the public until 1971. While not the very first independent recording studio that was opened in Nashville, it was one of only a few that existed in 1971. The vast majority of recording artists at this time were cutting their records at the Columbia and RCA recording studios.

At its height in the 1970s, Glaser Studios was grossing $1,200 per day for musician recordings and was generating $260,000 annually. In later years, the studio grossed $400-$500 per day if it was booked for the entire week. However, many times recording artists were allowed to record for free. Sometimes, this was to allow recording artists to experiment with new sounds; other times it was because the people who wanted to record in the studio simply had no money.

Claude Hill is currently a Regional Sales Manager for Calrec Audio LTD, a division of world-wide D&M Holding. Before that he worked at 3M, MCI, SoundShop, and was self-employed as a studio design engineer. Claude was the first head engineer at Glaser Sound Studios.

Hill was educated as an electrical engineer. He spent four years with the U.S. Army in a division known as the Army Security Agency, which did *electronic warfare*. According to the U.S. Army, electronic warfare involves "the ability to control the electromagnetic spectrum to gain and maintain the advantage in the operational environment." An example of this is the jamming of an adversary's radio-controlled devices without disrupting the U.S. forces' communications in a ground maneuver.

After the army, Hill worked for 3M and specialized in recording systems. This is what initially brought him to Nashville. He had heard that the Glaser Brothers were going to build a sound studio, so he made an appointment to demonstrate for them the 3M equipment he was selling around town.

Much to his surprise, when he arrived he found out that the Glasers needed an engineer to run their studio; they asked Hill if he'd be interested in taking the job. He said yes and left his 3M job to join the Glasers' new venture. At this point, there were only a couple of other studio employees: Marie Barrett (who later became Marie Hartford, John's wife), and June Johnson (who later married Tompall).

Hill was allowed to choose the equipment that would become the integral part of the new demo studio. While the initial studio, which was used by Tompall and the Glaser Brothers for their own demos, had only a 4-track recorder, Hill chose a *16-track* Flickinger console for the new studio. According to Hill, Dan Flickinger was a brilliant guy who specialized in hand-built consoles. The Glasers' bought a Model *Mod N20D*. Hill commented that some other Nashville studios also had Flickingers, but no two consoles were exactly alike. These consoles were extremely quiet and could truly capture what was going on in the studio. According to Hill, Flickinger's sound engineering consoles are still considered to be among the very best ever developed.

Initially, nearly $300,000 of equipment was purchased and placed in the Glasers' original recording studio. In addition to the 20-input Flickinger console, the Glasers outfitted their studio with: 40 microphones (including at least 20 each high-end *Neumann U47 FET* models, and several *AKG, Electrovoice* and *Byer* mics), 6 *JBL model 4320* main speakers (four across the front and two in the back to provide quadraphonic sound), *KLH Model 6* Monitors, a *Yamaha* grand piano (6 ft long), *UREI Model 1176LN* limiting amplifier and *LA-2A* tube-driven leveling amplifier for compression, a *Thomas* organ, a *Wurlitzer* electric piano, a *Hammond B3* organ, a *Mellotron* keyboard, a *Quantum* console, and various musical instruments—including a drum kit, piano and guitars.

The recording studio itself was housed in the top floor of a two-story building. There were two separate rooms on that floor for the recording studio and a control room. Professional offices filled the first floor of the building. The basement contained two live acoustic echo chambers that had *EMT 140* plates for reverb.

Tompall said, "Once our new studio was built, people heard about it and just began coming to Glaser Sound Studios to record their music. I never even put up a sign."

The general atmosphere at Glaser Studios was loose, laid-back, and comfortable. It was open 24 hours a day, 7 days a week, and no one was turned away unless there was a recording schedule conflict. This was an exciting, creative time. As artists began recording at Glaser Studios, they began telling their record companies that they wanted more artistic freedom, including the ability to record how they wanted, when they wanted, and where they wanted. Eventually, the record companies capitulated and allowed them to do just that.

Many people who had their start at Glaser Studios ended up having notable careers in the Nashville music recording business. Two such people were well-respected sound engineers Ron Treat and Kyle Lehning.

Vicki Mead worked at Glaser Studios and was Tompall's next-door neighbor while she was growing up. In fact, that's the reason she was hired by Tompall. According to Vicki, "Tompall told me, years later, that the reason he hired me at age 19 was because my mother went to his office and told him that he needed to hire me because I wanted to get into the music business. My mother was all of five feet tall but was a little dynamo, and Tompall told me that he was afraid to say no to her."

Vicki has many fond memories about working at Glaser Studio and about Tompall. She remembers that when she was 12-years-old, she used to wash Tompall's car, and he would give her a free record album for doing that. She also used to babysit for Jim and Jane Glaser, as well as for Chuck and Bev Glaser, when she was age 12 or 13. Chuck and Bev had six kids, and Jim and Jane had four kids, so there were always a lot of kids around. Washing cars and babysitting Glaser kids was how she grew up. Vicki said, "It was pretty fun."

Vicki said that all three of the Glaser Brothers treated her very well and considered her kind of a "little sister." They were very protective. She had a wonderful experience working for them and is forever grateful for it. She said, "I got to see an awful lot of stuff going on."

In 1969, Vicki worked for the publishing company, but there was also some overlap with the studio. One of her jobs at Glaser Publishing was to catalogue all press releases and other publicity about the Glasers. She would work all day in the office and then at night would go into the studio and sing demos for them. She was often at Glaser Sound Studio for 12 hours a day, and said she loved every minute of it. According to Vicki, "The studio was a very exciting, wonderful place to be. I got to meet Shel Silverstein and got to sing some of his songs."

Concerning Tompall, Vicki said, "he was a very, very handsome man, and I know that he had a genuine love of country music. I feel that Tompall always wanted what was in peoples' best interest. I don't believe that he ever set out to be unfair about anything. I never had an experience concerning him where he was unfair. He was very kind to me. As I said, I always had kind of a protective feeling from Tompall and never really experienced any issues with his temper. I would see him occasionally get upset, but it really didn't faze me since I was an army brat. I do recall one time that he got angry at me, and I called him on it. He backed right down."

Vicki continued, "Tompall is one of a kind, clearly. He was a huge talent who had focus and direction, was forward-thinking, and who went forward and accomplished quite a lot, especially in light of the fact that he and his brothers were these 'farm boys from Nebraska.' For them to come to Nashville and to accomplish what they did was remarkable. When you look at the percentage of people who do leave a mark in this business, they are already in a very select group. Tompall was a very, very smart man.

"One of Tompall's biggest contributions to country music was the fact that he could spot great songs. All the talent in the world will not make a difference if an artist doesn't have a great song to sing. Tompall had a great ear for great songs. But he also

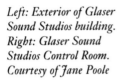

Left: Exterior of Glaser Sound Studios building. Right: Glaser Sound Studios Control Room. Courtesy of Jane Poole

had an outstanding, unique voice. It really beats the hell out of me why Tompall didn't become as well-known as Waylon and Willie. You know, there is a "mystery factor" in becoming a mega-star that no one will ever be able to explain fully. I know some really talented people who have not done nearly as well as Tompall."

Vicki got pregnant in 1972 and left the Glasers' employ shortly after that. Marie Barrett (later Hartford) took her place. Vicki recalls that Marie was a "breath of fresh air. She was so country, and so authentic, and could do nothing but tell the brutal truth. We all loved her."

Vicki married Kyle Lehning in 1970 and brought Kyle to Glaser Studio in 1972. After introducing Kyle to Tompall, Kyle was hired as an assistant engineer at Glaser Sound Studio. Vicki pointed out: "Kyle had a lot of opportunities because of Tompall, many just from being at Glaser Studios. When the studios were not being used, he was given free, unlimited use of the equipment. It was an incredible act of kindness and a vote of confidence that Kyle really appreciated...that we both really appreciated."

Kyle Lehning is an excellent musician and was formally

educated and trained in music, according to engineer Claude Hill. Although he started at Glaser Sound Studios as an assistant engineer, Kyle soon earned the chief sound engineer position. He eventually opened his own recording studio and has produced acts such as England Dan and John Ford Coley, Dan Seals, and Randy Travis. He even spent time as president of Asylum Records. Kyle had many memories about the time he spent at Glaser Sound and generously shared some of those with me:

> I began working at Glaser Studio in Fall of 1972 and left in January of 1976. I took over from Paul Skala (who took the reins from Claude Hill). Paul came to Glaser Studio via Dan Flickinger, inventor of the Flickinger console. Glaser Studio put in a Flickinger console in 1969, and to this day, I feel it is one of the best recording consoles that I have ever worked on. In fact, I recently pulled some tapes out that were recorded on the Flickinger and the sound was outstanding. The Flickinger consoles were installed at some of the best recording studios across the USA, including Muscle Shoals Sound and The Sound

Top: Flickinger Mod N20D Console. Bottom: Tompall doing some studio work in his later years. Courtesy of Jane Poole

Shoppe over in England. Sly Stone had one, Ray Stevens had one, and Wayne Moss (Barefoot Jerry) had one, so there were some around. However, for the most part, no two Flickinger Consoles were the same. The Flickinger console installed at Glaser Sound was similar to the ones at Muscle Shoals Sound and The Sound Shoppe.

I met my future wife, Vicki, in 1967 when my rock 'n roll band came to Nashville and we were looking for a female singer. She auditioned for my band through a mutual friend. We got married in 1970.

Vicki had been working as a secretary at Glaser Studio before we got married and I used to go to work with her sometimes, and just hung around and watched what was going on. I was fascinated with the whole recording side of things. At that time, I wasn't sure if I was going to be a musician or exactly how I would proceed in the music business.

Once we moved back to Nashville, even though I was a talented musician, I had the chance to watch some real studio musicians, namely Hargus 'Pig' Robbins, play on some stuff, and I realized that nobody would call me to play piano if they could call him.

So at that point I began thinking about getting on the other side of the glass. When Paul Skala left, I was given a chance to become the engineer at Glaser Studio. They gave a very green kid an opportunity to basically run their studio. It was an on-the-job training experience. While I had some natural talent, I didn't have the experience—but got it quickly. It turned into an 18-hour a day, sometimes 7 days per week, gig. There was always something going on at the studio, and there were many people besides the Glaser Brothers who used the studio.

Tompall, Chuck, and Jim were very generous when it came to using the studio. They were often on the road from Thursday morning until Monday afternoon, so if the studio wasn't booked with someone who was paying for time, I was able to use it with my buddies to experiment and try whatever I wanted to. Therefore, my growth curve was very quick.

There is no way to know the impact of what you are doing while you are doing it. It's only possible in retrospect. So now I look back and say, 'wow,' this was happening and that was happening, and I understand the kind of influence those things have had on me my entire life and career.

At the time there were not many independent recording studios in Nashville. There were some, but for the most part recordings took place at big studios where union engineers worked. It was that type of culture and environment. For a young guy like me to be in a highly equipped studio, and to have the kind of access that I had to it was pretty remarkable.

One of the rather unique things that Glaser Studios had was a *Mellotron*. This was an early sampler machine that provided sounds like the intro to the Beatles' Strawberry Fields song. It was expensive and cost around $4,000 in 1974. Tompall was not averse to spending some money for equipment in the studio that would put him in a little different category. The *Mellotrons* were controversial and the unions tried to shut down any studio that used them. Therefore, we had to be careful about when and how we used it.

Glaser Studios also had the first digital delay line. It had kind of a Pandora effect and would allow short delays and sounded interesting. It also cost around $4,000. We also added a *Quantum* board while I was there that gave us eight more inputs for mixing. Tompall agreed to many of my new equipment requests, so we could update the studio and keep it interesting.

My comments about Tompall now are in retrospect. My feelings about Tompall at the time... first of all, the truth is, he was a remarkably good singer. He had a really cool voice and could do a lot of things with it.

The blessing and curse of having his own studio was that he was able to not ever be happy. So consequently, since he had total access to the studio, he would sing way past what he needed to. He was way more talented than he gave himself credit for, in my opinion. He would sing and sing and sing and sing and sing and sing, and then sing some more. Then, he would come back into the studio the next day and sing and sing and sing and sing and sing and sing, and then sing some more. It just became kind of crazy how he went about doing what he was doing.

In the meantime, other people, like Waylon, would come into the studio and do one vocal and have a hit record. You know, Tompall is just a complicated guy. In a lot of ways, he had more autonomy than most other recordings artists. Elvis didn't even have as much autonomy as Tompall did. While Elvis had Colonel Tom, Tompall didn't have that constraint. Because Tompall was so far ahead of the curve on many things, I think he was able to help many other people more than he could help himself. For example, I know that in his relationship with Waylon he got Waylon thinking about the way he was doing things, and it helped spur Waylon onto the unique career that he ended up with. Tompall also helped Kinky Friedman's career.

I got to do a lot of work with Waylon, thanks to Tompall. I even got to play keyboards on the road with Waylon several times because Tompall was generous enough to let Waylon have me from time to time to take me with him. Tompall was a pretty open guy in that regard.

John Hartford recorded his album *Aereoplane* at Glaser Studio, and I got to watch it get recorded. That album turned bluegrass around into something else—into a new musical style.

Tompall handled the business side, and Chuck handled the publishing end of things, for the most part.

When I started I saw a lot of drinking and not much drug taking. But drinking occurred often. Tompall liked Jack Daniels, but unfortunately it did not like him. Drinking would literally change his personality. My experience of it was that when he wasn't drinking he was funny, sharp, smart, on it, had a fun sense of humor, and was generally fun to be around. You know, Tompall is a very bright guy.

Then, when he started drinking, it wouldn't take long for him to turn into someone that you wouldn't want to be around. He would become belligerent, angry, and almost the exact Jeckyll and Hyde opposite of the guy that you had just seen.

There was a running joke in the office—that you were never quite sure whether you were going to get Tom or Paul.

It was really a damn shame, but I don't think there was anything that anybody here could have done about it. This was before there was really anything much in the way of Alcoholics Anonymous; there wasn't a good understanding of how all that stuff was really affecting people. It was sort of a wild west, with people just out there doing it. I hardly ever drank, and I never took drugs, so I was sitting around there watching this in a different space than the people who were using were in. There was some pot smoking going on around there, but I kind of got out of there before the big-time cocaine stuff started happening. And that really changed things— at least it looked like it to me.

There was a lot of cigarette smoking going on in the studio. The place would just be full of cigarette smoke, and it was terrible for the equipment and stuff. But you need to remember that was just the way it was: everybody smoked, everybody drank, and eventually, everybody started doing cocaine. I moved on before this became a big problem.

While drugs were an aspect of the culture at Glaser Studio, there were many people who were not doing drugs. But drugs were around. They were around everywhere.

In retrospect, there were a few people that hung around the studio who were likely suppliers. I was thinking, 'What's this person doing here?' But I was naïve and I wasn't paying attention, and it wasn't what I was dealing with.

It was an interesting time with many people coming to the studio just to hang out. Chet Flippo, a Rolling Stone magazine journalist, used to hang out there. While there were many interesting people at the studio, I was very focused on what was interesting to me, which was trying to learn how to make a great sounding record. So I wasn't paying a ton of attention to a lot of other things that were going on. The beauty of it was that the Glasers let me do just that.

My opinion as to why Tompall didn't become better known is that he was his own worst enemy; I don't think there was any question about that. I think that he wanted to take control of his own career, that he needed to do that, and he probably needed a really good, trusted backboard. Someone who would help guide him. But there was no one who would tell him to stop. There was nobody who would say, 'Cut this song' or 'Don't cut that song.' There was nobody in that role for him when he became a solo artist after splitting from his brothers. He took sole control of everything...it is like the cliché of a surgeon operating on himself. He needed a little bit of help.

The one time that Tompall really got some help was when he did the album with Shel Silverstein that had 'Put Another Log on the Fire' on it. Shel wrote all the songs, and that album did okay. Tompall usually tried to write tunes and to do everything himself.

In the meantime, being the big brother and carrying the load of all of the Glaser brothers' business operations took its toll. Tompall had final say on expenditures. June appeared to be 'second in command' at the studio and could tell you 'yes,' 'no,' or 'I don't know.'

The place was just fascinating. You could write a book on Captain Midnight alone. He was always there…throwing knives in the backyard, or walking into the studio at just the right moment when some tense moment was going on, and he would say something that would sum up the absurdity. It usually resulted in someone recommending that he be killed immediately. Captain Midnight lived in the office an awful lot. He had an office with a hotplate in it. He was there all the time and he was one of my favorite people. He was a fascinating character.

I think that Tompall started something that is sort of ongoing today, kind of the 'independent-minded music maker.' Somebody who thought the system was somewhat rigged against the artist, and he was proved to be right about that. He was an artist advocate; he was the head of his own company, but at the same time was very artist-friendly and compassionate. He broke some rules and broke some molds. He was part of a trend that ultimately ended artists recording only at union owned and operated recording studios. We had Columbia recording artists who wanted to record at our studio because they felt there was a *vibe*, and something going on here that wasn't going on at their label's studio. And at first, those artists had to pay for a Columbia recording engineer to come and sit and read the paper while we worked because of the union rules. You could work at an independent studio, but you had to pay a Columbia engineer to oversee things to make sure it was done properly. Individually, the artists began saying, 'we don't want to do this,' and *it eventually changed the culture.*

I think that, plus the independent-minded approach to the whole thing, and encouraging artists to take more control of their careers, is a big part of why Tompall matters in the annals of country music.

I remember the first time that I saw Tompall and his brothers perform at the *Grand Ole Opry;* it was probably around 1971, and before I started working at the studio. It still gives me chills to think about how good they were. They were a stunning live act. When the three of them sang together, it was like...I'm not sure I have anything I can compare it to...they were that good. What they could do with their voices together was just amazing. They just sounded like one person who had three voices coming out of their face. It really was amazing. They got a standing ovation that night, and I was one of the people standing because they really deserved it.

I think that Tompall may have scared some folks in power because they saw that if everyone started going the way that he was going, there was going to be a very difficult group of people to manage...because they were going to be real independent-minded. So, there was probably some pushback in that regard. And maybe part of it was that Tompall had a hunch that things needed to change, but even as smart as he was, he didn't know just exactly how that should go. So there may have also been some clumsiness in the way in which he wanted to proceed about things. Nobody is that smart, really. I mean, generally you just kind of stumble through things.

I find it hard to think of any vocal group that could have out sung Tompall & The Glaser Brothers in pop or country. I honest to God cannot...and I'm talking about just three guys standing on stage singing live, with no studio trick or any of that. If any vocal group deserves to be in the *Country Music Hall of Fame*, it surely would be them. They never had enough consistent success to really become that well-known. I would be willing to bet, though, that anyone in the business old enough to have seen them would tell you the same thing that I'm telling you. But their sound was difficult to capture in the studio. I don't know that their records ever sounded as good as they did live.

I think that it was frustrating for Tompall, Chuck, and Jim to think that they needed each other in order to be special. A lot of what Tompall was trying to do was to prove that wrong, and he beat himself up severely, I think, in the process.

I was in a session with Tompall once where we started at 10:00 am and went until 2:00 am the next morning. At that time I told Tompall that I was going home and that I just couldn't do it anymore. He thought I was kidding. Hoover was there. Tompall ended up busting a bottle of Jack Daniels over the console, he was that upset at my leaving. It took a while to clean that booze out of the console. He and I then had a conversation and came to some sort of an agreement where he might be a little more reasonable, and I might be a little more patient. But I'm not sure that we really ever got there.

Willie Nelson was in Glaser Studio in 1973-1974 while producing Waylon's first album that was done there—and I engineered that. While I worked with Willie on this record a number of times, he has no memory to this day of producing it.

The fact that Tompall made the studio available for people like Shel Silverstein meant an awful lot. That brought the Dr. Hook stuff in. He had an open door policy at the studio and I think he was always willing to allow something to happen in there. The place did not have a lock on it. Folks came in and out all the time. It was not a fortress by any stretch. I think that attitude was pretty remarkable. You certainly could not just walk into a record company, or into a label's recording studio…those walls were hard to get through.

Waylon Jennings was a talented, interesting man, and very, very funny. I engineered three Waylon Jennings albums: *This Time*, *The Ramblin' Man*, and *Dreaming My Dreams* at Tompall's studio. When I would have one of the songs ready for Waylon to listen to, I would have to jump in my car and go down to the Burger Boy restaurant, where Waylon was playing pinball, and beg him to come back and listen to the mix. So he would come back and listen to the mix and say, 'Change this; that's good; fix that, and print it.' Then he would go back to the Burger Boy to play more pinball while I got the next mix going. You need to remember this took place before cell phones, email and all of the other technologies that we have today.

Tompall's wife June Glaser shared with me her conviction that Glaser Studios was haunted. To back up her claim, she said, "On several occasions I saw doors closing on their own, and I used to see bodies moving, but no one was there." Kyle absolutely agrees. He continued:

You know, I'm not the least bit superstitious, but that studio was haunted. I've never ever felt that way about any other place that I've been in. But, as an example, I was in the studio one Saturday night; I believe it was in 1975, all by myself sitting at the recording console. The studio was set up so that the door that led into the control room was all the way to your back while you were at the recording console. You couldn't see if somebody walked in. I was sitting at the console working on something about 2:00 am...the Glasers were on the road and there was absolutely no one else in the building...and all I can tell you is that my long hair towards the back of my neck started to stand up. I hit *stop* on the tape machine. I got up, I walked out the back door of the building, left everything on, left the whole place unlocked, and got into my car and drove home to Hendersonville. I came back the next day and shut everything down and turned everything off. But, as far as I'm concerned, there is no question that there was something else in that control room. I had a sense of a presence that wasn't there a moment before. And I had never felt that way before and I've never felt that way since. Sometimes you would hear noises, like clunking and banging, down in the basement. That didn't bother me. But that night was when I told myself, 'Yea, there's definitely something going on here.'

It was an incredibly rich time. A lot of things were being invented. The big country music boom was still in front of us, and those guys are the ones who started that whole thing. They really did. Tompall and Waylon and Willie and that whole crew caused people to start paying attention to that type

Tompall recording in Glaser Sound Studios in the early 1970s with Kyle Lehning in the foreground. Courtesy of Louis C. Glaser

of music in a way that hadn't been done before. They brought it to a new audience and opened an awful lot of doors for a lot of folks.

One of the things about Waylon was that the drugs he was taking really didn't change his personality. He didn't become an asshole...he was still funny, still smart, and he was still able to do a lot of different stuff. The problem that Tompall had was that booze did not affect him in a positive way. When he got drunk you just wanted to get out of there. But when he wasn't drunk, he was one of the most interesting, smart, funny and wise people that I have known. He always had such interesting takes on stuff. He saw things differently than other people saw them, but he saw them truthfully. He didn't try to distort things; instead, he saw things the way they were. He was a very, very smart guy. I have a lot of respect for him in a lot of different ways, and for Chuck and Jim, too. They gave me a great opportunity to be part of that whole scene. Also, if it weren't for Vicki, that never would have happened. I feel very lucky.

As painful as a lot of my experiences at Glaser Studio were, I would not trade it for *anything*. It was truly a fabulous time.

Drugs. Many people mention drugs and the fact that there were all kinds of alcohol and drugs at Glaser Studios. Tompall did not prohibit people from taking drugs in order to achieve the "enlightenment" that came about from an altered state of mind. But he certainly did not force anyone to drink or take drugs. In fact, there were many people who worked in the studios who didn't partake, and many who visited or booked studio time were clean and sober. However, there were a great number of people at Glaser Studios who drank, did drugs, or both—Tompall included.

Tompall did not hide the fact that during his music career he drank alcohol, usually Jack Daniels. He also freely admitted that he did drugs. The drugs included cocaine, for the most part, but he also took speed and various other pills on occasion. Mostly, Tompall said that he consumed cocaine during the two years from 1977 to 1978.

Tompall told me one humorous story involving cocaine possession. He shared, "Once, my piano player Bobby Woods and I were on a train in Holland. We had a considerable amount of cocaine with us and became aware that German storm troopers who were patrolling the train were on their way to our train car. These storm troopers did the military 'high step' just like in the movies, stomping between train car doors. Since Bobby and I knew that the troopers were heading our way, we dumped our coke down the toilet. Then, I started sprinkling a good amount of Jack Daniels whiskey throughout our train car so that it smelled like whiskey, *hoping* that it would lessen the possibility that the storm troopers would look for any other 'mood enhancers.' It worked like a charm."

I asked Tompall why so many performing artists take drugs. He said that one reason is that many want to recapture the feelings that they had when they first started performing professionally. Over time, basically, "the thrill is gone." It becomes difficult for many singers to retain a high level of excitement singing the same songs *over and over and over again.* Alcohol and drugs help singers overcome this monotony.

Another reason that musicians take drugs and alcohol is to aid in the creative process. While on drugs or alcohol, the brain processes information differently, and the creation that is "birthed" is different from what would have existed without the product that was used to achieve that altered state.

The last major reason that drugs are consumed by musicians is that some drugs (i.e. speed) allow musicians to continue to function on very little sleep. Sometimes, shows are unavoidably close together. Between the lengthy travel times, preparations, and other things that suck up blocks of time, there is little opportunity to sleep. Drugs can help performers keep going.

During my interview of Tompall he emphatically said, "drugs are bad." Tompall quit drugs in 1978—and stopped playing pinball on the same day, although he did continue to drink alcohol for quite some time after this date. Tompall had been clean and sober for many years when we spoke. However, he made it a point to state that, "Many people didn't realize that I had an extremely good memory while I was drinking."

Those who recorded at Glaser Sound Studio were offered a unique experience. In addition to the laid-back, informal atmosphere, Claude Hill had figured out how to play music from the studio through a low-power FM transmitter into a car's FM stereo radio so recording artists could hear what their songs would sound like over the radio before making the final cut of their recording. After a recording session was finished, the artists would go outside

Glaser Studios and broadcast their recording onto an open FM band. They would then sit in a car in the parking lot and listen to the playback of their tape. This helped them decide how to mix the final cuts. If a song wasn't mixed to sound good on the FM radio in the parking lot, most likely it wouldn't sound good on the normal home stereo or car radio. "Listening to a song in the studio and on the radio were two different animals altogether," according to Mickey Jones, a member of the First Edition, and someone who recorded at Glaser Sound Studios.

In addition to being a drummer for the music group, the First Edition, Mickey Jones has been a Hollywood character actor now for several years. Mickey has been in many movies and has played a recurring role on the television series *Home Improvement*. He can be seen as one of the actors appearing on the FX television station series *Justified*.

Mickey has many fond memories of Kenny Rogers and the First Edition's recording of "The Ballad of Calico" at Glaser Studio in Nashville in 1972. This was a six-week project and Mickey said, "Glaser Studio was the best studio in Nashville." Other comments Mickey shared include:

> When the *Grand Ole Opry* was at the Ryman, I attended several times as the Glaser Brothers' guest. Because of the Glaser Brothers, I was given a chance to perform at the Ryman when the Glaser Brothers hosted the show.
>
> Tompall was always a gentleman and very kind to me. However, there were nights when I would run into Tompall at the King of the Road Hotel, when he would say in a low voice, 'Shh. I'm Fred Harper tonight, not Tompall.' 'Fred' did some serious 'roaring' over the years. He'd be gone for days on end having a great time.

Tompall brought me into the studio to play drums on some of his individual recordings. This took place in the early to mid-1970s (around 1972-1975). Tompall knew exactly what he wanted in the recording studio.

I feel that the three brothers harmonized well, but that they were not the most electrifying act together. They basically came out and sang. But Tompall, away from his brothers, and in the studio, was electric. He really was on fire in the studio. I feel that Tompall liked his own personal studio time the best of all.

The studio made Tompall come alive. I have nothing but good things to say about Tompall.

The house next door to the Glaser Studios was owned by the Oak Ridge Boys (Joe Bonsall, Duane Allen, and William Lee Golden). The First Edition recorded a song at the Glaser Studio and played it for the Oak Ridge Boys. The Oak Ridge Boys loved the song and went on to record it. It was called 'Elvira' *and was exactly the same as The First Edition's version.*

I have many great memories of Glaser Studios.

Glaser Publishing published quite a few of my songs, ones that I wrote and recorded at Stax Records.

At the height of the Glaser Brothers' careers, I don't think there was anybody any better at what they did.

Tompall had a unique voice.

Today, it is possible to get away with poor vocals on a recording due to the recording 'tools' available (such as *Pro Tools)*. That wasn't the case back when Tompall and the Glaser Brothers were recording. Recordings had to be perfect back then and Tompall and the Glaser Brothers were at perfection.

Waylon and Tompall were the ass-kicking couple of Nashville.

Once, I went up into a room at King of the Road where Tompall and Waylon were partying. I was around 30-years-old (just a kid back then), and I was not a party guy. They were a couple of guys who were doing what they loved to do—party and make records.

When The First Edition first saw Glaser Studios, they fell in love. It was not as fancy as some recording studios, but it was *cooler and better* than the high dollar studios (such as RCA). Those fancy studios were just *too shiny* for me.

Kenny Rogers was able to make his own decisions on 'Ballad of Calico' and was basically his own producer. We brought in John Hartford to play fiddle and Doyle Gresham to play steel guitar on this album.

Few are aware that many different types of recordings were done at Glaser Studios—including commercials—not only country music artist recordings. Many people associated with the *Hee-Haw* TV show also frequented the studio, including Buck Owens and Roy Clark. Some of the custom sessions for *Hee-Haw* were also done at Glaser Studios.

The Glasers had approximately 60-65 fulltime songwriters under exclusive contract when Claude Hill worked as a sound engineer at Glaser Studios. Each of these songwriters would get about three hours per month in the studio, and were also given 3-4 musicians to work with to create their demos. A lot of the demos done during this time used only a few of the 16 available recording tracks. Some of the songs were good enough for the Glasers to record themselves, and others were good enough to pitch to other singing artists. In those days, in addition to Tompall, the main pitchmen for Glaser Publishing were Johnny Russell (who became one of the main personalities on the *Grand Ole Opry*) and Bill Holmes. They would take Glaser Publishing songs to producers and others in Nashville with hopes of getting them to license (or buy) and record the songs, thereby generating publishing company royalties.

Concerning the Glaser Brothers "sound," Claude Hill said:

> When singing together with his two brothers, in close proximity to one another (which did not always happen), standing close to one microphone, there was no trio better *anywhere*. I don't care who else you name, including the Gatlin Brothers and others. There was no one better than the Glaser Brothers when they were in tune with one another artistically. When they wanted to be together and to sing together, regardless of the venue, there was no one better. There is no one that I have ever heard that was better. And there are a lot of great artists that I wish they could have performed with. The vocal harmonies they did were just so unique and almost haunting, in a way.
>
> Tom would sing straight lead, Jim sang the tenor parts, and Chuck's part is what makes the trio sound so truly unique. However, Chuck didn't always know what to sing. So Jim used to tell him to 'do this' or 'do that.' When he did, it would sound marvelous. Chuck's part is unlike what anyone else in any other trio sang. I don't care if it was Peter, Paul and Mary; the Limelighters; or anybody else. It doesn't matter if it was country music, folk music, or

whatever. It was what gave the Glaser Brothers their incredible, unique sound.

Hill remembers that there were times that the three Glaser brothers were not getting along. "I feel that one of the biggest tragedies was the fact that the three brothers were not always united. They let issues develop between them that I don't know the details of. However, I do know there were times when they were not speaking to each other. In fact, there were times when we would do a session and Tompall would come in and sing his part, a couple of days later Jim would come in and sing the tenor part, then a few days later Chuck came in to sing his part. But typically Jim would come with Chuck and coach him some on what to sing to get the magic done. I would then mix the recordings. They always sounded good, but not as good as when the three of them would sing their parts at the same time."

Hill made several other general comments based upon his memories from the time that he worked at Glaser Studio:

Sometime around 1971, producer Buzz Cason brought one of his songwriters over to the studio. That songwriter stood in back of the control room and listened to the first of his songs being recorded. That songwriter was Jimmy Buffett.

Kris Kristofferson was mainly around Glaser Studio when the Glasers covered his songs. These included 'Sunday Morning Comin' Down,' 'Bobby McGee,' and more.

There is only one Tompall Glaser. He is a true artist. He is his own person. He knows who he is. He worked very hard at trying to be a good performer.

Tompall is a great songwriter, and he has always been in tune with what is considered country as a writer or performer. He is the real deal.

The Glasers (whether Tom by himself or the Glaser Brothers) would always make a song their own. They would never sing a cover exactly as it had been done before; it would always be new, unique and different. They never followed the pack, which is one of the worst things about Nashville.

I never went on the road with the Glaser Brothers, but I heard many stories about those touring days. They travelled mainly in a station wagon pulling a 2-wheel or a 4-wheel trailer that contained their instruments. I heard that these road trips were 'adventures' and I'll leave it at that. Jimmy Payne, Bill Holmes and others were band members at that time.

Tompall is truly an artist. As such, I don't feel he was the world's greatest businessman. He's a very likeable guy, despite trying to put on an outlaw or renegade image. He's a prince of a guy.

Tom was his own worst critic. There was one song, 'Aint it All Worth Livin' For,' where Tom spent 56 hours trying to get the sound he wanted. The Glasers' gave me a terrific career opportunity to be a part of the Nashville music business in the 1970s. I gave them everything that I had and then I moved on.

Hazel Smith was a long-time employee of Glaser Publishing. She initially started as a receptionist and later worked as Tompall's publicist. She fondly recalls her time spent working for Tompall, and she shared some of her key memories.

Hazel said, "Tompall has a big heart. For example, one

night, as I left the office and was driving on highway 40-East to my parent's home in North Carolina, I didn't realize that a tornado had hit Chattanooga, Tennessee. In addition, a bridge located on 40-East had frozen over. Suddenly, I hit the ice, and as a result my car turned over six times. I called Glaser Studios and reached Tompall. He immediately drove about an hour to my location, picked me up, and took me back to my home in Nashville. On the way back, however, he couldn't resist scolding me just a little bit for driving too fast for the road conditions."

Hazel remembers when Waylon Jennings first moved to the Glaser Studio office. Tompall and Waylon both felt that the existing country music industry needed to change. One of the changes that they wanted was to make recorded music sound just like it did when an artist was on stage.

Once, when Waylon and Hazel were in the studio recording booth and could hear Tompall singing, Waylon turned to Hazel and said, "Tompall really is a *great* singer." She has never shared Waylon's statement with Tompall but wishes she had.

In these days Tompall and Waylon were close friends and nearly inseparable. Hazel said, "Tompall frequently dressed in cowboy attire and he would sometimes play pinball all night long. One time, both he and Waylon Jennings were in a Burger Boy restaurant. Waylon was in the back playing a machine, and the other machine was located at the front of the restaurant. So Tompall grabbed the front pinball machine and moved it back and forth until it finally came to rest in the back of the restaurant. He then played that pinball machine right next to Waylon's machine." As I have heard elsewhere, the owner of the restaurant was not at all happy with Tompall because he damaged both the room and the pinball machine in the process.

Hazel confirmed that the recording studio was basically open 24-hours a day and that there was not a single window in the building. None of the doors in the studio were ever locked except the doors to Tompall's office and to June's office.

Hazel recalls that Johnny Cash stopped by Glaser Studios when he got out of Folsom State Prison, and that Johnny was driving a brightly colored gold Cadillac at that time.

In reference to the Outlaw Tours that took place after the *Wanted! The Outlaws* record came out, Hazel said that Tompall found it hard to start touring on his own. In her opinion, he was used to having his brothers Chuck and Jim by his side as they had been ever since childhood.

In Hazel's opinion, Tompall didn't become a household name the way Waylon and Willie did, because Tompall spent more time in the *business of music* rather than performing. Also, in her mind, he was somewhat shy or reserved compared to other big-name artists. Hazel commented that it is hard to "do it all."

When reflecting on what Tompall should be remembered for, she said, "*First*, when Tompall was onstage, there was no one better. *Second*, he had quite a head for business."

Some notable albums that were recorded at Glaser Sound Studios include: Waylon Jennings' *Honky Tonk Heroes* and *Dreaming My Dreams*, John Hartford's *Aereoplane*, the platinum compilation album *Wanted! The Outlaws*, Kenny Rodgers and The First Edition's *The Ballad of Calico*, Dr. Hook and the Medicine Show's *Dr. Hook and the Medicine Show*, Billie Joe Shaver's *Old Five and Dimers Like Me*, Grand Funk Railroad's *Phoenix*, Jimmy Buffet's *A White Sport Coat and a Pink Crustacean*, Kinky Friedman and his Texas Jewboys' *Sold American*, and many, many more.

Record producer Buzz Cason began working with Jimmy Buffet, and in 1973 they recorded Jimmy's third album at Glaser Sound Studio. This is the point when Jimmy's backing band began to take shape. Greg "Fingers" Taylor, Jimmy's long-time harpoon (harmonica) player, and Doyle Gresham, Jimmy's current steel guitar player, played on this album. Doyle happened to be the steel guitar player for Tompall & The Glaser Brothers' band back then, both on tour and when they recorded, and he also played as a studio musician for others.

Jimmy Buffett(www.margaritaville.com) needs no introduction. He is recognized world-wide as a unique singer, songwriter, musician and author, and he considers himself among Tompall's friends. Jimmy provided the following comments about Tompall:

Tompall was introduced to me by Don Light when he was trying to get me a record deal in my early days in Nashville. He, along with a few other people like Chet Atkins, Glenn Sutton, and Bob Beckham, liked my stuff, but no record deal appeared. With nothing much happening for me in Nashville, I headed for Key West. Let's just say it worked out. In the next few years, I would take trips back up to Nashville to see Don, who was my manager, and to hang out. Re-kindled my friendship with Tompall and some others around that time, by then I believe they had built Glaser Brothers Studios, which came onto my song line. I think I did some demos there during that period and that is when I first heard Doyle Gresham play and loved what I heard.

Those were the days of hanging out at Ireland's, Mario's, and the Exit/In when it came along, and needless to say I would run into Tompall on that trail. When Don Gant finally signed me to a record deal on ABC, based on our friendship and the fact that I really liked the comfort of Glaser Brothers Studio, I requested that we record there, which we did. We did my first album for ABC Records, in three days. Tompall was around for a lot of that record. I think this might have been just the beginning of the 'outlaw' thing, which I was not much a part of as I had moved to Key West and only visited Nashville occasionally, but it was always a pleasure to run into Tompall when I did.

Tompall said that he remembered Jimmy Buffet and that he liked him. Both of them were working to "do their own thing" in Nashville, although in different ways. Tompall did comment that Jimmy liked his weed while Tompall liked his booze and that people using these two different types of mood enhancers sometimes did not always see eye to eye on things.

In addition to the constant flow of famous musicians in and out of the Glaser Studios, one rather infamous person actually *lived* at the music studio. His name was Roger Schutt, but he was best known by his moniker, "Captain Midnight." During my interviews with people who know Tompall, nearly every single one of them mentioned that character, Captain Midnight. He was a well-recognized, popular rock/shock jock (DJ) in Nashville for many years during the period when Tompall and The Glaser Brothers were releasing records, and he often played their songs over the airwaves. According to Tompall, he got fired from the radio station after making fun of a Chinese wrestler. He became nearly penniless after this, so Tompall let him live in his office building. Captain Midnight lived there for almost *eight years.*

Midnight had the ability to diffuse tense situations and he was someone who was generally fun to be around. This was in spite of his penchant for throwing steel-tipped darts down the long hallway, regardless of who was walking through, and tossing big knives in the parking lot. One of his well-known sayings around the studio was, "I've been up for seven days and it feels like a week."

I liken life at Glaser Studios to the "Camelot" of old, a kingdom where Tompall reigned as king; princes and knights, such as Waylon Jennings, Bobby Bare, and Cowboy Jack Clement were constantly coming and going, and court jester Captain Midnight was around 24/7.

Midnight's life at the studio came to an abrupt end one day when Tompall overheard him talking to someone else in the hallway and badmouthing Tompall, saying things like, "Tompall wouldn't know a #1 country song if it hit him in the face." Tompall immediately confronted Captain Midnight and booted him from the building. Tompall said, "I told him that I may have some enemies, but I'm not paying any of their expenses. Take your shit and get the hell out of here." Shortly thereafter, Midnight got married and moved into a house with his new wife.

However, according to Hazel Smith, when Midnight died in February of 2005, Tompall attended his funeral. He was in a wheelchair at this time but sang a heartfelt song at the funeral, even so.

One person who frequently hung around Glaser's studio in the late 1970s into the early 1980s was Dave Hickey. Hickey earlier provided his insight relative to Nashville's culture in the days he lived there. During this time, Hickey was dating Marshall Chapman, a young woman from South Carolina who was then recording at Glaser Sound Studio. Dave is an interesting person and someone you might not expect to find at a recording studio. Hickey looks back fondly at his time spent at Glaser Sound Studio and had several memories to share.

Hickey first came to Nashville with an assignment to write a book about Waylon and Willie. He never got around to it since he existed in a "fog of cocaine and dope" during his time at Glaser Sound Studios. He considers the time he spent there as a "studio internship," and mentioned that because he lived only two blocks away, he would sometimes sleep in the studio.

According to Hickey, "Glaser Sound Studio became 'ground zero' for the Outlaw Movement (a phrase that Dave claims to have coined), due to the fact that people like Tompall, Waylon, Willie and Neil Reshen were there during this time. This was the moment that country music artists discovered that they didn't need to ask Chet Atkins' permission before they could go to the bathroom. The old-time studio system (Acuff-Rose, etc.) could be bypassed. Everyone took control of their own destiny. They had their own publishing companies, studios, managers, etc. They weren't beholden to record companies or to Billy Sherrill's idea of what a good song was."

Bambi Golden, Tompall and June Johnson in 1975. Courtesty of Willis David Hoover

In Hickey's mind, the "Rebellious Center of Nashville" during this time included Roger Miller, John Lomax, Waylon Jennings, Willie Nelson, Billy Joe shaver, Tompall, Billy Swan, and Kinky Freidman, among others. However, Tompall was the "improvisario of the scene" and the scene was very valuable to a great many people. Tompall was a force to be reckoned with, and he was willing to take chances. A lot of studio time was provided pro bono and involved experimental types of activities.

Tompall has many unique qualities, according to Hickey. For instance, he was very aware of the songs he would sing and that they became an extension of his persona (which wasn't true of Waylon and Willie). Also, Tompall has the ability to sit in a room, and everyone in that room considers him to be different from any other person in that room. He has an uncanny ability to "please everybody but still win."

Hickey felt that Tompall desired to do something distinctly different that was not related to the Glaser Brothers. In this regard, he put together some great musicians who worked with him when he was a solo act. One was black drummer Charles Polk who lived in his limousine parked outside the studio. Another was Mel Brown, a great jazz guitarist. Tompall was willing to experiment in the studio.

Hickey said that drugs were the culture of this time period (pre-1985). Glaser Studios certainly wasn't a "drug alley," but drugs were certainly there. Tompall got into cocaine later in his career, but he (Hickey) doesn't think that Tompall was into speed the way Willie and Waylon were. Waylon once said that "speed is pot for people who have to work two shifts per day." Hickey also remembers that a professional cleaning company once came in to clean up all the smoke from pot and cigarettes that had become attached to the underside of the studio soundboard.

Concerning Tompall's style, Hickey feels that "Tompall would sometimes disenfranchise the men in the audience at his concerts, unlike Waylon Jennings. While Waylon sang to everyone and was considered just 'one of the gang,' Tompall was much more assertive and masculine, and he did what Elvis did—he sang just to the girls."

In Hickey's opinion, Tompall didn't become as well known as Waylon and Willie because "the obligation of having the recording studio created somewhat of a burden for Tompall, and he was not willing to leave and go on the road for eight weeks and live in a bus, etc. It just wasn't his thing...and that is the thing that makes performers successful. However, Tompall seemed to be comfortable with the way things were." Also, Hickey felt that Tompall wasn't really comfortable with the place he found in the group that included Waylon, Willie, and Kris Kristofferson. If there is a tragedy to the story of Tompall, maybe this is it. Hickey compared Tompall's place in this group to Bill Wyman's place in the Rolling Stones, opposite of Keith Richards and Mick Jagger.

Hickey said that Tompall was a private person and a very proud man. He was not the type of guy that shared personal information. The rule of thumb in our group was, "if you want a friend, buy a dog." Most conversations took place among them as if it were one band member to another.

Hickey laughed as he recalled sitting around Tompall's office one night with a few other people. Tompall turned to him and said, "You think you're my equal, don't you?"

Another person who spent time in the Glaser Sound Studios in those days was Robert "Bob" Kirsch. Bob has had quite a varied career in the music business: he was a writer for *Billboard Magazine* for four years, and he later worked at ABC-DOT records. In fact, he wrote the album liner notes for Tompall's album *The Great Tompall* that was released on the ABC-DOT label.

Bob and Tompall had been friends for many years. Bob said that he always visited Glaser's studio when he visited from his home in Los Angeles. Tompall was "exceptionally kind to me," said Bob. "He would give me free reign to do as I pleased." So, Bob hung out, talked to a lot of people, observed records being cut, and made friends. He also occasionally traveled on the road with Tompall's band. It was a great time, according to Bob.

Bob said that Tompall is a legitimately great singer and could also be a great songwriter when he put his mind to it. Audiences loved to hear him sing. Bob commented, "I don't know what he was missing [that prevented him from reaching mega-star status], but my guess is that it was him. He was impatient. He had a temper. He would say things that he would later regret, and I'm not sure he really meant the things that he said. You know, after half a bottle of Jack Daniels it is likely that we'd all say things we'd later regret."

But, while Tompall never made it "really big," Bob said everyone in the music industry knew what a really great singer he was. The Glaser Brothers were looked upon with great favor by the music industry. They were champion singers and harmonizers. All the great Marty Robbins songs included the Glaser brothers as backup singers.

People admired what Tompall had done. He put together a center where artists could come together; he was the very first to do that. To the outside world they may have looked like a bunch of misfits, but they were determined not to get kicked around by the system. And in the end, they weren't.

According to Kirsch, Tompall had a good sense of humor. Kirsch remembers one time when Tompall and Waylon were staying at the Century Plaza Hotel in Los Angeles. Their assigned room service delivery man was an elderly man. He would bring things to the hotel room and would always call Waylon "Mr. Jenkins." It drove Waylon crazy, but he was too nice a guy to correct the old timer. Tompall thought it was hilarious and made it a point to call for room service about twelve times per day. Each time, the old fellow would say, "Thank you, Mister Jenkins," before leaving. Waylon would turn red and Tompall would then laugh like crazy. He continued calling for room service each of the three days that he and Waylon were at the Plaza.

In Bob's opinion, Tompall became a victim of his own self-created reputation. He was a nice guy, but sometimes it seemed that there was no filter between his brain and his tongue. Most of what he said was 100% correct, but people would take offense to it. Tompall knew what he wanted but he was difficult. Waylon was somewhat more sophisticated and didn't make as many enemies.

Bob was present when Tompall recorded on ABC Records (now part of the Universal conglomerate) with producer Ken Mansfield. Ken had an extensive music background, including promoting the Beatles, running Barnaby Records and producing some of Waylon Jennings' songs. ABC Records hired Mansfield to produce Tompall. At the completion of his Mansfield-produced album, Tompall told him, "Everything about this album sucks. Even the hat I had to wear for the cover photo was too small." To which Mansfield replied, "Well, it fit when we started."

Bob said that, yes, Tompall had an ego, but all people who are bright and are visionaries have egos. "If you want to earn your living standing in front of a lot of people on a stage, you *need* to have an ego," said Kirsch.

Nashville was a very controlling town when Tompall opened his studio. They gave recording artists three hours to record three songs, and this was their "session." The producer picked the songs.

There were very few singer/songwriters. The system then was made up entirely of people who worked at the music labels.

One of Tompall's major contributions was his involvement in publishing. He changed the way things were done. Tompall knew the importance of publishing right from the start. He was a smart guy, according to Kirsch.

Kirsch continued, "Tompall's greatest legacy was breaking the hold that record labels had on artists and their recording studios. In the days before Glaser Sound Studios, record labels dictated what would be recorded and the amount of time that could be spent to complete an album, i.e., two days from start to finish. Many times artists had not even seen the song they would be recording until they got into the studio. Even the producers may not have seen the song yet. The same session musicians played on all the recordings. While they were great musicians, the best ones often ended up running record labels (like Chet Atkins and Jerry Kennedy) and were no longer available for sessions. Also, if you're the same musician playing song after song, week after week, the records eventually all start to sound alike.

"It has gone full circle today. Record labels are once again calling the shots and it is difficult to break into the music business. Labels are manufacturing stars now. They look at their stable and determine what is missing, such as a 'group' act. Then they devote time to fill that needed niche. Everyone else tends to get overlooked. For example, a female soloist who recorded for RCA a few years back was given four different producers to record with during a four-year stretch. RCA issued one single promotion song at the end of these four years, but it didn't do very well, so they dropped her.

"One of the big differences between today and back in Tompall's heyday is that today's recording artists all write or co-write their own songs. Before Tompall, staff writers at the publishing companies wrote the majority of songs that got recorded."

Continuing, Bob Kirsch said that in his opinion, Tompall had "more forward thinking ideas than Waylon. Waylon basically knew what he wanted to do and was sick of being pushed around by the labels. But a lot of it was that Waylon was concerned about his career. Tompall was concerned about the entire industry. Of course, Tompall was concerned about his career, as well, but he took a larger view. He didn't think that people in Nashville were being treated properly.

"Tompall appreciates people for who they are and what they can do. He doesn't base his opinions on race. As such, he was one of the first, if not the first Nashville artist to include persons of color in his band: the black jazz musicians— guitarist Mel Brown and drummer Charles Polk."

Kirsch remembers when Polk first joined Tompall's band— that after their first recording session together, Tompall and the entire band went out to dinner. Polk had what seemed like 30 drinks, got inebriated, and had to be carried up the steps to his apartment. Tompall said, "Charles, this isn't going to be a nightly occurrence, is it?" And it wasn't, according to Kirsch.

Tompall's concern for the musician was expressed in the studio, too. The equipment was more up-to-date than at many of the studios, in Bob Kirsch's mind. And they actually paid attention to the recording process. "When a record was being made at Glaser Sound Studios, it wasn't said, 'That's good enough' or 'We're backed up on time...let's go.' Tompall didn't need to have union employees. At Tompall's studio an artist could spend days recording a song, if that was what he wanted to do," added Kirsch. Artistic freedom was in full bloom at Glaser Sound Studios.

Tompall was not only doing things differently, he didn't feel he had to kowtow to the music industry for any reason. He felt that he was outside of that environment, and he wanted to stay outside. Kirsch recalls Tompall and Waylon had a big fight because Waylon was nominated for the Male Vocalist of the Year at the CMA (Country Music Association) Country Music Awards in 1975. Waylon won and Tompall told him that he didn't want Waylon to go to the awards. Tompall said, "Waylon, this will show those bastards that we don't need them." However, Waylon went and he accepted the award. Tompall subsequently hit the ceiling.

Even though Glaser Sound Studios had developed a reputation as a haven for artistic recording flexibility, other factors had an impact on its existence. One of these things was ownership of the studio. When Glaser Sound Studios opened to the public, it was equally owned by each of the three brothers. However, ownership of the studio changed as the brothers went their separate ways. As tensions mounted among the three men, they split up as a group in 1973, reunited in 1979, and then separated once again for the final time in 1982.

According to a *Billboard* article that appeared on page 33 of the 8-18-73 edition:

> *Agent Don Light said that The Glaser Brothers, one of the most consistent selling acts of the MGM country roster for more than five years have "suspended functioning together" at least for the time being. The Glasers began recording 15 years ago with Decca (now MCA) and stayed with that label until a move to UA, then MGM. The Glasers jointly own a recording studio, a publishing company with a massive and successful catalog, a production firm which has been involved with many major artists, and an art, advertising, and promotion operation. Just how this will affect their membership in the Grand Ole Opry isn't known at this time. Bud Wendell, manager of the Opry, said he hasn't heard anything officially.*

A business is like a marriage. It involves a relationship between the owners and is subject to both good times and bad. Sometimes, for many different reasons, marriages fail and a divorce results. Tompall said that his father had mentioned to both Chuck and Jim that they should reconsider staying in business with Tompall, and feels that his words played a part in the group's first break-up.

Ironically, it was during a trip back home to Nebraska to attend their father's funeral that Tompall, Chuck, and Jim's first reconciliation occurred.

From my perspective, it may be easiest to use the words *irreconcilable differences* in reference to the Glaser Brothers' breakup. To this day, none of the Glaser brothers is willing to openly share his feelings related to the trio's breakup. Tompall said that it hurt too much to discuss this part of his life, so we will just leave it at that.

9

Songwriting

Have you ever written a song? Many people, including me, have done so. It's pretty easy to write down some lyrics and toss together some accompanying musical notes. But, chances are the song you wrote is *garbage*. I recall reading the liner notes on one of Harry Chapin's albums. He mused that he had to throw away his first 300 songs before he'd written anything good! It's not easy to write a good song, and it's harder yet to write a hit song. Yet, that is exactly what Tompall Glaser did.

Tompall wrote several impressive songs during his music career. He wrote his very first song when he was 12-years-old, called "Tear Stains On My Letter." Looking back, he said, "I didn't know what the hell I was writing about at that age." He didn't remember writing more songs until he went into the army, where he wrote a couple more.

In 1966, Tompall and well-known Nashville songwriter Harlan Howard collaborated on the song "Streets Of Baltimore." Tompall wrote the lyrics and music for everything except the chorus, while Harlan wrote only the music for the chorus. Tompall said that while he wrote nearly the entire song, it was important to have Harlan Howard involved back then because "he could get songs cut, and I couldn't."

While talking about Harlan Howard, Tompall mentioned that he and Harlan flipped a coin for the publishing rights to some songs. Tompall won the toss for the publishing rights for "Gentle On My Mind" and Harlan won the toss for "Streets Of Baltimore."

Bobby Bare was the first to record the "Streets Of Baltimore." He changed the words in one of Tompall's verses from "shutters painted green" to "in a neighborhood serene." Bare also deleted one verse of the song in order to shorten it for his recording. Tompall changed the song back to his original lyrics and replaced the missing verse when he recorded the song with his brothers Chuck and Jim.

Tompall said that he first thought of lyrics for the "Streets of Baltimore" when he saw a well-dressed, pretty young woman standing in the *Grand Ole Opry* one night. She was looking fine, and other men were taking notice. Tompall observed that she was with a poorly dressed man who appeared to be some type of laborer—he had dirty hands and grease under his fingernails. It looked to Tompall like the man was working hard to keep his woman in style, and they looked out of place together. Tompall thought that the man looked tired and guessed that he probably spent money he didn't have to take her to the *Grand Ole Opry*. Tompall said, "She was looking for a way out and he was the door."

Tompall imagined that the man had left his farm, got a factory job to earn money to make his wife happy, discovered his efforts weren't enough to *keep* her happy, then left her and went back to the farm, leaving his wife in the city that she loved so dearly. When Tompall wrote his last two lines, "While my baby walks the streets of Baltimore" he meant to reflect the fact that the woman became a "streetwalker" (hooker) in the city of Baltimore after her husband left her.

The "Streets of Baltimore" is a true American Classic. In fact, the song has even been the subject of a college course in American Literature. A wide variety of artists have recorded the song, including Charley Pride, Gram Parsons, Darius Rucker with Hootie and the Blowfish, Coldplay, the Statler Brothers, the Little Willies (featuring Norah Jones), as well as Tompall & The Glaser Brothers, and many, many more. Gram Parsons' version of this song has been featured in HBO's series *The Wire* that takes place in the city of Baltimore. However, the person who is most identified with the song, and who had the biggest hit singing it, is Bobby Bare. It has been said that Harlan Howard sent this song to Bare within 24 hours after it was finished.

Concerning the art of songwriting, Tompall felt that when someone writes a song, it is important to say something you really *have* to say. "A song should be something you know, but haven't heard put that exact way before."[2] Ken Hatley (www.khainc.com), an accomplished musician and composer who runs Ken Hatley and Associates, a music industry licensing and music clearance company, first met Tompall in 1967 while he was spending time with Jack Clement. He ended up spending several years hanging out at Glaser Publications. When he thinks about songwriting, Ken remembers Tompall's advice: "Do not try to write like someone else. Be yourself."

Ken remembered that one day he and Captain Midnight were listening to songs. It was a Monday, and on Mondays big mailbags full of cassette tapes would be delivered to the office. These were the songs of hopeful songwriters. He and Captain Midnight were shaking the cassettes to their ears and laughing out loud, saying that they didn't hear a hit song in the bag. Tompall overheard them and got upset. He said, "Remember this—there are millions of songs out there, hundreds of great songs, but very, very few hits, so you may be missing the needle in the haystack. The very tape you don't listen to may be the one that becomes a hit. Listen to a song until you lose interest. If it hasn't got your attention in the first eight bars, then move on!"

[2] *Billboard Magazine*, 8-31-74, p. 24

Other comments from Ken Hatley pertaining to Tompall include:

> In my opinion, Tompall was responsible for starting the whole outlaw movement, including Waylon and Willie's careers. The mainstream was not accepting Waylon and Willie's music, and Tompall got behind Waylon during this time frame.
>
> I liken Glaser Sound Studios in Nashville to 'Greenwich Village' during the outlaw movement years.
>
> Tompall was both the orneriest and the most kind-hearted person that I have ever met. He was a perfectionist, and he used to be tough on Jim and Chuck. He had no reservations saying what he felt, but he told people why he felt the way that he did.
>
> Tompall is humble and sensitive. However, he did not want to be known for being kindhearted.
>
> Tompall was a big inspiration in my life. One of the things that he told me concerning music was, 'Things will get tough. You can choose to be a baby and give up or not. Music is a lifelong endeavor.'
>
> I remember seeing Kris Kristofferson, Eddie Rabbit, Willie Nelson, Shel Silverstein and Mel Tillis hanging out at Glaser Sound Studios.
>
> Joanie James wrote a song about Tompall called 'Pinball Cowboy.'
>
> I still have a bubble gum machine that Tompall gave me in exchange for a painting that I gave him, which he put in his office.

Many people do not realize that Tompall is a prominent country music songwriter. In fact, Nashville television and performance star Marty Stuart talked in length about Tompall's gift for songwriting, as well as sharing several other fond memories about his friend Tompall:

> Tompall's greatest contribution to country music, in other words, 'why did he matter,' was the fact that he was a trailblazer. He kicked doors down for others. It should never be overlooked how important Tompall was.
>
> I'm not sure why Tompall did not become a household name to many people; however, he is a household name to me. Maybe because he designed it that way...I don't know for sure. The first two records I ever owned were Flatt & Scruggs and Johnny Cash, and I began listening to these when I was five-years-old. My second Johnny Cash record was *The Sound of Johnny Cash*. There was a song on there called 'Mr. Lonesome.' And when everyone else was listening to the Beatles, I was listening to 'Mr. Lonesome' over and over and over again. I saw the name T. Glaser on the record and always wondered who T. Glaser was, and I held onto that thought.
>
> The same thing with my listening to Flatt & Scruggs records. The first song of theirs that really got to me was, 'I Don't Care Anymore.' Once again, I saw the name T. Glaser. When I finally made it to Nashville and got a job here, I found out that T. Glaser was Tompall Glaser. Some of my most favorite songs ever were written by Tompall.
>
> The Glaser Brothers' harmony was undeniable...I got that. However, what separates Tompall is that he is a writer, publisher, innovator, free thinker, Bohemian, renegade, and a rascal in general. He paid the price for all of that, and he opened

the doors for a lot of people to play the kind of music that we play.

The best thing that Tompall did was to help me find a sound that enriched my life from the Mr. Lonesome days forward. I know that there were so many times, especially in the early 1970s, when he loaned people money, gave them a place to stay, and gave free studio time away to people who were 'always going to pay him,' but never got around to it. If those kinds of things are called good deeds, then his bank account is full now.

Tompall, when I look back at it...several years ago at Hank Snow's funeral...Hank was a very private man, and Tompall got up and spoke. The thing that came to my mind was that they were both kind of wild (like playing Cowboys and Indians around the house with real guns), but they were both guarded and private individuals, as well.

I respect that, so I've never intruded beyond the line of Tompall's privacy. What Tompall needs to know from my mouth is how much I love him and how much I respect him and honor him for being who he is. Tompall and the Glaser Brothers have stood the test of time. When me and my band, the Fabulous Superlatives, work on harmonies, we always go back to the Glaser Brothers. And when I think of country music 'standards' I always think of the standards set forth by Tompall & The Glaser Brothers. That gives me a lot to work off of.

Claude Hill, the former Glaser Studios engineer commented that "Tompall is a great songwriter and he has always been in tune with what is considered country as a writer or performer. He is the real deal."

Concerning songwriting, Willis David Hoover said that Tompall "taught me a lot, but I wonder if he even knows that he did. I remember once I was working on a song and he said, 'What are you trying to say there...what does that line mean?' I told him what I was thinking, and he said, 'Well, then, say it that way. Don't beat around the bush... come right out and say it.' That was great advice."

Songs written by Tompall during his professional career include:

- Running Gun (co-written with Jim Glaser)
- She Loved the Wrong Man (Big Ben Colson)
- A Girl Like You
- Mr. Lonesome
- I Don't Care Anymore
- Stand Beside Me (Tompall said this song was written in only a few minutes)
- Streets of Baltimore (co-written with Harlan Howard)
- Charlie
- Bad, Bad, Bad Cowboy
- Mama Don't Let Your Big Boy Play Outside
- (For Every Inch I've Laughed) I've Cried A Mile
- Back in Each Other's Arms Again
- Barred From Every Honky Tonk
- A Lady Needs a Bastard (co-written with Shel Silverstein)
- Velvet Wallpaper
- I Got Troubles
- When It's My Turn Again
- Gospel Medley
- Let It Be Pretty
- Date With Loneliness
- Molly Darlin'
- Silence and Tears
- Let Me Down Easy (co-written with Jim Glaser)

Songwriter Willis David Hoover with Tompall in 1977. Courtesty of Willis David Hoover

- Lovely Lucy (co-written with Lee Fry)
- Yesterday's Love
- As Far As I'm Concerned (co-written with Harlan Howard)
- The Same Old Memories
- Lonely Christmas
- Tompall in "D" on the Ukulele
- As Good For You
- Date With Loneliness
- I'm Losing Again (co-written with Dewey Brown, Charles Glaser and Jim Glaser)
- Blow Out the Candles
- Big Jim Folsom
- One Way Give and Take
- I Hear Bells
- Words Come Easy
- The Feeling In Our Hearts (That Makes A Home)
- I Backed Out
- Five Brothers
- Where Has Everything Gone Now (co-written with Way-

lon Jennings and Lynda Whitmore)
- An Ode To My Notorious Youth
- You're Making A Fool Out Of Me
- You're In My Heart Again
- I've Cried a Mile (co-written with Harlan Howard)
- I Can't Remember
- Look At Me (co-written with Marylene Smith)
- Duncan and Brady
- Before You Go
- I'm Losing Again
- That's How It Goes
- Sad Country Songs
- I Can't Remember
- Tired of Crying Over You
- Oh Little Mary (Let Me Be)

Tompall said that once he had written a song he would often try to sell it by singing it for *Grand Ole Opry* performers in their dressing rooms. He said that he would "make a pest out of myself" and would often get an immediate response from his listener, that the person either liked it, or did not.

Sharing another example of how one of his songs got recorded, Tompall recalled that he once gained access to legendary performers Earl Scruggs and Lester Flatts on their travel bus. He gave them an impromptu audition of his song "I Don't Care Anymore." They later recorded it. As far as he knew, he was the last person allowed to audition for them in that manner.

Tompall, June and others having fun at the office in the early 1970s. Courtesty of June Glaser

10

Tompall On His Own

Many people don't realize what a traditionalist Tompall was during his first decade or so in Nashville. For example, he was a member (and frequent MC) of the *Grand Ole Opry*, along with his brothers, Chuck and Jim. He was a director of the Country Music Association (CMA) in 1970, 1971 and 1972, serving alongside Tom T. Hall, Don Nelson, W.W. "Bud" Wendell, Wesley Rose, Jerry Bradley, Frances Williams Preston, and Hubert Long. Until the day of his death, Tompall emphatically stated, "I absolutely love and am passionate about country music." For him, it has always been all about the music.

But after spending many years in Nashville, Tompall became frustrated. He had several ideas about new ways to make music, but he found himself running smack dab into the rigid establishment of the time. The existing power structure in Nashville would have no part of the changes he wanted to implement, even though Tompall felt that the changes he wanted to see would *enhance* country music, not *destroy* it.

Tompall said, "We believed that we were as good musicians and singers and talents as anybody that was called pop and that we ought to be an industry unto ourselves; that we should have the ability allowed to us by the record companies to sell a million records if we reach one million people who wanted to buy them." He said life was hard for country artists back then. He explained, "In order to get more money, you had to have a hit record. In order to have a hit record, you had to have the record company promote it. In order to promote it, you had to record what they wanted."

After the Glaser brothers separated in 1973, reporter Bob Kirsch wrote an article about Tompall for *Billboard Magazine*. It was published in the August 31, 1974 edition and titled "Tompall Glaser Goes Out On His Own; Still A Stubborn Renegade." In this article, Tompall explained his attitude toward the Nashville establishment and some of his reasons for the breakup of the Glaser Brothers act:

> *"When I got to Nashville 12 years ago, I just couldn't go along with the way things were being handled. I did want to make it in the business, but I couldn't see things like giving a guy a pair of cowboy boots for half an interest in a song."*
>
> *So says Tompall Glaser, for more than a decade a third of one of the most successful country music groups in history, the Tompall & The Glaser Brothers, and now set to carve a solo career for himself.*
>
> *Glaser earned a "renegade" reputation for himself back in 1962, when he produced himself, formed a production company, began watching his own booking and thinking about the studio he and his brothers were soon to build—all things that artists in country music traditionally stayed away from. Nevertheless, he did make it in a big way.*
>
> *Glaser says, "When I got to Nashville, everything was sewed up by a few people and I didn't like that*

idea. Consequently, my brothers and I were never on the inside circle.

"I respected and do respect most of the people in Nashville," he continues. "What I really resented were those in power not allowing things to be done any way but theirs. Working away from that was and is like any other liberation movement. The older ones say 'no way' and the younger ones can't see any other way but the new way."

Citing an example of how the system worked, Glaser points out that he once wanted to produce himself. "That wasn't cool with people, so I formed a production company. Then they weren't talking to me, they were talking to a company, and that fit into the structure. That was cool."

About a year ago Glaser released a critically acclaimed LP, "Charlie," with a wide variety of material ranging from religious to cowboy to ballads to pure country. Shortly afterward, the brother act split up.

"We just got too heavy for each other," Glaser says. "We were in business together 15 years, and all our individuality had gone into the group. Each of us was only a third of our identity, which is necessary if you want to be a good group. You can't impose all of yourself on the others. But we decided to hang it up and move on.

"Now," Glaser continues, "I feel like a new artist and, in reality, I'm starting all over again. I have to come up with my own sound, because who wants to buy a third of The Glaser Brothers?"

He's now getting set to score a country musical film which he says will be "realistic and have some representative songs" for producer John Hancock. Working with him will be Shel Silverstein (who wrote all the material for his next LP), Waylon Jennings, Willie Fong Young, Kinky Friedman and Billie Joe Shavers.

Tompall performing in the mid-1970s with his Ovation guitar, which was a gift from Waylon Jennings. Courtesty of June Glaser

He's also continuing his producing and his business interests, and will be writing more. "I don't write that much," Glaser says. "What I respect in a song is somebody saying something they really have to say. A song should be something you know, but haven't heard put

175

that exact way before. As for being commercial, I want to reach people, and I can't imagine creating something just for your own amusement and unleashing it on the world. You can't do things just for yourself, because if you are an entertainer your identity is how a lot of others find entertainment or solace or whatever."

Glaser will work with as many as five producers on an LP because "I want a producer to bring me a feel along with the song. And you never learn anything unless you allow yourself to get inside someone else's head and vice versa. A couple of producers can add variety to an LP, and when I work with a producer, we work on everything together. You can't think of everything yourself and you end up in a shell if you don't get involved with other creative people."

Glaser works in his own Nashville facility, and is not adverse to spending a good deal of money on an LP. "A lot of people say the country industry can't survive with $50,000 LPs," he says. "I say it can't survive without them, if the album merits it."

Tompall, as he soon may be calling himself, minus the Glaser, says, "I don't like it when concert audiences are surprised over how good an artist sounds compared to his records. The record should be every bit as good as the performance. Things should be natural in sessions, too. The ideal thing is one take. Have the singer and the players learn the song together and then tape that take. It's something that only happens once, and it's better than artificial perfection. It's the creation of a feel and a mood."

Glaser's studio is busy, with Waylon Jennings and Kinky Friedman cutting their albums as well as material for the Heart Warming gospel label and a number of commercials.

*"A few years ago," he says, "we needed to get away
from the strictly three-chord punk honky tonk things and
Hartford's 'Gentle On My Mind' did that. Then better
budgets were needed and we got that. The industry will
not grow until those with the information start to share
it, and this is happening. There will be more changes, and
those who are not heroes to the old crowd will be heroes to
the new ones."*

During Tompall's early years as a solo act, he and his band
played in Sweden (as part of a tour arranged by English promoter
Mervyn Conn of Wembley fame). Tompall's drummer Larry London was not able to play with the band. He had signed an endorse-
ment contract with a drum manufacturer stating that he could not
play any drums that did not contain this manufacturer's logo. At this
concert, a drum set manufactured by a different company was set
up on the stage, and the concert was to be televised. So, Tompall
worked it out with Kenny Rogers to have Kenny's drummer step in
to play with Tompall's band. During this same tour, one of Tompall's
band member's parents became gravely ill. Tompall paid all travel
expenses, so he could return to the United States to be with his sick
parent.

One person who held a very special place in Tompall's heart
is Jane Poole (formerly Glover). Jane was an ardent fan of Tompall's, especially during those years when he performed without his
brothers. Jane was the former secretary of the Tompall Glaser Appreciation Society in Great Britain. In essence, she served as president of the organization. Jane has a deep appreciation and unbri-
dled admiration for Tompall. She published a newsletter and stayed
up-to-date with current events in Tompall's life. At one point, Jane
even became a "roadie" while Tompall was playing at various clubs
throughout England and other European cities. She arranged places
for him to play, made certain that travel-related itineraries worked
smoothly, and acted as a gracious hostess while Tompall, June, and

the band travelled in Europe. Jane shared her memories and her feelings about Tompall:

> I first saw Tompall on stage at Wembley Arena, London, around 1974. At this time he was going solo without Chuck and Jim. I thought then WOW what a voice. I followed his career in the country music press avidly. I also met a man by the name of Tony Peters who ran the London-based end of Acuff-Rose publishers. He knew Tompall and introduced me to him.
>
> I was totally in awe of Tompall and can't remember anything that was said. I then went to see him at every opportunity I could in U.K. and in Holland. I am sure that I was a real pest in those days to him and June, but I thought that he was terrific. I asked him on several occasions if I could run his fan club, but it took him about 10 years before he agreed. I was over the moon. I know it took both Tompall and June a long time to trust me totally, and I think that this came about when I was invited to join Tompall, June, and the band on tour.
>
> I was always aware that there was a line that I dare not cross with him and tried never to take advantage of his generosity. Like when we were on tour, if he was sitting on his own at a bar or table, I didn't sit down with him until I was invited to. I also knew that his personal/private life was just that and didn't ask him about it. I tried to keep my questions to his showbiz life. Even after all these years, I find it easier to talk to June and get tongue-tied talking to the man himself. His voice still gives me a buzz!!
>
> I still enjoy a good relationship with them both, and June and Tompall welcomed both me and

my husband Frank when we came over to Nashville to see him four years ago. Tompall was in hospital at the time and really quite sick. I felt very privileged that he wanted to see me but so sad to see a man who had been so vibrant just lying there.

I remember times when we were on tour that after the show Tompall would 'hold court' at the hotel. The band and I would sit in a bar and listen to Tompall telling amusing stories about his life on the road and the people he met and worked with. There was one magical evening when we were in Scotland. It was in the early hours of the morning, and the hotel had kept the bar open for him and the band. His bass player on this tour was Ken Smith who also did vocal backings and Tompall and Ken sang 'Cool Water.' Everybody came out from behind the bar to listen. I only wish that I had been able to record it. Just after that the band started telling jokes, and Tompall stopped them and turned to me and said, 'Jane, time for you to go to bed.' I knew not to argue!!!

One time I took him and June to a radio station in London to meet up with a presenter named Bob Powell, whose show was aired live on a Sunday morning. As we went in, I fell down a slope and cut my leg. Then on the way out, June fell and did the same thing. Tompall looked at us and said 'Goddammit! I can't take you two anywhere.' June laughed and said to me, 'Well, he WAS concerned about our well-being.' Until that day, Bob Powell had never acknowledged my existence, but after that he was always extremely friendly towards me.

On the tour in 1987, Tompall raised money on behalf of the Rotary Club in England for POLIO

PLUS. The Rotary Club is run by business men and women in order to raise money for worthy charities, and this was the Rotary Club's charity for that year. It was to vaccinate children in third world countries against polio, measles, and whooping cough. Tompall was able to hand over enough money to vaccinate about 10,000 children.

He was also very generous with his time towards fans and journalists. They were often invited back to the hotel for a talk and drinks. Needless to say, they were extremely thrilled. I know that he has helped struggling musicians with advice and with his expertise regarding their careers. When I went to see him in Holland, he arranged for me to be picked up at the Amsterdam airport on at least three occasions and taken to where the show was being held.

As for his contribution to country music, well, I feel that his talent, knowledge, and total generosity towards others has to play a big part. I have never thought that he was 'marketed' enough by the record companies and that his talent was never exposed enough. I guess though, that he was happy with what was happening, as he liked his privacy. I know that his U.K. fans were always hungry for more!

The album *Charlie* was Tompall's first attempt as a *solo* artist. It received positive reviews from song critics. This album was recorded under the MGM/Curb Records label before Curb was the huge Nashville name that it is today. Tompall remembered that Mike Curb was a hard-working guy in the years that they worked together. Tompall said that Mike would sometimes take "No Doze" in order to keep going (but nothing stronger), and that he respected Mike as a person and what Mike has accomplished over the years.

Simply put, Mike Curb is a Nashville institution. To fully

appreciate what he has accomplished thus far in his life, visit his biography page at www.mikecurb.com/about/bio.cfm. However, here is a brief snapshot of his many accolades: he was lieutenant governor and governor of California; he is president of Curb Records (a well-known independent record label), and he has written more than 400 songs. Curb is also a song producer, chairman of the Mike Curb Family Foundation, and the chairman of Word Entertainment. In addition, he has been awarded stars on both the Nashville Music City Walk of Fame and the Hollywood Walk of Fame.

Here are some of Mike Curb's comments about Tompall:

My most memorable experience was working with him on the soundtrack ...tick...tick...tick..., which was an MGM film, and I was amazed at how this soundtrack expanded his audience and how quickly Tompall and his brothers adapted their music to the film industry.

Tompall always cared about everyone he was working with; he made sure that everyone felt that their role was important, and he inspired everyone who worked with him.

I believe that Tompall Glaser & The Glaser Brothers were the original outlaws in country music. I believe that they inspired Waylon Jennings, Willie Nelson, Kris Kristofferson, and others who made great contributions to the outlaw country movement.

When I signed their record contract in late 1969, it was two weeks before I signed Hank Williams Jr., and four weeks before I signed Mel Tillis. This would make Tompall & The Glaser Brothers the first major country music signing for Curb Records in Nashville.

As he worked towards releasing *Charlie*, Tompall decided to begin charging an upfront flat fee to record companies to produce his albums; then he let the record companies keep royalties generated from sales. For instance, it was not unusual for him to receive payments of $250,000 or more to produce a record. He would then spend up to $25,000 just for the production costs for the album itself, i.e., for session musicians, producer time, and other costs.

Tompall released *Charlie* in 1973, followed by an album simply titled *Tompall* in 1974, and in 1975 he put out *Tompall Sings The Songs Of Shel Silverstein*. However, in 1976, what I describe as a sentinel event took place. Hospitals use these two words to describe "an unexpected occurrence involving death or serious physical or psychological injury, or the risk thereof." Basically, it involves a single event that a major outcome can be traced back to. In my mind, the release of *Wanted! The Outlaws* album in 1976 was a sentinel event because this one album forever changed country music.

In the mid-1970s, RCA vice-president and head of the Nashville office, Jerry Bradley, came up with the idea of assembling several country recording artists together in one album. He wanted to give the album packaging an old-time western flavor so he thought up a weathered parchment "wanted" poster with singed corners and bullet holes throughout. The album featured Tompall Glaser, Willie Nelson, Jessi Colter and her husband, Waylon Jennings. "Outlaws" was a moniker that was already in use for Tompall and other artists who were recording at Glaser Studios. Bradley incorporated that word into the album name *Wanted! The Outlaws* and featured photos of the artists in black and white on the cover. Waylon's photo was featured on top with the other three situated below. Bradley's intent was to showcase Waylon with the hope that he would become a bigger star after the album's release.

The album was released in January of 1976 and went gold ($1,000,000 in sales) soon thereafter. The album then went platinum (sales of one million units). *Wanted! The Outlaws* was the first country music album to achieve this impressive feat.

Two of Tompall's songs were included in the *Wanted! The Outlaws* album: "T For Texas," Tompall's version of a song written by Jimmie Rodgers, and "Put Another Log on the Fire" that was written by Shel Silverstein.

"Put Another Log on the Fire" (aka the "Male Chauvinist National Anthem") reached #21 on the *Billboard* chart and was Tompall's last hit record.

Red Young (www.redyoung.com) is a talented professional musician who has toured with some of the biggest names in the music business. He grew up in Fort Worth, Texas, and has been playing the piano since he was three-years-old. In 1976, he was part of the Tompall Glaser Outlaw Band that toured with Waylon Jennings, Willie Nelson, and Jessi Coulter after the release of *Wanted! The Outlaws* album. He shared several memories about his time with Tompall:

> In 1976, on a trip back to Nashville, Lee Emerson (who wrote several songs with Marty Robbins) gave me a call about the possibility of being a keyboardist on an upcoming tour with Tompall Glaser in a package called *Wanted! The Outlaws* with Willie Nelson, Waylon Jennings, and Jessi Colter, with occasional opening acts of Steve Young or others. The band consisted of Mel Brown on guitar, Charles Polk on drums (both having recently played with Bobby "Blue" Bland), Ben Keith on steel guitar (from Neil Young's Band), with Ted Reynolds on base, Fred Newell on guitar, and Tompall on vocals and guitar. It was a very eclectic band with blues, jazz, and country all coming from the same people. As the opening act to audiences of up to 25,000, seeing this band start with 'Ode to Billy Joe' as an instrumental with Big Mel Brown on guitar, Red on piano, and Ben on steel guitar was quite a stunning effect on the audience of

hippies and rednecks. The hit song for Tompall was
'Put Another Log on the Fire' and with Willie and
Waylon, 'Good Hearted Woman' and the album that
featured all performers was the first country album
to go platinum. Tompall gave me a platinum record
even though I didn't play on it because he was so
happy to get it! There were many stories of the three-
week tour of five buses containing three bands and
road crews and many I can't recall.

The tour started in Salt Lake City, then
Denver, Albuquerque, El Paso, Tucson, Phoenix,
Hollywood Bowl, Fresno, San Francisco, Reno and
other places, ending in Norman, Oklahoma. When
we hit the West Coast, the Hells Angels were our
security guards. They would continually ask us if
we needed any women, drugs, alcohol. And our
answer would be '...Yes!!...' We used to joke about
Ben Keith saying he would take anything that would
make him feel different from what he was feeling
right now... it was a hell of an experience, and some
good memories and good music played. Shows were
typically five to six hours long: Tompall would do
one hour, Jessi (backed up by Waylon's band) one
hour, Waylon one and one-half hours, then 'Good
Hearted Woman' with both Waylon and Willie, and
then Willie's band for the next three hours. Sometimes Willie would play first and sometimes Waylon. One night Willie's band was the 'Good Hearted
Women' dressing up in dresses. It was a great time
and a *great way* to start my touring career.

After the tour, after a few weeks in Ft Worth,
I came to Nashville and stayed in the Hall Of Fame
along with my Triumph Motorcycle and van for two
months. I thought Tompall had told me he was go-

ing to take care of the accommodations, but I misunderstood and had to sneak out late one night. But during the time I was in Nashville, we started working on the *Outlaw Band* album with 'You Can Have Her,' 'Release Me,' 'Tennessee Blues,' 'Come Back Shane' (Tompall's song to Waylon), 'It Ain't Fair Medley,' 'Sweethearts Or Strangers,' 'Let My Fingers Do The Walking,' and 'I Just Want To Hear The Music.' It was a very loose recording with much Jack Daniels and other inspirational enhancements, a lot of hanging out at Tompall Land (Glaser Sound Studio on 19th Avenue South), and many characters coming and going like Captain Midnight (who actually lived at the studio), June, Colleen, and others coming and going.

One of the songs, 'I Just Want To Hear The Music' had special guests Buddy Spicher and Johnny Gimble. We cut for the whole band live: Charles Polk/drums and Ted Reynolds/bass, with Ben Keith on steel and dobro. Mel Brown on guitar and me on piano and Hammond organ. Since this was a one-off session (most Nashville sessions ran on time at 10, 2 and 6, and ran for 3 hours, but when at Tompall's place we just went however long we wanted). But with the extra players Buddy Spicher and Johnny Gimble, things didn't jell right away as we hadn't all played together before. Tompall started the session and since it didn't hit the stride this group of players should have had, excused himself to go to work on the lyrics. After an hour of sitting around and talking with just the musicians, one by one the guys went in the studio and started jamming: first Johnny, then Buddy, then Mel, then me, then the whole crew and we just played for an hour or more.

We were having fun playing whatever came to mind that we were capable of and interacting and inspiring each other to play. At the beginning of the third hour, Tompall showed up, and I'm sure he knew what had been going on in his absence because he was not far away. We cut the track in one take, and at the end of it went on for at least five minutes longer than it is on the album. Tompall knew that this caliber of players are not ones to just sit around and do nothing until he returned, so by leaving, it allowed us to know each other as players of great capacity. When he returned (as if on cue), we were ready to play anything that was put in front of us.

I remember once during the recording session I wasn't playing simple enough for Tompall's idea for what the piano should be playing. He told me, 'I'm going to cut off your fingers one at a time until you're left with only one...' 'You mean I'm playing too much?' 'Yes!'

There was another song on the album called 'You Can Have Her,' which Tompall called Disco Billy as Disco was coming out at that time. The producer Ken Mansfield (who had produced albums for Waylon among others) wanted to add some things to the track. I suggested horns and he knew some guys in Los Angeles. I wrote the parts for them since I had been in the Air Force Band and done some arranging for horns, and Ken took it and did a session with them in LA with Jim Horn and others. It was my first recording of arrangements I had written. And it sounded good.

Apparently, I sang background vocals on some of the songs. I had written vocal arrangements in Houston at Sugar Hill with Tracey Balin on many of the Freddy Fender recordings from 1975-76, so I had my arranging abilities in high form, and I probably used that skill on the recordings as well as I was credited with being a singer.

With the Outlaw Band, we played some gigs I can't remember very well, just bits and pieces. One was at Old Hickory Lake with Mickey Newbury. It was a benefit for someone I can't remember. We did one gig at Charlotte's Web in Rockford, Illinois, in which we flew in a small private plane. I remember a couple of other trips, one to the Palamino in North Hollywood, and Ben Keith took us on a tour of places where he had lived in San Fernando Valley. Tompall insisted on using the 'Marty Robbin's Door' that they had to build for Marty so he wouldn't have to walk through the crowd to get to the stage; he could simply walk from the outside right on to the stage. Another memorable trip was to San Francisco and a performance for a few nights at the Boarding House where Steve Martin recorded his first live album, and many other performers had played as well. Hells Angels did a lot of hanging with us along with some of their women and associates. It was a memorable time.

Shortly after the last California trip, I decided that instead of moving to Nashville and pursuing my career there, I would go to Los Angeles—I had an offer to join Sonny & Cher's group, and several friends of mine were in the band. One other reason for the decision was that the last time I stayed in Nashville, the Cumberland River froze solid and the coal barges couldn't come down river to bring the coal that heated the power generators. So we didn't have electric power in Nashville, leaving many places without electricity or heat for much of the day or night. It left much of the city, including me, freezing. That put me over the top and sent me heading toward the warmer area of California.

The last time I was in Nashville with Tompall, however, I stayed in the Days Inn on Murfreesboro Road and hooked up with longtime friends Delbert McClinton and new acquaintance Greg 'Fingers' Taylor on a session that had both of them playing harmonica. It was a good time, but also reminded me I needed to go west.

Tompall played in a variety of venues at this point in his career. He recalled that once he and his band were playing in an auditorium directly below where Joan Rivers was performing. Joan sent someone down to tell Tompall to turn down the volume on his band's amplifiers because his music was disrupting her show. Tompall told her representative that he would turn down his volume if she would quit talking about her hysterectomy. He had heard her talk about her operation every night, for what seemed like hours during her show, and Tompall was getting sick and tired of hearing about it!

It is fitting to mention Waylon Jennings when discussing the years that Tompall was a solo performer. Waylon was also becoming fed up with the status quo in Nashville. He wanted more artistic freedom to produce records the way that he felt they should sound. Waylon heard about Glaser Sound Studio and one day just showed up with his band, ready to record.

Waylon was completely broke and facing bankruptcy when he first arrived at Glaser Sound Studios in the early 1970s. In fact, June Glaser remembers that he was at the point of hiding his car so it wouldn't be repossessed. But Waylon and Tompall hit it off and had a shared vision about what they felt country music should be. So, in exchange for a 40% interest in publishing royalties from Waylon's company, Baron Music, Waylon was given a rent-free office at the studio and all of the recording time that he wanted, at no charge.

Jennings liked the feel of the Glaser studio and recorded several albums there. His first was *Honky Tonk Heroes* in 1973, co-produced by Waylon and Tompall.

After the *Wanted! The Outlaws* album's 1976 release, three more albums were cut by Waylon at Glaser Sound Studios for Waylon's record label, RCA Records. During Waylon's recordings at Glaser Studios, Tompall recalled that RCA Records became upset because union engineers were not used in the recording process and his studios had nevertheless charged RCA $119 per hour, which was the full hourly rate at that time. While Tompall never charged Waylon for studio time, he did charge RCA when a record was cut. It took a very long time, but RCA did eventually pay what they owed for the studio recording sessions.

Tompall and Waylon's arrangement worked out fabulously until 1976, when Waylon's manager at the time, Neil "Mad Dog" Reshen accused Tompall of not paying Waylon and Jessi Colter all of the publishing royalties due to them. The issue went to court, and Tompall sought $300,000 in damages from Jessi Colter and Waylon Jennings for breach of contract in management of the publishing rights to over 100 songs. There were suits and countersuits, but the final outcome resulted in more than just dollars paid. A close friendship came to an abrupt end. Later, Waylon fired Reshen because Waylon's finances were in shambles. In his autobiography, *Waylon: An Autobiography*, he states, "Neil had to go…my damn business was screwed up."[3]

One recurring statement from the people I interviewed for this book was that Tompall is an honest person who never cheated anyone, and he was someone who had always treated people fairly.

Once the lawsuits were underway, Tompall and Waylon no longer spoke to one another. While they performed on the same stage during their West Coast Outlaw Tour, newspaper reviews

[3] Waylon Jennings with Lenny Kaye, *Waylon: An Autobiography* (Grand Central Publishing, 1996), 276-277.

Waylon with Tompall in Tompall's office in the early 1970s. Courtesy of Louis C. Glaser

made little mention about Tompall Glaser's portion of the show. Part of the reason for this may well have been that Tompall's time on stage didn't sound as good as when Waylon, Willie, and Jessi were on stage. One person I interviewed claimed that the sound people who were used during the tour took Waylon's side in the disagreement and may have sabotaged Tompall's sound more than once.

But know this: Tompall loved Waylon. He was heartbroken when they went their separate ways, and he even wrote a poem to express his sentiments, titled *A Cowboy's Lament*, which is included in this book. In this 1976 poem, Tompall muses about watching a friend who has "just done you in." Concerning Waylon, Tompall's wife June said, "I always liked Waylon, and I have never harbored any ill will towards him. Waylon worked very hard to get where he was, and I've always respected him for that."

Few may know that Jimmy Bowen is a former pop star since he is generally thought of as a genius music producer. As a producer, he has worked with a variety of different performers, including Frank Sinatra, Dean Martin, Sammy Davis, Jr., Mel Tillis, Hank Williams, Jr., George Strait, Garth Brooks and, yes, Tompall Glaser.

When he first moved to Nashville, Tompall gave Bowen an office. "I spent up to 18 hours a day in Tompall's studio," recalled Bowen, "listening, absorbing, and producing. Tompall was the best supporter, teacher, and friend I could have had. He'd take me down to his office, which was the biggest mess I've ever seen. He had tapes, 45s, and gold LPs scattered all over, but he knew exactly where everything was." Bowen added, "there was one night when no one got advance word of a drug bust, and everyone in the studio flushed contraband substances down the toilet. The public utilities must have noted a huge momentary usage of water and an accompanying sewer volume increase." In 1978, Bowen started Elektra Records Nashville division and signed the newly regrouped Glaser Brothers.

Jimmy Bowen has strong feelings about Tompall and spoke to me at length about him. Here are excerpts from his comments to me:

> When I first came to Nashville from California, I spent one year with Tompall. He taught me everything about Nashville: who the players were, good contacts, people to stay away from, who was trustworthy, and who was not. Tompall saved me about five years by sharing his knowledge about Nashville.
>
> One question that has really struck me is, 'Why didn't Tompall become a household name like Waylon and Willie?' My answer strikes the very essence of who Tompall is. In music, you have the music side and the business side. Tompall and I were alike in that we both liked *both* of these sides of music. Waylon and Willie just wanted to do their music. But you need to know that Tompall is a household name to many people...he touched a lot of people. I feel that another consideration is the fact that a person who is part of a trio probably does not have a burning desire to be a huge solo artist, especially

when they have other things (such as publishing and running a studio) to occupy their time.

We were all part of that era when Nashville was starting to make a change, when the artists were starting to take control of the songs they wanted to record. Tompall loved the publishing side, and he loved the studio, which you can hear in the beautiful harmonies that he and his brothers made.

Tompall is unique, as are the other two outlaws (Waylon and Willie), as well as Dolly (Parton), and others who were part of that time of country music change. Tompall got into the available recording technology of that time, including multi-track recordings. He loved having people at his studio recording and many times would let them record for free.

Tompall taught me about country music. I first came from Los Angeles to Nashville because I did not want to work with rock and roll or pop groups. I wanted to make music for adults and felt that country music was the way to do that.

I first met Tompall when I ran MGM Records in LA. That is when I first got a sense of who he was, and what he was, and that he had a passion and a vision for country music.

I had come to Nashville a few times in the past to look for good songs, so I was familiar with some of the people who ran country music at that time.

Tompall taught me the *music* of country music. He said things like, 'Bowen, you don't know how a steel guitar should sound,' and 'You don't know how a fiddle should sound,' and Tompall taught me about these things, at least the way that Tompall felt it should be. I synched in with Tompall immediately on the music end of things.

I learned so much when I was with Tompall—it was just like going to college for a year and learning about a subject. I feel I would not have been successful in Nashville without first understanding the roots, the soul, of Nashville country music. And that is what Tompall taught me.

Tompall enjoyed what I was bringing to the music, and I enjoyed what Tompall was teaching about it and his opinions about how fast a change could move or should move.

Tompall is a very deep thinking guy. He filled me in on the inner workings of the Nashville music community. Nashville is a very small community.

When I emerged after spending that year with Tompall and got back into the business side of it, I knew all the players.

My time with Tompall was incredibly valuable for all of the luck and success that I experienced while I was in Nashville.

Tompall enjoyed helping me. He enjoyed helping other people. He was part of the change in Nashville; he loved seeing it happen. He got a joy out of seeing an increase in artistic control in music.

I did produce songs for Tompall and my opinion of him during our sessions was that 'he was a pro.' He had been around and knew the process. He knew that it was his music, not mine. I have always felt that my job as a producer was to help an artist do what they wanted to do. The time I spent producing Tompall was great fun and very enjoyable. We had more laughs for more hours than we ever should have in the studio, and we tried everything new that came along. We did not do a lot together, but what we did do was great fun.

Part of the reason that I wanted to work with Tompall in his studio was that I didn't want to own my own Nashville studio. Many Nashville music producers did own their own studio, and that is why I mistakenly got painted with the same broad brush. My opinion is that owning a studio does not foster a good relationship between the artist and the producer.

Tompall's music studio was his laboratory. He loved it. He never made any money off his studio; he owned the studio for another reason.

Country music needs people in it who love country music so that as times change, and that music changes, it always keeps some of its soul...its roots. I'll tell you this: Tompall cared more about country music than anyone else in Nashville.

While I was still in Los Angeles, somebody suggested that I needed to check out Tompall's music studio when I got to Nashville, that it was somewhere where I might like to work. Back then, Nashville had studios like RCA Studios and Columbia Studios, and these were like the LA and New York studios. Great big, mammoth things, but very sterile. I didn't feel comfortable there, so I sought out Tompall's studio. Tompall's place was somewhere where you could walk in and kick off your shoes, and the lights would not blind you like they would in other recording studios.

Most of the time that Tompall and I spent together while in Nashville was at the studio. During that year that we were together, we only hung out two or three times outside the studio. One reason was that Tompall really loved to play the pinball machine, and I didn't play pinball.

In addition to producing Tompall, I produced Mel Tillis at Glaser Studios and Merle Haggard, as well as other recording artists.

I remember that before I arrived at Nashville, session drummers were responsible for carrying their own equipment into and out of the recording studios. I felt that after the drummers spent an hour carrying items in and getting set up, it was difficult for them to give a lot of energy for a three-hour recording session. So I found a cartage business in Nashville that had not done a lot with the music industry, and they started carrying in the drums and setting them up. When I first began submitting bills for the cartage, the bill processor had never heard the term before. She asked what the 'carta' bills were for over at Glaser Studios.

By fighting the country music establishment of the time, Tompall was considered a 'bad boy.' Any time you go against something that has been established a certain way, whether they are right or wrong, it is their life and they profit from it. They always resist change, whatever it is. I don't know why the artists were not given control, but Tompall was part of the reason for this change happening.

During this period when Bowen was spending a great deal of time with Tompall in Glaser Studio, Jerry Lee Lewis announced that he "had it out" for Jimmy Bowen. Because of this, Tompall began carrying a gun, bringing it with him to his studio. Tompall thought then, and a great number of people agreed with him, that Jerry Lee Lewis was "a crazy man...*seriously wild and crazy.*"

Joe Osborn is an amazing bass guitar player who spent much

of his music career in the 1960s through the 1980s as a session player. He spent several years in both Los Angeles and Nashville and played with such diverse artists as Neil Diamond, Ricky Nelson, the Beach Boys, The Association, Simon & Garfunkel, The Fifth Dimension, The Mamas & The Papas, Johnny Rivers, Kenny Rogers, Mel Tillis and Hank Williams, Jr., as well as Tompall Glaser. Joe is credited with discovering the brother and sister act, The Carpenters.

Joe said that he met Tompall at Glaser Studios shortly after Jimmy Bowen arrived in Nashville. Joe had done quite a bit of work for Bowen while he was in Los Angeles, but moved to the Nashville area at the end of 1974. He worked with Tompall on sessions that Bowen produced during this time frame.

Osborn did a lot of hanging out at the studio and Tompall and he became friends right away. "It may have been drinking that became our common ground, or the fact that I was just about as mean as Tompall, but we really hit it off. I really enjoyed working with Tompall a lot, and we spent quite a bit of time together talking about all sorts of things," said Joe.

Osborn remembers: "When recording at Tompall's studio we would usually work from 6 pm to midnight. After that, we would go downstairs to the office and put on the rough mixes of the sessions and listen to that, have some drinks, and talk about everything." Tompall was like the other artists Joe had worked with in the past. He wanted to get the sound "just right." No, worse, in Joe's opinion: "You never know how long it will take to get a track recorded. Three hours was a normal session; then the musicians would take a break and return for another session. They kept at it until they got it right, but usually they would stop around midnight. Most times, musicians wouldn't care if they had to stay longer because they billed by the hour.

"Tompall had a temper, but I never really saw him get on anybody seriously about anything; nobody messed with Tompall too much.

"I had started to become quite busy in Nashville as a session player. When Bowen contacted me to play for Tompall in his studio, I suggested some other musicians they might also want to consider using. For Tompall's sessions we ended up with Larry London on drums, Reggie Young, and Bobby Wood. Sometimes Pig would come in to play piano, and Bobby Thompson or Jimmy Capps would play guitar."

In 1978 Tompall toured England. He performed at the Country Music Festival in Wembley, England, as well as four other countries. Joe Osborn recalls, "I was part of Tompall's band that included Reggie Young, Larry London, Bobby Thompson, and Buddy Emmons on steel guitar." He continues, "All of Tompall's shows in Europe were packed. He got a very good audience reception. The studio band played with Tompall, which helped. Buddy Emmons was England's #1 steel guitar player at the time, so he got a lot of attention. Tompall felt some resentment about Buddy's popularity, especially one night when Tompall felt Buddy was getting too much applause. Well, you know Tompall has a big ego, so I can understand that.

"Tompall certainly had the talent to be as big a star as anyone. He was the best singer in the Nashville bunch, no question about that. He was a great singer and entertainer. Tompall would talk about when the Outlaw band broke up. They kind of left him behind. But I think that the reason they no longer included him was because of his attitude, his temper, and that sort of thing. I think that he just didn't have their temperament and their way of looking at the whole picture. I think that was a lot of it. They couldn't take his sometimes belligerence. Tompall didn't want to admit this, so he just talked about them leaving him behind. He just kind of did it to himself, really. Tompall was his own worst enemy. It certainly wasn't because he wasn't a talented musician and singer.

"We did some things in the studio that were not even released. These songs were some of the best stuff I've *ever* heard Tompall do. I don't know if it was his relationship with the label that was behind the songs not getting out, or what the cause was.

"That whole Outlaw thing was really about artists saying

we are sick and tired of being told what to do. And Tompall was certainly a leader in that idea, and he practiced what he preached. I don't know if Waylon ever got as serious about going his own way as Tompall actually did. And Willie didn't seem like a fighter to me. Tompall probably stuck to the idea a lot closer than the two of them did, so he was definitely a big factor in all of that and probably influenced other people who felt the same way. Most of the people just went along with the program, and Tompall didn't want to do that; and he was right, of course. The way that different music comes about is when you break out of the mold. And he wasn't in that Nashville mold.

"I love Tompall. He is one of my favorite people. I dealt with his paranoia and insecurities. He would ask me questions like, 'Why would you want to hang around me?' And I would respond, 'Maybe it's because I like you.' Sometimes, he would get hung up on making a deal because he would be afraid that he would make a mistake. Tompall didn't trust many people, but he is one of my most favorite people that I ever met. He was a complicated person in a good way. He was a super intelligent person. We had wonderful conversations on such a wide variety of topics. He had a very broad base of knowledge, and whatever subject came up he was able to contribute to the conversation.

"Tompall was a partier. One night he was drinking sake in a Japanese restaurant, and he called me up and said, 'Joe, come on over here when you get done.' So I showed up after my session, it must have been around 10:30 pm. He was already wiped-out, so he started doubling me up on shots of sake to catch up with him. I said, 'Tompall, I'm already as drunk as you are!' And he said, 'I know, but you're not as belligerent.' "

Richard S. "Kinky" Friedman is an author, singer, songwriter, politician and newspaper columnist, among many other things. One of his best known recordings was the album *Sold American* that was produced in 1973 by Chuck Glaser. Kinky is one of the most interesting people that I interviewed for this book. He is philosophical, intelligent, and opinionated. More about Kinky can be found at www.kinkyfriedman.com.

Here are Kinky's reflections about Tompall Glaser:

The story of Tompall and his brothers is somewhat of a Greek tragedy.

It's very hard to calculate the importance of the Glaser Brothers, and the driving force behind the Glaser Brothers was Tompall.

Tompall's stubbornness was legendary, but he had great instincts and was right nearly all of the time.

The *spirit* of Tompall was important; he had a lot to do with the outlaw movement.

I know that Tompall took people and country music seriously, but not himself.

Captain Midnight would have been homeless if not for Tompall.

Waylon Jennings learned a lot from Tompall. Waylon did not take himself seriously. He kept in mind that if he had not given up his airplane seat to Buddy Holly, he would have died. Waylon had a lot of swagger. For instance, he used to wink at the audience. I feel that Waylon picked up this attitude from Tompall.

The Glaser Studio was a place where a person could make music the way they wanted to. It was kind of a Camelot, and it was a hub for many different people—myself included.

I liken the Glaser Sound Studio to the Statue of Liberty because they took in all people. The Glaser Brothers had a lot of influence on country music because 'they did it first.'

Tompall kept his music studio open 24-hours a day.

Tompall encouraged people to 'sail against the wind.' Because of this, the establishment did not like Tompall. The existing music establishment frowned upon country music artists trying something different. In fact, Johnnie Cash couldn't even get a record deal at one point.

Tom had the money and the power to make change happen. As a performer, he was not as musically talented as some, but he inspired the attitude and spirit of the outlaw movement. I see him as the stage manager/puppeteer of the outlaw movement.

The Glaser Brothers broke the Nashville establishment chains—and paid the price.

The question will get asked whether the Glasers created the outlaw mood, or whether they were just there at the right time. In my opinion, they helped *create* the outlaw movement in a *big way*.

I feel that if Tompall would've had a chance to be a record company executive, he could have done something marvelous. I also feel that Tompall would've been a great movie studio head a few decades ago—because of his creativity, and due to the fact that he worked well with other people. Listening to ideas was not done in Nashville, but Tompall did.

Tompall was *significant*, not just important, to country music. The president is important, as are senators, mayors and other politicians; however, they are not significant, in my opinion. Tompall has had a profound impact and influence on the world around him. Sometimes this was overt, and sometimes not.

Tompall helped architect a movement that allowed Waylon, Willie, and others to be heard.

Today, the big publishing houses are whorehouses. Back when Tompall had his studio running, there were four great songwriters: Kris Kristofferson, Shel Silverstein, Willie Nelson, and Roger Miller. I feel that many songs of today are just rehashed songs written by these four people. Today's songs are 'derivative' and they suck.

The crowd is always wrong. Given a choice, they always choose Barabbas over Jesus. Jesus was considered an outsider, just like Tompall.

Bob Dylan said that Art should subvert Culture. That is what Tompall did.

Tompall charted the way for people for years to come, and he did it as an outsider looking in. For example, he didn't go to the record companies, etc.

Because Tompall was head of Glaser Publishing, he frequently interacted with the performance rights organization, Broadcast Music, Inc. (BMI). Frances Williams Preston was the president and CEO of BMI from 1986 to 2004. She had a storied professional career and was well known throughout Nashville for her leadership and acts of altruism. Between the time that I began writing this book and when it was published, Ms. Williams Preston passed away. Her death was a huge loss for country music and the entire Nashville community. However, I was privileged to speak with her before her passing, and here are her recollections about her interactions with Tompall:

Tompall was always very nice in all of my dealings with him. This included discussing contracts, etc. He was very well-mannered...which was not what I expected from a hillbilly! Tompall was kind to people, in general, based upon what I observed. I believe that his greatest contribution to country music was the fact that he was always fresh and always stood out from others in country music at the time. Concerning why Tompall didn't become more of a household name, I'd have to say it was because he was so busy. He ran the companies that the Glaser brothers owned and did not have time to devote strictly to performing.

Del Bryant took over the helm of BMI from Frances Williams Preston in 2004 and is currently BMI's president and CEO. Mr. Bryant has a long and rich Nashville background, having been raised by parents who were successful musicians and songwriters. In fact, his parents, Felice and Boudleaux Bryant, wrote the hit bluegrass song "Rocky Top," which is the official Tennessee State song. In addition, they wrote hit songs for the Everly Brothers, such as" Bye Bye Love," "Wake Up Little Susie," and "All I Have to Do Is Dream." The Bryants also wrote "Lay Down the Gun" and "She Loves the Love I Give Her," which were among the first songs recorded by Tompall, Chuck, and Jim (late 1958 and early 1959).

Like many performers in the 1960s, the Bryants brought Del with them when they performed at the *Grand Ole Opry*, and Del could often be found in the backstage area of the *Opry* which is where Tompall first met him.

Del said he remembers that Tompall & The Glaser Brothers gave exciting performances at the *Grand Ole Opry*. He also commented that Tompall seemed to change after he experienced a major cut on his upper lip. Del had no idea what had happened to Tompall's lip, but said that Tompall began sporting a beard soon afterwards to hide his prominent scar.

When I asked Tompall about this scar, he said that it was the result of a train accident. Tompall said, "I owned a Chevy Corvair and was driving it home from the office one night. As I crossed the railroad tracks a train struck my car and totaled it, badly injuring me in the process. I sued the railroad and obtained a settlement from them." Upon reflection, Tompall said that this incident likely did change him. "You don't come that close to death without it having an impact on you."

In Del's words, "If things would have *twisted a bit differently,* Tompall would have been *a huge phenomenon.*"

Danny Finley (Panama Red) is a guitar player who could often be found around Glaser Studio in the 1970s and who occasionally played guitar for Tompall Glaser. More information about Panama Red can be found on his website at www.panamaredmusic. com. Here is what Panama had to say about Tompall:

> Tompall was always generous, sharing his knowledge in all areas, including financial, music, and more. One thing that Tompall imparted upon me was the statement that 'Simplicity is the key to life. You will likely get the same answer from someone whether you spend a lot of time in preparation beforehand or not.'
>
> I feel that Tompall never got the musical recognition that he deserved. Tompall's greatest contribution to country music was probably in the music business end of things. When I first got to town, I spent a considerable amount of time in Tompall's studio and was often present when Tompall 'held court.' I remember that Tompall always paid on time. All of my memories and feelings about Tompall are positive.

Billy Swan (www.billyswanmusic.com) is a singer and songwriter. Although he has accomplished much in the music world, he may be best remembered for his hit record "I Can Help," which hit #1 on the *Billboard* Chart in 1974. Billy spent time at the Glaser Sound Studio and shared his memories about Tompall:

I first saw Tompall, Chuck, and Jim in the 1960s while living in Nashville. I got closer to them when I started hanging out with Kinky Friedman, who lived in an apartment above me on Broadway.

Kinky and his brother, Roger, were working out of Glaser Studios and I would see Tompall at the studio during the day and would also occasionally see him later in the day at the Burger Boy playing pinball with Waylon Jennings.

Tompall had considered me to play keyboard on 'Put Another Log on the Fire,' but it never came together. However, I was one of the singers in the chorus of this song and can be heard singing near the end of this recording.

I remember seeing Shel Silverstein and Waylon Jennings often at Glaser Studios, as well as John Hartford.

Kinky Friedman had an office at the studio and recorded *Sold American* there. I was part of Kinky's band, The Texas Jewboys, for a while.

Tompall was one of those guys who would do it 'however he wanted to do it' and Waylon was the same way.

Among Tompall's greatest contributions to country music were publishing, singing, and giving songwriters a chance. For instance, I don't know where Kinky would have gone to do his songwriting and recording if Tompall had not given him the opportunity to do it at Glaser Studios. Tompall had a great voice. He also had good taste, a different taste when it came to picking out songs. He was always willing to give people a chance.

Glaser Sound Studios was a great place to hang out, it was always 'cool.' It had a very relaxed atmosphere and was always 'loose.'

Tompall did three songs for a Marlo Thomas movie soundtrack in 1976. He sang two of the songs, and the other one was an instrumental titled "Tompall in D on the Ukulele," which was just short of one minute in length. According to Tompall, he tuned his ukulele up one octave to achieve the sound he wanted. To the best of his knowledge, no one had done this before. After the release of this song (as part of a Marlo Thomas movie soundtrack), there was a resurgence in the use of ukuleles. Tompall attributed this to his record since the ukulele had been very much a forgotten instrument up to this time.

Gary Vincent, and his wife, Carol, are the owners of Vincent Productions, a music and film production company. The Vincents' business is a joint venture with actor Morgan Freeman and well-known Mississippi attorney Bill Luckett.

Gary said that Tompall was his mentor as a musician. He was living in Pittsburgh and decided to "bite the bullet" and go to Nashville to be a songwriter for a living. According to Gary, "Tompall was gracious enough to let me be a fly on the wall and to hang out at Glaser Studio during those crazy days when they were making all those records. He gave me my start, really."

Gary said that he had some luck and had a hit song with Mickey Gilley (Back in the Doo-Wah Days) and when that happened, Tompall tried to work on him as an artist. "He actually worked with me for quite a while trying to get me a record deal in Nashville. At the time, Jimmy Bowen said I sounded more like Jimmy Buffett than a country artist, so I never did get a record deal. However, having Tompall's tutelage was just incredible. He was very, very gracious in giving me my start.

"There were so many people spending time at Glaser Studios when I was there. Billy Ray Reynolds was recording there a lot. Captain Midnight was always around, and he was a blast. Joe Osborn was a close friend of Tompall's and was there often. I also consider Joe to be one of my mentors. He is a brilliant, brilliant musician and hung out in LA during its music heyday. He was a triple-scale guy as a base player. Joe taught me how the business works and how to record in the studio. Between Tompall and Joe Osborn, and also Billy Ray Reynolds, I got quite an education at an early age."

Gary also mentioned that when Tompall heard something he liked, he would stand up for it. He feels that this is part of the reason for Tompall's "Outlaw" moniker. Gary continues:

> Tompall was such an individual as far as what he liked and his passion for what he would get behind. It wasn't so much about his behavior, but because of his musical choices. Tompall had the vision before Waylon and Willie made it big. And people like Shel Silverstein— he was *so* bizarre. And John Hartford and Kinky Friedman. Tompall was always getting behind something that was different but good. Tompall's vision was accurate so that whenever he said someone was great, I would believe him because he really did have a great ear. Not only did Tompall recognize talent, he also groomed it and stood behind it. I feel this was his greatest contribution to country music. There are so many people who got their start and who did well in the music business because of Tompall. Without him, you may never have heard of many names, in my opinion.
>
> I think that Tompall's passion was being in the studio working and recognizing talent, more so than touring and playing music on the road. But understand that Tompall sure had talent. There was no one who could sing like him. He could take the listener on such a ride with his voice; he could bend

it, shape it, and use it however he wanted. He had so many tricks that he could do. I graduated with a voice degree and have heard many great singing voices, but I've never heard one like his. He could do acrobatics with it…he was so good!

Gary felt that Tompall liked a lot of different types of songs and put a wide variety of songs on his records. Perhaps his fan base was not as tight as some other country singers because he was less "in a box" than most.

Gary said that when country music legend Don Williams couldn't get a record deal, he thought it was time for him to leave Nashville. So Gary moved to Mississippi and now has a joint venture with Morgan Freeman in a film company, and Gary works a lot with the blues. Gary's tastes have changed over time, and the music business has changed so much that he said he doesn't recognize it any more.

Gary Vincent went on:

I remember that I used to think that I could play fiddle. I could play the stuff that I wrote and was pretty good at playing it. So one day Tompall said, 'Hey, you play fiddle so come on in to this recording session and play your fiddle.' So I got into a Tompall Glaser studio session on a song he was doing and joined the likes of Charles Cochrane, Joe Osborn, Buddy Emmons, and Gene Chrisman who was there, and all of these other great musicians. So I started noodlin' around on the fiddle. About halfway through the song Tompall stopped the session and walked out of the control room into the big room and said to me, 'Fiddle player, my ass!' And that was my last session as a fiddle player for Tompall Glaser. Shortly after that I put the fiddle down.

I was in Hawaii and had the chance to visit with Hoover. Hoover told me that one night he and Tompall went into the bar where they used to play pinball all the time and Tompall told the bartender to line up ten gin martinis with olives all at once and put them in a row on the bar. The bartender did so and Tompall began drinking them one at a time. He got all the way to the 10th martini and picked it up and looked over at Hoover with this shit-eating grin and said, 'I bought this one for you.'

Marshall Chapman (Dave Hickey's former girlfriend) has a great sense of humor and strikes me as someone who is extremely comfortable in her own skin. She spent a lot of time with Tompall at Glaser Studios singing background on some of Tompall's songs and cutting records of her own.

Marshall is a songwriter, dynamic performer, and author of several books; the most recent is *They Came To Nashville*. She has been in the music profession for an impressive forty years and has a staunch following. More information about Marshall can be found at her website www.tallgirl.com. She considers Tompall a friend and shared several memories:

I had a brief crush on Tompall. However, Tompall kept me stiff-armed and nothing ever happened between us. Besides, he was about 15 years older than me, so he probably had more sense. (Laughs)

The first time I ever saw Tompall was at a country music concert in Greenville, South Carolina. I was in junior high school; this was around 1964. Some friends had driven us over from Spartanburg to hear George Jones. Tompall and his brothers happened to be on the bill. When they came out—I remember Tompall was wearing a cowboy hat. Anyway, he and Jim had those dark eyes and dark curly hair. They were all rather exotic looking. With their soaring harmonies that had a sort of South-of-the-Border feel and their exotic looks, I thought they were Mexicans!

I remember one time going into Tompall's office, and there was a group of people sitting in there. All of a sudden Tompall gave me a spanking! I mean, he grabbed me, threw me over his lap, and proceeded to smack me on my behind. (I imagine I did something to provoke this.) After about three smacks, I took my free hand and swiped it across his wall, knocking several of his gold records to the floor. We were all laughing. It really was a hysterical scene.

I used to 'roar with the boys' (Tompall, Waylon, and others) back in those days, which meant we'd stay up all night playing pinball. I'd be out roaring with Tompall and Waylon, but come Sunday morning, Jessi [Jessi Colter, Waylon's wife] would haul my ass into church—so I had the whole experience.

I always thought Tompall had sort of a 'Richard Burton' quality, as far as his persona. They both had those dark, brooding good looks, curly hair, and sex appeal. Burton had that rich speaking voice, and Tompall...he could sing like a god. What a voice!

There was a sweetness about Tompall. I'm not sure what others would say about him, but he was always sweet and kind to me.

The band that played on *Tompall and His Outlaw Band* was one of the most talented and diverse bands ever to play on a Nashville-recorded album. To put a band like that together in the mid-

1970s was really a gutsy thing to do. I've always said 'the '70s were when the '60s hit the South.' Anyway, Tompall recorded one of my songs, 'Let My Fingers Do The Walking,' on that album, which thrilled me no end.

I remember another time when Tompall decided to go on a health kick. So he went jogging. Mind you, he was no typical jogger (laughs); he was wearing the ugliest damn jumpsuit you ever saw, and not running shoes but cowboy boots. And smoking a cigarette. That was Tompall's idea of a workout; jogging in cowboy boots while smoking a cigarette.

As a trio, Tompall & The Glaser Brothers were unique. They were, like, the Supremes of country music! Their harmonies were just incredible. Whenever I hear them today, like, on YouTube, I'm blown away by the sound of their voices singing together. I'd have to agree with whoever called them the Bee Gees of country music.

One time I did a show with Tompall early in my career. I'd just been signed to Epic records, and *Tompall and His Outlaw Band* had just been released. My band and I were the opening act. I mean, Mel Brown was playing guitar with Tompall, Ben Keith was on steel, and Buddy Emmons was playing with me, so it was a helluva night for music lovers.

My favorite Tompall recording is 'Tennessee Blues.' Many artists have recorded that song (written by Bobby Charles), but I like Tompall's version the best. He really caught the feel of that song. Damn. Makes me cry every time I hear it.

I was there in the studio when Tompall recorded *Tompall and His Outlaw Band*. It was an exciting time. We all felt like this would be the album to put Tompall up there with Waylon and Willie. It really felt like a masterpiece. I still think it's a great record.

Why did Waylon and Willie become more popular than Tompall? I've often thought it may have had something to do with Tompall's relationship with an audience. Tompall had that incredible voice, but tended to stay *within himself* when he sang. He'd kind of hide in his voice, whereas Waylon and Willie would look an audience right in the eye and just lay it out there! I'm not sure Tompall really enjoyed performing as much as he enjoyed the rest of it—the singing and recording. Who knows? Maybe he missed his brothers. But Waylon and Willie really seemed to enjoy performing.

I've always loved Tompall. He may be a rascal, but he's a lovable, talented rascal!

11

Unconditional Love

Dorothy "June" Johnson is Tompall's soul mate. She has been an important part of his life since she first worked for Glaser Publications and remains steadfast in her love for Tompall to this day. Tompall and June had been married for 33 years and lived in a house in Nashville that she had purchased years ago while working for WSM radio.

June was raised on a farm in a large, close-knit family in Alabama. While close to all of her siblings, she has always had a special relationship with her sister Robbie Ledlow that continues to this day. June knew at an early age that she did not want to stay on the farm. Therefore, she focused on obtaining an education that would allow her to get a city job.

When she was in her early twenties, June worked at WSM radio in Nashville. WSM began in 1925 as part of a Nashville life insurance company; the call letters stand for "We Shield Millions." Likely its biggest claim to fame is that WSM started the *Grand Ole Opry* radio show shortly after its inception in 1925, and the *Grand*

Photo courtesy of Jeff Selmonto, Claba, Brazil

June and Tompall's wedding reception. Courtesty of June Glaser

Tompall and June marriage ceremony. Courtesty of June Glaser

Ole Opry is now the longest running live radio show in the nation.

One of June's jobs at WSM was to make certain that the acts performing on the *Grand Ole Opry* show were ready to go on stage at the appropriate time. She said, "When I first met Tompall, my heart stopped. It continued to stop whenever I would see him...and it still does to this day." June also commented that, "I fell in love with Tompall the first time I saw him performing on stage at the *Grand Ole Opry*, and right then and there I said to myself, 'I'm going to marry that man someday.'"

Tompall and Rosemarie Glaser divorced in 1975. June emphatically says, "I didn't steal Tompall. His marriage was over when we first started seeing each other." When Tompall first got divorced, he moved into his office. Those were rough days, according to Tompall. He said there were many times that he would spend a few days away from his office to "think about things." When he did so, he would check into a Nashville hotel under the pseudonym "Fred Harper," and would tell only June and a few other select people where he was in case of an emergency.

June worked at WSM for 12 years and was then approached by SESAC (Society of European Stage Authors and Composers) to join their organization. SESAC was one of three organizations in the USA that worked to protect artists' rights. The others are ASCAP and BMI. Her job was to monitor which performers played what songs. Later, she was offered an opportunity to work as a manager for SESAC earning a salary of $150,000 per year, but she declined because she didn't like the person that she would be working for. Instead, she went to work for Tompall and the Glaser Brothers. When she first joined the Glasers in 1972, they would often not have enough money to pay her salary. June said there were several times during her stay at the Glaser organization that she worked for free until royalty checks and other payments came in.

June remembers that when Tompall first met her dad, her dad was feeding the chickens on his farm. Tompall went over and began helping with the chicken-feeding chores and said some things to her dad. He liked Tompall right away.

After Tompall divorced Rosemarie and had lived in his office for a while, he moved in with June. A couple of years after this, in 1979, June Johnson and Tompall Glaser got married at her sister Robbie's home. June was raised as a Southern Protestant and Tompall is a Catholic midwesterner, so many people said that their marriage would never last. Those people have been proven absolutely wrong.

June ran the Glaser businesses. She was in charge of the books, scheduling studio time, obtaining copyrights, tracking royalties, and everything else that pertained to running the day-to-day operations. Several of the people that I interviewed commented that she had great business acumen.

One thing that few people know is that June wrote two songs and Tompall recorded one of them.

During the years that June spent with Tompall, she protected his time while he was at the recording studio, stood by his side when he had disagreements with Waylon and others, and was his "shoulder to lean on" when life got tough. During Tompall's road tours, June frequently accompanied him, especially when Tompall was performing as a solo act. She worked the promotional material sales tables and did whatever else needed to be done to make the touring experience successful and profitable. June has always been fervently devoted to Tompall.

Tompall in 1982 (49 yrs. old) at the 80th birthday party for his mom, Marie. L to R: sister, Eleanor; brother, Chuck; Marie; borther Bob and Tompall. Courtesty of Eleanor Ryan

12

Tompall's Later Years

In 1986, Tompall spent time producing two recording artists, Mac Wiseman and Ethel & The Shameless Hussies. They took their name from the Ray Steven's tune "The Streak" where he says, "Ethel, you shameless hussie."

Mac Wiseman is a bluegrass singer and guitar player who is revered as a cult figure in bluegrass music. He was part of Lester Flatt and Earl Scruggs' band, the Foggy Mountain Boys, and also played with Bill Monroe's Bluegrass Boys band.

In 1986, Tompall (along with Bill Holmes) produced *Travelin' This Lonesome Road* for Wiseman. Tompall played guitar in the studio sessions. Other notable musicians who appeared on the recording included John Hartford (banjo and guitar), Doyle Gresham (steel guitar), and Uncle Josh Graves (resonator guitar, also known as *dobro*).

Mac said that this album was part of a series of seven albums released by MCA Records and performed by different artists. They refused to release any singles from any of these al-

Tompall performing in Norfolk, Nebraska on September 13, 1986. Courtesty of Eleanor Ryan

bums. One day Mac got a call from Tompall saying that MCA had called him about the royalties' statement for *Travelin' This Lonesome Road* and told Tompall that he owed them $9,000...and then he laughed.

Mac said that Tompall was a good friend as well as a good producer. He mentioned that Tompall loved to go fishing, a fact confirmed by Clint Miller. Tompall would sometimes fish by himself, other times he would take people with him. Mac said that once Tompall went fishing with David Akeman, who was known by the moniker "Stringbean." Stringbean was a regular fixture on both the *Grand Ole Opry* and on the *Hee-Haw* television show. Stringbean liked to fish from a canoe, which requires a good sense of balance. Tompall stepped into the canoe and immediately turned it over. Stringbean commented, "Tompall, we'll need to do this again sometime soon" and guffawed.

Mac recalled being a part of some shows with Tompall when Tompall performed with his brothers. These shows were in the Midwest as well as overseas at the Wembley Festival in England.

Mac said he recalls Tompall & The Glaser Brothers "really tore it up" at Wembley and were very well received by the crowd.

Kacey Jones and her band, Ethel & The Shameless Hussies, received some acclaim during the years from 1986-1989, achieving some chart successes on a couple of occasions by breaking into the top 100 country charts. Tompall (along with Jimmy Bowen and Bill Holmes) produced this band's first album, which was titled *Born to Burn*.

In late 1987, Tompall toured England. He produced a cassette tape under his own label, *Nashville Talking Network*, due to the lack of time to get a different type of media made. The cassette tape contained several songs from the 1930s and the World War II era. He recorded the following songs for this album:
- The Rogue
- Tears on My Pillow

Tompall participating in a Fishing Rodeo in 1989. Courtesty of June Glaser

Tompall recording in the studio with his ukulele. Courtesty of Jane Poole

- Forever and Ever
- Shackles and Chains
- My Pretty Quadroon
- Lean on Me
- I'll Hold You in My Heart
- True Love
- Open Arms
- I Love You so Much It Hurts
- Chattanooga Shoe Shine Boy
- You Can't Borrow Back Any Time

More details about this record production and Tompall's final major European tour in November of 1987 can be found in Chapter 14, "Jane Poole's Road Diary."

Glaser Sound Studios began in 1969, opened to the public in 1971, and was sold by Tompall in 1988. In addition to the fact that the economy had taken a negative downturn, the value of the studio itself steadily declined. When Tompall first built the studio he had state-of-the-art equipment. Over time, recording technology changed, and his equipment had become outdated. In addition, some recording artists had begun to put recording studios in their own homes.

Bear Family Records is an independent record label based in Germany. It was founded in 1975 by the visionary Richard Weize and is run by him to this day. Bear Family Records specializes in reissuing older music that many times is no longer available in the marketplace. It has produced recordings of artists such as Johnny Cash, Doris Day, Jim Reeves, Petula Clark, and many others including, of course, Tompall Glaser.

In 1994, Bear Family released a CD of Tompall's songs called *The Rogue*. It contained his World War II era songs, as well as some unreleased material that was recorded for ABC Records under the title *Unwanted Outlaw*.

This CD included these tracks:
1. The Rogue
2. Tears on My Pillow
3. Forever and Ever
4. Shackles and Chains
5. My Pretty Quadroon
6. Lean on Me
7. I'll Hold You in My Heart
8. True Love
9. Open Arms
10. I Love You So Much It Hurts
11. Chattanooga Shoe Shine Boy
12. You Can't Borrow Back Any Time
13. Like an Old Country Song
14. Sad Country Songs
15. What a Town
16. Don't Think You're Too Good For Country Music
17. Unwanted Outlaw
18. The Man You Think You See

19. When I Dream
20. Burn, Georgia Burn
21. Billy Tyler
22. Carry Me On

In 2006, Bear Family released *My Notorious Youth: Hillbilly Central #1* that contained a compilation of previously released Tompall material, with the following tracks:

1. Charlie
2. Mr. Lonesome
3. Ode to My Notorious Youth, An
4. Loneliest Man
5. I'll Fly Away Medley: I'll Fly Away / I Saw the Light: I'll Fly Away / I Saw The Light
6. Cowboys and Daddies
7. Big Jim Colson
8. Bad Bad Bad Cowboy
9. Gideon Bible
10. Let It Be Pretty
11. Sold American
12. Texas Law Sez
13. Broken Down Momma
14. Pass Me on By
15. Willy the Wandering Gypsy and Me
16. Lay Down Beside Me
17. Take the Singer with the Song
18. Honey Don't You Know
19. The Good Lord Knows I Tried
20. Breakdown (A Long Way from Home)
21. I'll Fly Away Medley: I Saw the Light / I'll Fly Away / Love Lifted Me: I Saw the Light / I'll Fly Away / Love Lifted Me
22. Love Stoned
23. Will the Circle Be Unbroken

PROGRAMME

8.00pm: Introducing The Corn Dogs

Rick McKay Band

Gary Perkins

9.15pm: Interval

9.45pm: The Corndogs

TOMPALL GLASER

11.15pm: Finish

Tompall Glaser with Waylon Jennings, 1970

Ray and Eileen would like to thank you for attending this concert and hope you enjoy it.

Special thanks to Gordon 'Sounds like Nashville' CRMK 898fm and Jack Shepherd who kindly lent us his Tompall Glaser record collection.

Program Excerpt From Tompall's Final "Farewell" Performance in 2000 in England. Courtesty of Jane Poole

The last Bear Family CD produced was also released in 2006. It was titled, *Another Log on the Fire, Hillbilly Central #2* and contained the following tracks:

1. I Ain't Looking For the Answers Anymore
2. Roll On
3. Mendocino
4. Country Gospel Good Book Rock' N' Roll
5. Put Another Log on the Fire
6. Musical Chairs
7. Grab a Hold
8. Echoes
9. Old New Orleans
10. Custom
11. If I'm There
12. Oleander
13. The Wild Side of Life

14. We Live in Two Different Worlds
15. I Can't Remember
16. When It Goes, It's Gone Girl
17. The Hunger
18. Time Changes Everything
19. If I'd Only Come and Gone
20. Good Hearted Woman
21. West Canterbury Subdivision Blues
22. Tompall in D on the Ukulele
23. Broken Down Mama
24. Loving You Again
25. T For Texas

Tompall's last professional recording of new music was a CD consisting of gospel songs, titled *Outlaw To The Cross*. It was produced by Clint Miller and released in 2007 under the Clint Miller Music record label.

Clint Miller has been involved in the music business for a number of years (www.clintmiller.com). He is a songwriter, performer, recording artist, and a record producer. Clint has worked with artists ranging from Johnny Cash and Tompall Glaser to Kenny Rogers and Waylon Jennings. He has also rubbed shoulders with the likes of Charlton Heston, Glenn Ford, Bob Barkley, Sonny & Cher, and many more. Clint shared the following comments about Tompall:

> Tompall is my hero, one of my best friends, I love him to death, and I am privileged to know Tompall Glaser. He is an amazing man. The first time that I met Tompall, I was with Mel Tillis at a bar. Mel mentioned that Tompall was in the room, and I went over and introduced myself. We hit it off and have been friends ever since.

Whenever I got to Nashville, Tompall was the first person that I would call. Often, Tompall would come visit me at the hotel, have dinner, and the two of us would have lengthy talks. These talks would go for hours on end, and we referred to them as 'round-table discussions.'

The two of us were an interesting combination: We had fun, we shared music, we shared life, and the ups and downs of life. We shared joy, we shared sorrow, and the other kinds of things that people share when they are friends.

When I first met Tompall, I was unsaved and was having my own worldly problems. It was in 1984 that I received Christ, and as the years went by, our conversations remained consistent and leaned the Lord's way. Of course, music was always a part of our conversations, and we discovered a mutual love for gospel music.

As the years passed, Tompall made the comment that he felt he had another album in him and that he would really like to record a Christian album. Tompall asked me if I would be interested in producing it. I said, 'Of course! Can we start yesterday?'

From that day forward, we started planning the material to include what the title would be, and so on and so forth. In coming up with a title, I thought what would be more appropriate than *Outlaw to the Cross?* Tompall liked it, so that is how we got the title.

The project took some time. The first decision was that some of the recording would be done in Escondido, California, including the basic tracks. Tompall flew to California, and both he and I had a great time. Tompall even sang at my church...and the people loved him, of course!

The thing that blew me away at the time was just how beautiful Tompall's voice still was...it was unbelieveable!

Ten of the song tracks were recorded in California; then a friend by the name of Gary Vincent (who was very instrumental in this project) let Tompall use his recording studio, which is located about 30 minutes outside of Nashville.

Tompall did not want the pressure of recording songs as quickly as possible for this project. Rather, he wanted to record when he felt like it, to do some fishing when he felt like it, and he did not want anyone to tell him when he should do what. So, Tompall headed to Gary Vincent's place with his fishing pole and fished for a while, then sang for a while, then fished for a while, and on and on for a total of 8-10 months.

Gary Vincent did a great job. When he was done, I had the Jordanaires in the wings to sing on this CD because I wanted this to be a label-quality, top-notch CD. We moved the project at that point to David Ferguson's studio in Nashville. David was Johnny Cash's exclusive engineer. Charles Cochrane was then brought in to provide keyboards for the recordings.

We waited for the Jordanaires to finish their part. When they were done, Ray Walker from the Jordanaires told me, 'This is the best that I have ever heard Tompall sing.' And the rest of the Jordanaires agreed with that statement, which is a huge compliment coming from the Jordanaires.

David Ferguson then did the mixing and mastering on the CD, and then we spent a lot of time on the packaging. A photographer was sent over to Tompall's house to capture some photos of Tompall, and the project was completed at that point.

Outlaw to the Cross is my favorite CD of all time, and I feel that it is the best work that Tompall has ever done!

I feel that Tompall opened the door for what is happening in music today. There was a time when the whole country music scene and industry was very closed and non-independent, and Tompall was the original outlaw. He had the attitude, 'I'm going to do music the way I want to do it and if the labels don't like it, then…' [you know what Tompall would say about that]. He built a beautiful studio and at one point had John Hartford, and later, Waylon over there at his studio. He had an agreement with Waylon that he could play pinball and record for free, as long as Tompall got part of the publishing. In summary, I would say, 'Tompall kicked the doors down.'

I feel that part of the reason that Tompall did not become better known by the public was because 'family politics' took a lot out of him. I also think that the labels didn't know what to do with him at one point, as well, which was a similar situation to what Johnny Cash experienced when he was released from Columbia records in 1972.

Tompall had a great streak of kindness in him. For example, it is not uncommon for him to call me just to check up on me with some regularity. In this industry, that's a pretty big deal. Also, in the studio with the musicians, he was probably the kindest, most considerate person that I have ever worked with. He was 'mega-concerned' that everyone was happy, that everyone had a soda pop, and so forth. People mean a lot to Tompall and he wanted them to be happy.

Tompall was a lot more open-minded and flexible with his music then many people probably expected. For example, he came in with one vision for our album *Outlaw to the Cross*, and when I shared my vision with him he said, 'You know what, I like yours a lot better. Let's go with yours.'

Tompall Glaser's rivers run deep. Far deeper than the average person would be aware of. For example, one night we (my family and I) were out to dinner with Tompall, and he mentioned that when he was playing in Las Vegas, Johnny Cash had pretty much just been kicked out of town. Johnny came to him and wanted to see if there was anything that Tompall could do to help him get back into Vegas, so to speak. Tompall immediately put up a sign saying, 'Johnny Cash Performing Here Tonight.' That was Johnny Cash's re-entrance into Las Vegas. It was a very bold thing for Tompall to do. He put himself on the line by doing that. I always thought that was an amazing story and one that not many people know about.

The last time that I saw Kris Kristofferson I gave him a copy of Tompall's *Outlaw to the Cross* CD. Kristofferson then told me that he probably wouldn't be where he is today without Tompall Glaser.

Glaser siblings on 6-13-09 at John's 80th birthday party in Omaha:
L-R: Chuck, Jim, Eleanor, John and Tompall

Up to the day of his death, Tompall's relationship with Christ remained a work in progress. Tompall told me, "I have always known who He is, but I am not ready to talk about His message and His meaning to me at this point in time."

13

Jane Poole's Road Diary

Tompall's last major tour of England in November of 1987 consisted of playing in some of the larger bars in the English countryside. He specifically requested this type of venue so that he could perform in close proximity to his fans. As mentioned earlier, Jane Poole was the secretary (president) of the Tompall Appreciation Society in England. Her former married name is Jane Glover.

As a result of gathering information for this book, I had the privilege of getting to know Jane. Believe me, she is one terrific lady! Jane is happy, upbeat, and is the kind of person who says, "If I can help you in any way, whatsoever, just let me know. I would be happy to do so."

As secretary, Jane gathered a great deal of Tompall memorabilia over the years. She also provided frequent newsletters to members of the Tompall Glaser Fan Club.

The newsletter was one of Jane's more time-consuming endeavors. In her February 1988 newsletter she provides the Tompall Appreciation Society members with all the details of Tompall's tour

Nigel Barrow, Jane (Glover) Poole and the Tour Bus. Courtesy of Jane Poole

Jane Poole, Tompall and Bob McKinlay while on tour in England in 1997. Courtesty of Jane Poole

of England, which took place from November 3rd to 27th in 1987. This particular newsletter was basically a diary of the activities of Tompall and June; Nigel Barrow, the tour bus driver; Jane; and the band members.

The band members who toured with Tompall during his November 1987 tour were Bill Holmes on bass guitar, Jerry McEwen on lead guitar, Richie Simpson on drums, and Tony Taliaferro on keyboard.

Jane's detailed notes about Tompall's last tour of England provide a great deal of insight not only into the reality of what it's actually like for a singer to travel from town to town putting on shows, but they also give us a unique look at Tompall as a country music legend. I am indebted to Jane for sharing her work with me and for allowing me to include it in this publication.

Please note that Jane speaks (and writes) in that delightful "English dialect," and I am printing her words just as she wrote them.

Very special thanks to artist Gwen Aylmer, who painted the portrait of Tompall. Gwen's portrait served as the cover of Jane's February 1988 newsletter and is also found on the cover of this book.

Gwen Aylmer portrait of Tompall, used with permission of the artist.

113 Aragon Road
Norden Park
Surrey SM4 4QG

Dear Members:

Hello once again and a belated welcome to another year.
As I mentioned in the last newsletter this edition has
been devoted entirely to reports on the "87 Tour". It is
much longer than I had envisaged and producing it has
proved far more time consuming than I expected, hence
the delay.

As you will see this newsletter is divided into two parts.
The numbered pages contain my account of the tour
and the blue pages are a mixture of letters, reports, and
articles sent in by society members. In between there is a
selection of photographs taken on tour. There are one or
two details, particularly in the first section, which I have
touched on in previous newsletters. I have repeated them
here to help set the scene and to provide a self-contained
account of the whole tour, including how it came about
and the early arrangements.

Whilst naturally I made some notes at the time, I now
regret that these were not more comprehensive. The
intensity of the tour, coupled with the all round elation
that I felt throughout, has tended to play tricks with my
memory. So regretfully I cannot guarantee that I have
remembered the names of all the many members whom
I met, several of them for the first time, and all those

who so kindly helped. If I haven't mentioned you by name, or if by chance I've got you down at the wrong venue, please accept my apologies.

My special thanks to those of you who sent me reports and contributions for this edition, and particularly to Grahame Nobes for his poem. He did in fact originally ask that it be put in anonymously as he wasn't entirely happy with the end result. I am sure that you will agree, however, that it is an excellent contribution, and I am pleased to report that he is now willing to own up to it. My thanks also go to CMP editor Craig Baguley for allowing me to reproduce an article that was written for Country Music People.

I hope that you all enjoy what follows, and I look forward to meeting up with as many of you as possible at Wembley next month.

Yours truly,

JANE GLOVER

BUILD UP TO THE TOUR

It all started when Wally Whyton went to Nashville in October 1986 and whilst there talked to Tompall about the possibility of a UK tour. Before that of course I had been nagging Tompall for ages trying to convince him that he was assured of a fantastic reception over here, but it was Wally who got it off the ground. Tompall told Wally that he would like to tour providing a suitable promoter could be found, one who would arrange a tour that took in the small country music clubs. He wanted to sing for, and meet, the real country music fans. I remember phoning the Glaser Studios whilst Wally was still out there in Nashville, and Tompall told me what was happening. I then couldn't wait for Wally to get back to start the ball rolling.

When Wally did return to the UK he approached Lee Williams. Lee confirmed to Wally that he was interested in promoting a Tompall tour and as he expected to be in Nashville in December, he would discuss the arrangements with Tompall then. By then, my impatience had got the better of me, and I had made telephone contact with Lee and offered to help in any way I could. I had also phoned Tompall again to tell him that Lee Williams was "his man" and that he would be in touch in December. It happened that Lee was unable to go to Nashville at that time, and the initial negotiations took place by telephone over the next couple of months. In February 1987 Tompall finally gave the "go ahead" and the fun began.

One of my first tasks for Lee was to prepare the publicity for the venues and to send out promotional copies of the album *The Very Best of Tompall & The Glaser Brothers* which Starblend Records had kindly made available. I met up with Lee for the first time at Wembley Festival that Easter. We met almost by accident. Lee was walking towards the arena with Larry Adams of Radio Kent. I stopped to say hello to Larry, an old acquaintance, and he introduced me to Lee. I then spent the next half an hour chatting to Lee about the arrangements for the forthcoming tour.

In another of my phone calls to the Glaser Studios, June explained how they were looking for sponsors at their end for the air flight, and she asked me to check out the possibility of sponsors for the tour bus etc., over here. At the same time Tompall asked me if I could get the necessary time off to accompany them throughout the tour. Up until then I had only had it in mind to drive to as many venues as I could reasonably get to. Well you don't turn down invitations like that, and so I confirmed right away that I would and then set about making sure I could get the time off.

It meant saving up almost all of my leave allowance, which although not in itself a hardship, did mean that my husband Peter and I had no real summer holiday together. With the weather as it was, however, we didn't really miss much. Also I changed offices in June, and I was able to ensure before taking up my new post that I could be spared for the four weeks in question.

Finding sponsors to help with the cost of the tour bus proved much more difficult than I at first imagined. After exploring many of the likely companies, including Miller Lite, Budweiser and Jack Daniels, I was discussing the problem with the publicity promotion officer for our local hospice, and it was she who suggested an approach to Age Concern, or the local Lions or Rotary Clubs, all of whom have national organizations, and usually their own buses.

I made enquiries and all three were interested. Eventually we linked up with the Rotary Organisation. We chose Rotary because their international campaign "Polio Plus" fired our imagination. It seems to involve achievable goals and represented such a worthwhile cause. And, of primary importance, there would be no administrative expenditure and every penny collected would actually go towards immunisation. Rotary showed us a video that had been made to promote the campaign and also arranged for a copy to be made available in Nashville for Tompall and June to see. They were both very keen to become involved, and so the necessary arrangements were set in motion.

I attended a number of meetings with the Rotary Club

people over the next couple of months. As you would expect they are very successful business people, were pleasant and cooperative throughout, and eager to get involved in any venture that would lead to money and publicity for Polio Plus. But at the same time, as the saying goes, what they knew about country music was about the equivalent of what Cyril Smith knows about hang-gliding. They had never heard of our Tompall, nor Willie Nelson or George Jones for that matter, and in fact our starting point was that one of them had vaguely heard of Dolly Parton!

My first task, therefore, was to convince them that Tompall was of sufficient standing to fill the venues and make their involvement worthwhile. I did this by taking to our first meeting armfuls of books, photographs, and articles, and I also gave them a copy of the album *The Very Best of Tompall & The Glaser Brothers*, and insisted that they listen to it before I met with them again the following week. That did the trick.

By September most of the venues had sold out of tickets, and Lee and I had discussions about a driver for the tour bus. Initially I tried to find a driver from amongst the society members, knowing that one or two were drivers by profession. And of course being Tompall's "roadie" was an attractive proposition. However, although those I approached were more than willing, nobody could get the necessary time off for the whole of the tour, and the problem was passed back to Lee.

One of my other tasks had been to find a small hotel that could be suitable for the tour party as their London area base. I eventually settled on the aptly named Thatched House Hotel at North Cheam, Surrey, and this turned out to be a good choice. Everybody was happy there and in the end it was used more than was originally planned.

The hotel was situated about half a mile from Sutton, which has an attractive shopping centre, and only a quarter of a mile from the picturesque Cheam Village. It was only about twelve miles to the centre of London and within easy reach of the motorway and main roads we would be setting out from for most of the venues. The hotel was being extended during their stay and, although this resulted in a degree of inconvenience, it did mean that the band was able to watch the "thatchers" working on the roof, and this they found fascinating.

October was now here and there were only four weeks to go! Final arrangements were made with the Rotary Club Officials and I set about assembling over 1000 souvenir brochures that were to be sold at the venues. I well remember that my dining room was awash with papers and boxes, and we had to eat all our meals in the lounge.

Tompall and June had decided that T-shirts and records would be sold at the venues, and I placed orders for these by telephone. Tompall had also decided to release an album of new material especially for the tour, and as you now know this was released in cassette form on Tompall's own label NTM (Nashville Talking Machine). It was released as a cassette because having it pressed over here was easier than bringing albums in from the States, and in the time available a cassette was the only viable proposition. Tompall asked me to approach Gwen Aylmer to see if she would be prepared to allow her drawing of him to be used on the cassette insert. Gwen was only too pleased to agree and in fact was extremely flattered.

The actual master tape was not completed until three weeks before the start of the tour, and June phoned me about the final insert details shortly afterwards. I then passed them on to A-Z Music, the company that was producing the cassette.

Lee had notified me that, through one of his contacts, he had got us a driver for the tour bus. The driver's name was Nigel Barrow, from Stockport, and as you will hear later he was a devoted Tompall fan. I had to pass on the driver details to the Rotary people so they could make the necessary insurance arrangements. The insurance charges were of course somewhat higher than the norm because of the presence of such valuable "cargo".

During October the only London area venue, which was

scheduled for the Peak Frean CMC at Sidcup, [a biscuit bakery co.] fell by the wayside. June knew that I was keen to take my friends and family to a show, and prompted Lee to look for a replacement venue somewhere in the London area. Lee could not have done better because his replacement venue turned out to be my local CMC [country music club] at North Cheam, no more than half a mile from where I live, although I must confess I'd never been there. I contacted the venue organisers right away, made an initial request for forty tickets, and arranged to deliver the promotional material the next morning on my way to the office. The organisers were themselves thrilled at the prospect of Tompall appearing at their club.

In my letter accompanying the advance publicity I had asked all the venue organisers to let me have directions to their clubs. In fact only three of them did and so I had to chase the others by phone. Lee also originally asked for each venue organiser to arrange the hotel accommodation for the visit to their area. However, having established a contact in an agency which specialised in arranging accommodation for tours, Lee took over this responsibility. Unfortunately this agency appeared to have one or two administrative problems: one hotel they booked turned out to be about 120 miles from the venue. On the credit side though, several hotels were really classy, and well suited to my taste if not to Tompall's pocket! Also by booking through this agency the schedule of where we were to stay was not in our possession until the day that Tompall arrived, which meant last minute phone calls for the directions.

The last few weeks before the tour I hardly seemed to be off the telephone, and by the size of my recently received phone bill I probably wasn't! Still it was all in a good cause, and as the days crept by the excitement mounted. There still seemed such a lot to do. My good friend Paula Glaser came to the rescue on the final weekend when she came over from Barnet and helped me sort out the T-shirts into different colours and sizes and to staple together the last of the souvenir brochures.

On Monday 2 November I officially started my four weeks

annual leave and my first job that day was to collect the "Very Best Of" albums and cassettes from Starblend Records in nearby Wimbledon.

Nigel was arriving from Stockport around lunchtime and I met him at Norden Station. We had described ourselves to each other over the telephone to aid recognition, and I was looking for a man of medium height with dark curly hair and a mustache. Being a lady, I had glossed over my most recognisable features and asked him to look out for a lady carrying a dog. We almost missed each other because our dog, a Yorkshire terrier, is so tiny she was hardly noticeable tucked under my arm

We then went off to New Malden, about five miles away, to collect the tour bus. For those of you who didn't see the bus I have included a photograph of it later in this Newsletter. In its full glory the tour bus was bright yellow and painted up with the Polio Plus and Rotary International campaign signs. Having booked him into the Thatched House Hotel and parked the bus, Nigel then came back to our house for a meal and to watch my videos of Tompall in concert. As you can imagine, with two devoted fans in tandem the subject of "The Man" dominated the conversation. To be fair though we did let my husband make the occasional contribution, providing of course it was in praise of Tompall.

I eventually took Nigel back to the hotel about 9.30 pm. By then it had become very foggy in the London area and we crossed our fingers and everything else for that matter, that it would be clear by the morning. We had visions of the flight being diverted to Manchester or somewhere else miles away. I had an earlyish night but was much too excited to sleep. Had I remembered everything; I went over and over the list in my mind.

ARRIVAL DAY

Tuesday 3 November was here at last and our first prayer had been answered: the fog had gone. I met with Nigel at the hotel and we set off for Gatwick Airport at 7.45 am. The flight was due in at 9 am but we had arranged to meet Lee at 8.30 am in the arrival lounge.

As soon as we got under way we encountered our first problem—the heater on the bus wasn't working. Luckily it was a mild morning and didn't matter too much at that stage, but nevertheless it was an irritation that we could well have done without. We parked in the coach park at Gatwick and made our way to the arrival lounge where we met Lee for coffee. We chatted to Lee about the final details whilst waiting for the indicator board to show us that the flight had landed. Time seemed to drag, but eventually the flight came in 30 minutes late.

Tompall came through the doors from customs first, followed by June, Bill, and the rest of the band. I was over the barrier to greet them "like greased lightening" as the saying goes! I had met Bill, Richie, and Jerry on previous visits; Tony was here for the first time. They brought more luggage than I expected, including a large metal trunk, and poor Nigel strained his back whilst loading it all onto the roof of the bus. He ended up having to make three visits to an osteopath, who fortunately practised from the house next door to the Thatched Hotel; he had to wear a corset for the early part of the tour.

Tompall and June travelled back in the car with Lee, and the band and I came back on the bus. Although, as I've said, it was quite a mild morning they had obviously left much warmer temperatures behind them in the States, because they were all dressed as though they were going to the North Pole. Where on earth did Jerry get that hat!

We got to the hotel about 12.30 pm and over coffee Tompall, Lee, and June discussed the final tour arrangements. June had brought a whole film of photographs of the inside of the Glaser studios for me, plus some that had been taken at her home. We seemed to talk about all sorts of things for the next hour or so and time went very quickly. I have always found June so easy to talk to and this was no exception. Around 2.30 pm, with the arrangements settled, they all went to catch up on some sleep and I came home.

Having dropped us off at the Thatched Hotel, Nigel had gone to collect my husband, and they had taken the bus back to base to have the heater looked at. It was arranged that this would be repaired the following day. Whilst there, the problem of the extra luggage was discussed, and the Rotary people kindly agreed to our also borrowing one of their trailers to tow behind the bus. This trailer, which was shaped like a mini caravan, proved a real bonus because it relieved Nigel of much of the lifting, and everything fitted in so much more easily.

That evening I had arranged that Peter and I would take Tompall and June out to dinner at the local carvery in a pub called The Plough. The Rotary Club officials were of course keen to meet Tompall, and I had arranged for this to take place prior to our meal. Thus Rotary at 8 pm, carvery at 9 pm. We collected Tompall and June from the Thatched at 7.45 pm and this was the first time Peter had met either Tompall or June. He had been warned to be on his best behaviour! We met up with the Rotary people as arranged, and they were favourably impressed with Tompall's knowledge of their campaign and the problems of the Third World countries. We had a very nice meal in a relaxed atmosphere, which made for a thoroughly enjoyable evening. Tompall was impressed by the decor and quality of the carvery, and in fact went back there on a couple of occasions later in the tour.

Nigel and the band had stayed in that evening resting up for the hectic days ahead.

* * *

On Wednesday 4 November Tompall had an interview arranged with Wally Whyton at the BBC's Country Club Studios in central London. I thought that it would be quickest and most sensible for us to drive to Norden and complete the rest of the journey by tube. Quickest it might well have been, but I lost "Brownie Points" when it came to being sensible, because of course the underground is now a complete no smoking area.

I then lost further points when I missed our turning leading to Charlotte Street. At this stage I vowed never to be without my map book for the rest of the tour—and I wasn't. It became my constant companion, along with my ring binder containing all the relevant tour data on people, places, venues, directions etc.

I eventually successfully guided us to our destination where we were met by Wally and his producer Colin Chandler, and taken to the studio. Two interviews were taped, one to be broadcast the following evening on Country Club, and the other, which covered their plans for Christmas, went out the week before Christmas. As part of the first interview Wally produced a hand carved belt given to him many years before by Tompall, which they had both outgrown by several inches. It was used as first prize in a competition which, as most of you will know, was won by member Tommy Sexton.

I took Tompall and June back to the Thatched around 2.30 pm and by now Tompall was beginning to feel the cold. We concluded that he needed a scarf to help keep out the wind, and I managed to find one at home that served him well for the rest of the tour.

Whilst we were doing all this Nigel and Peter had gone off to get the heater on the bus repaired and to have a tow bar fitted so that the trailer could be attached. Driving the bus with the trailer proved no problem for Nigel, but it did produce the occasional headache on tour when we had to park in a limited space. Still overall, as I've said, it was a real bonus.

I spent my evening making last-minute phone calls, finishing my packing, and once again I went to bed too excited to sleep.

ON THE ROAD AT LAST

At 10.20 am on Thursday 5 November the moment I had been looking forward to for so long finally arrived, and we set out from the hotel for the first venue at Dunstable. As we headed off around the M25 the tour party took up what was to become their familiar seating positions. Tompall sat at the front next to Nigel, and June sat in the seat behind. Tony, Jerry, and Richie sat in the middle, with Bill and me in the back two seats together with our provisions box: bread, chocolates, coke, and spring water. We were all dressed in our Tompall sweatshirts which he had bought us especially for the tour.

I'm sure it would help to set the scene if at this stage I gave you a little more background information on the band.

I will be providing a more detailed pen picture of BILL HOLMES in a later newsletter, but for now just the edited "highlights". W.R. "Bill" Holmes was born in St. Louis, Missouri and moved to Nashville in 1968. Almost immediately he began working with Tompall, Chuck, and Jim, and he has been associated with the brothers on and off ever since. In 1985 he became Tompall's business partner in the Glaser Studios.

In the band Bill plays bass guitar and is easily recognised by his greying hair and beard. Bill has made a number of trips to this country over the years, but now readily admits to not enjoying the "touring scene" as much as he used to. Despite this he loves the English people, our countryside and heritage, and lists amongst his particular likes our bakery products, chocolate, and Scotch Whiskey. His dislikes definitely include what we do to our meat in cooking it!

Whilst on the road Bill always sat at the back of the bus, often with a book in his hand, but sometimes he would just sit there singing to himself, whilst playing Tompall's ukulele, not caring whether anyone was listening or not. At the venues he could often be found mingling with the fans, both before and after the shows, just talking and signing autographs. His laid back style was very much appreciated by fans and venue organisers wherever we went.

Bill is very intelligent, talented, and has a terrific sense of humour. He respects other people and their views, and is always willing to listen to comments on both his and others' music. I never once saw him lose his cool throughout the tour and there were occasions when he might well have done so. No doubt this stems from his philosophy on life which is that things go wrong no matter what you do, so there is no point in getting upset about them.

JERRY McEWEN was the band's lead guitarist, and some fans will remember him from the 1985 Wembley Festival when he was part of the Glaser Brothers band that backed Tompall, Chuck, and Shaun Neilson. You can identify Jerry from the video of the show. Tompall would introduce Jerry on stage as the only musician he knew in Nashville who was actually born there.

Jerry was the smallest member of the touring party; I had remembered him as being much taller. In fact, when I met them at the airport, I didn't recognise him. His hair was longer this trip, but it was his height that confused me. He later explained that in 1985 he spent most of the trip on roller skates. He says it's the best way to get around; of course, they made him appear another six inches taller than me.

Jerry, who used to play in Crystal Gayle's band, is engaged to Rosie Carter, the daughter of Johnny Cash and June Carter. Rosie phoned Jerry almost every day, and on the occasions when we did not stay at the originally scheduled hotel, she would phone my husband for up-to-date details.

Jerry smokes almost continuously. He is a "born again Christian" and very sincere in his beliefs. He is also a very kind person. He was always on the lookout for my welfare, and not once did he miss checking that I was all right, and whether I needed anything when the band arrived for a show.

On the tour bus he could never sit still for very long. He was always organising himself and his luggage. And he was probably the ringleader in the continuous good humoured teasing of me that took place. He even tried to persuade me to go on stage during the middle of one performance. He also promised to teach me to play the guitar, but we never really found the time to make a start. It was probably just as well as I've a feeling that it would have been a long job!

RICHIE SIMPSON hails from Memphis and was the band's drummer. He has also been here before with the Glaser Brothers, and with Lynn Anderson and Roy Orbison.

Richie is somewhat large of frame and on tour he became known as "mean bastard". There were many, many photographs taken during the tour, but despite his size, seldom was there a clear one of Richie on stage, because he was always at the back hidden behind his equipment.

Offstage he was probably the quietest of the group, but with a wry sense of humour. He smokes cigars and was rarely seen without his camera. Richie is married to Connie, and she was to join us for the second half of the tour. They have one child named Jackson, and he stayed at home with Connie's parents when Connie joined the tour. Richie normally roomed with Bill, until Connie joined us of course!

TONY TALIAFERRO (pronounced TOLLIVER) was the band's keyboard player and this was his first time in this country. Because of this Tompall would introduce him on stage as Tony "Virgin" Taliaferro.

Tony is 30 and still single. He has striking good looks, long blond hair, and a great voice. Tony originates from a small town in Texas, but is now living in Nashville. He used to play in the Randy Travis band whilst Randy was known as Randy Rae, but now wants to make it as a solo artiste. Tompall is convinced that Tony is star material. He always opened the show for Tompall by singing the first three or four numbers, and his contribution was warmly received by the audiences.

At the start of the tour Tony was enthusiastic about everything, particularly our heritage, and he rarely stopped talking. He would prefix all his sentences with the word "Gollieeeee" and he tried unsuccessfully to get me to speak likewise. As the tour progressed, however, and the cold weather got to him, he gradually became quieter.

On the bus he was always bursting into song, and it was he who introduced the "Jane Song" that the band would launch into at various moments both on and off the bus:

We've got a girl called Jane, with no last name,
She's a homely little thing,
But we love her just the same.

Tony also became noted for his partiality to coke and his dislike of British food, especially our sandwiches which were referred to as "butter sandwiches". Americans have mayonnaise rather than butter, and in the end I bought him a large jar of Hellman's to shut him up. Returning to his liking of coke he always seemed to have a pint of coke, complete with ice cubes, in his hand whenever he boarded the bus, and as he also had the weakest bladder of the whole party, he was the one who was responsible for most of our comfort stops.

Tony hates people smoking and so he and Nigel, who is also a non-smoker, roomed together for much of the tour. Mind you, that pairing produced its own problems because Nigel apparently snores a lot. One night Tony had to wake him six times to ask him to stop so he could get some sleep. Nigel had his own back the next morning by going early to breakfast, plus a couple of other excursions, without his room key. He then made Tony get out of bed to let him back in—three times.

NIGEL BARROW was our driver and roadie and the only other English member of the entourage. He in fact, got the job of driving the bus by a stroke of luck. Steve, the driver Lee Williams often uses, was not available for the whole of this tour. Steve had used Nigel as a stand-in before and offered the job to him. Nigel willingly accepted.

Nigel normally works for the local authority at Lyme Park, Stockport. Lyme Park is a large National Trust Estate containing a listed building, and Nigel and his wife Audrey live in the grounds. He has an adopted son who is currently away in the army.

Nigel had never met any of the band before the tour but had been a big Tompall fan for many years. In fact, before landing the dubious honour of driving us around, he had already bought tickets for three of the venues! Nigel was once a member of a country music band in Stockport, and he and Jerry often spent time together singing and playing guitars in the hotel rooms.

He is a caring person, and particularly in the early stages, was nervous that he would do something wrong and let Tompall down. He needn't have worried because he played his part well, and his skill in handling the bus and trailer impressed us all. At the end of the tour, Tompall took him out to dinner to express his personal gratitude for looking after us all so well.

Nigel had obviously developed his driving skills whilst driving his tractor and trailer around Lyme Park. Unfortunately Lyme Park had not given him the same opportunity to develop his sense of direction, and once or twice we got lost or missed a relevant turning. Needless to say the band weren't going to miss an opportunity like that, and poor Nigel ended up being teased more than I did. When he wasn't sure which way to go, Nigel would often turn to me for assistance, to the point where it became a standing joke. On one occasion we stopped en route for Nigel to go to the toilet, and Tony shouted after him "do you want Jane to come with you with the map book"! Tony also nicknamed him "van driving bastard"— bastard became the "in" word throughout the tour. But Nigel took it all in good part and never once during the whole tour did he lose his temper. His way yes, but his temper no.

* * *

We made good time to Dunstable and arrived without incident around half past twelve. We checked in at the very pleasant and tastefully decorated Highwayman Hotel. We were met on arrival by the proprietor, a warm friendly man, and I could feel a sense of excitement in everyone now that we were underway. The rooms were superb, each with a TV and telephone, and I remember thinking "if all the hotels are like this I'm going to get to like this touring life."

All the hotel staff were extremely helpful and couldn't do enough for us. After settling in we went to the bar to have something to eat, and Jerry and I shared a toasted sandwich. With our stomachs now content we set off to the venue for our first sound check. The venue was at the Queensway Hall in Dunstable, a large modern hall holding about 400 people. We were met on arrival by Bill and Jenny Atkinson, the venue organisers, and also by the support group Clovis. Tompall was in a great mood, laughing and joking with everybody. A sound check became something of a full dress rehearsal lasting for three hours. It was probably necessary at this stage of the tour, but as you would expect, it became less so as the tour progressed.

We all went back to the hotel to change, and I returned to the venue almost straight away to set up our "promotional stall", something which I was to go on to do at each of the subsequent venues. I became responsible for setting up the stall, with a little help from my friends, and a format developed whereby I would do this in time for the doors opening, and then act as "minder" until June joined me on her arrival with Tompall and the band. Her presence at the venues was always appreciated by the fans, many of whom were highly delighted to meet her. June and I, and when she joined the tour Connie as well, shared the task of selling our stall produce, which included the tour cassette, records, T-shirts, photographs and posters.

Bill Holmes came back with me on this occasion and helped me set up the stall at the back of the hall. The siting of the stall was of course of prime importance, partly to maximize sales, but of equal importance so that June and I could see Tompall on stage. In the main we succeeded, but there were exceptions when we had to take it in turns to sell and watch.

The hall layout consisted of a number of large tables, each seating around 16 people, with a central wooden dance floor in front of the stage. Member Paula Glaser was there and she helped me by selling the souvenir brochures. Also there to see the show was friend and part-time record dealer Pat Mansfield who, as many of you will know, has been a valuable source of supply for Tompall records. Two of the Rotary Club officials had made the trip to this venue; they thoroughly enjoyed the performance, and were well pleased with the sincerity of Tompall's appeal from the stage on behalf of Polio Plus.

Clovis got the show under way at 7.30 pm with Tompall and the band coming on around 9.15 pm. The band opened up with a couple of numbers from Tony before Tompall made his eagerly awaited appearance. The audience was not that receptive initially until, after four or five numbers, Tompall invited them to dance if they wished to. This seemed to be the cue that they were waiting for, and in no time they were dancing and shouting for more.

Tompall sang a selection of "Outlaw Songs", plus old hits and songs from his new cassette, finishing with "Put Another Log On The Fire". Audiences these days have come to expect this song to be part of any Tompall performance, and although no longer one of his favourites, he accepts that his fans would be disappointed if he didn't include it in his act. For an encore he sang "Lovin ' Her Was Easier". Tompall's section of the show finished about 11 pm and afterwards he came back to the promotion stall, where he signed autographs and met the fans, for the first of many such sessions on this tour.

We arrived back at the hotel just after midnight, and we sat in the lounge eating sandwiches that the hotel had kindly left for us. Tompall and the band spent some time discussing the show and what changes they might make. Tompall thought that, as had happened on that evening, it was a good idea for the support group to come back on after his spot, leaving him time to sign autographs and meet the fans, before it got too late and both we, and the audience had to leave. We were aware that our schedule included a lengthy drive back to the hotel after a couple of the future shows. He therefore asked me to set about phoning the venue organisers for the subsequent shows to arrange for him to appear at 9-9.30 pm wherever possible.

I was in bed by just after 1 am but couldn't sleep and was up again by 3.30 am playing Tompall's new tape. What a lovely way to spend the early hours.

* * *

The following day Friday 6 November we were up early and I went along to breakfast at 7.30 am. Afterwards Nigel came to my room, and we went over the directions to our next hotel and to the evening venue. I phoned home to check all was well, and also phoned one of the Rotary Club Officials to let them know how the Polio Plus collection had gone.

We were on the road at 10.30 am heading for our next port of call which was at Marlborough in Wiltshire. The bus was so full of sandwiches from the venue the night before that Richie suggested we start a catering business by setting up a stall by the roadside. After writing his memoirs of the last three days, Bill sat reading and Jerry started to organise himself. Tompall sat at the front talking to Nigel, and I sat next to June going over the previous night's sales and getting the books up to date.

It was a longish journey of approximately 120 miles and mostly motorway where the traffic was particularly heavy. We had started out in drizzle, but it was getting foggy by the time we got to our hotel. The hotel "The Bear" at Marlborough was a late arrangement; the one booked by the agency turning out to be in South Devon! It was under new management and a bit on the small side. In addition it was the only hotel that didn't have a phone in the bedrooms, something I feel is a necessity.

Parking was also a problem and Nigel in fact had to park the bus nearly a mile from the hotel. The centre of town was taken up by a street market, and as the main A4 road runs right through Marlborough, there are double yellow lines all over the place. However, Marlborough is a very pretty town, full of character, with a high proportion of old and preserved buildings, and the party found it an interesting place to look round.

We set off for the sound check at the White Horse CMC, Burbage, which was about 5 miles away at 4.30 pm. The actual venue was the village hall which was surprisingly hard to find, down back lanes, and by now the fog had gotten much thicker. We eventually found the hall where we were met by Nick and Audrey Chandler, the venue hosts. By coincidence it was Audrey's birthday that day. On this occasion, I stayed at the hall after the sound check to keep an eye on the promotion stall, which was nicely situated at the rear of the club and in full view of the stage.

The hall officially holds just under 200 but there seemed to be more than that there. The show got under way at 7.30 pm with a support group called Bobbie and Nashville Pride. They had a terrific German born fiddle player who later joined in with the band to play "Faded Love".

Tompall and the band returned about 9 pm and went on stage at 9.40 pm. By then there was a terrific atmosphere and this turned out to be one of the best receptions of the whole tour. The audience joined in many of the songs including "Drinkin' Them Beers", "Good Hearted Woman", "Put Another Log On The Fire," and one of the songs from the Tour '87 cassette, "For Ever And Ever". Tompall really appreciated the response and applauded the audience. The tour tape sold well and June and I could hardly keep up with the rush.

After the show Tompall signed autographs and chatted to fans for well over an hour. Society members there included Norma Hughes and husband, Terry Cousins and wife, Dave and Ann Johnson, Graham Nobes and Tony Wride. All managed to meet Tompall and get his autograph, and Norma also got her long awaited kiss. Also there were Lee Williams on the first of several appearances and Richard Holt from Wiltshire Hospital Radio.

We left Burbage well after midnight. Tompall, June, and Bill went back in Lee's car, with the rest of us on the bus. Tony complained about being cold, and of course it was with us coming out of a warm environment late at night, and so I decided that the next day I would invest in some travel rugs.

Back at the hotel we all settled down in Tompall and June's room, where June, Bill, Tony and I initially sat on the floor counting the Polio Plus collection. I eventually went to bed about 2.30 am leaving the others still talking, but one of the problems resolved that evening was the name by which the band would be known. They were already being referred to at the venues by a variety of names, including "The Outlaws" and "The Glaser Band", and so they decided to settle on the title "The Third Outlaw Band" to make life easier for all concerned.

I had a much better night sleeping soundly until 6.30 am.

Saturday 7 November started with a damp miserable morning, but the weather improved gradually during the day. I had breakfast with Nigel about 8 am and Jerry, June, and Tompall came down just as we were finishing. Nigel went and bought the rugs for the bus and some postcards, and I paid the Polio Plus money into the bank. Most of the party had a brief look around Marlborough before we moved off around 11 o'clock.

We were heading south towards Ringwood and, as it was a relatively short journey, we had decided to stop off at Stonehenge on route. Stonehenge, as you will probably know, is the site of the famous prehistoric megalithic monument believed to be connected with ancient sun-worship rites. Several of the stones are still in their original positions, the largest being 21 feet high and buried 8 feet into the ground. The surrounding area is National Trust property and they provide guides to explain the history etc., to tourists and visitors.

All found the visit interesting and informative. Tony was

particularly impressed and there were lots of "Gollieeeees" that day. He also got talking to a couple from Texas who lived only a few miles from his home town. We took a number of photographs, a couple of which I have included in this newsletter, and Jerry bought so many souvenirs that there nearly wasn't room for him on the bus. I also introduced Jerry to the bread pudding on sale at the gift shop whilst we were there, and he really enjoyed it.

The National Trust guide referred to the famous Wiltshire "white horses" in his talk, and Tompall wanted to see one at close quarters. There are a number of these white horses, which are the result of horse-shaped carvings made 200 years ago in the chalk based hillsides, so that when the turf was removed the shape of a large white horse remained. Incidentally, you can now see where the White Horse CMC of the previous evening got its name.

And so having asked directions, we set off to seek out the largest of these white horses situated a few miles away. Tompall and Nigel had both asked for directions and had been given conflicting replies. Two separate people had given Nigel his directions and we foolishly plumped for the version he had been given. We might have known that nobody dares to lie to Tompall! So after half an hour or so driving up and down country lanes, thoroughly lost, we finally fell back on Tompall's directions and found what we were looking for. It was still worth the effort, and Tompall was keen to look into the history of the area later in the tour, but shortage of time prevented this.

All this had held us up somewhat and we did not arrive at our motel until 4.15 pm. By then we were feeling weary and somewhat concerned that we would be late for the sound check. My first task on arrival, therefore, was to phone the venue to say that we would be a bit late arriving. The motel was about 6 miles to the east of the venue, which was at the Avon CMC, Ringwood. The motel was a large modern building situated on the corner of a roundabout on the main A31 road. It had a very pleasant atmosphere and was very spacious, with each room containing three beds.

We set off an hour later for the sound check only to get lost once again. After a long frustrating journey, which should have taken 15 minutes, but in fact took over an hour, we ended up having to phone the venue to check the directions again before we finally arrived. The sound check over, I stayed at the venue and set up our stall at the side of the stage. The band went back to the motel to eat and prepare for the evening. They were accompanied by the venue organiser John McNulty, to ensure that they did not get lost again, and he also volunteered to go back to the motel again at 9 o'clock to guide them back to the club.

The supporting artistes for the show were the Les Mitchell Band and Maureen Lewis. Unfortunately the acoustics at this venue were not as good as at most of the others, but the audience reaction helped make up for this, and they were clearly thrilled with Tompall's performance.

Avon CMC is the home club of Ros Ray and Colin Fearnhead of 2CR Radio, and Ros presented Tompall with a bouquet of red roses, and June and me with bouquets of carnations. We of course asked Tompall what he had that we hadn't that qualified him for roses—as if we didn't know! Ros got a good interview for her radio show, which her listeners have since told her was one of the best she has ever done.

Other Society members there that evening included Frances and John Sexton from the Isle of Wight, Jenny Gorrick, Norah Vincent, Maurice Bowers, Tony and Shelia Harmes, and Paul and Gwen Aylmer. All met Tompall afterwards and got his autograph, and Jenny Garrick also got the kiss she had been looking forward to for so long—have you washed your cheek yet Jenny?

Sadly Frances Sexton is very ill with lung cancer, but despite the associated difficulties, she would not have missed the occasion for the world. And when Tompall put his arms around her, and wished her better health in the future, it gave her much more of a tonic than anything medicine could provide. I can think of many fans who would be similarly thrilled to be hugged by Tompall, but

I also know how much it meant to Frances—a very special moment and one she will always treasure.

Gwen and Paul Aylmer were invited back to the motel for a drink, and for Tompall to say thank you to Gwen for the use of her drawing of him for publicity purposes. They discussed art in some detail, and I know Gwen was pleasantly surprised with Tompall's knowledge of the subject. Gwen presented Tompall with one of her oil paintings of him, which he then asked her to sign. Paul has told me since how thrilled they both were to have been able to spend so much time with Tompall and June, and how Gwen keeps looking at the cassette cover still unable to believe that it features her drawing.

It was 3 am before we got to bed that night, but everybody was feeling pretty pleased with the way things were going.

The tour schedule now provided a couple of days break, but Sunday 8 November required an early start because Tompall was booked for an interview with Bob Powell on his London Country Show at Radio London. He had guested on Bob Powell's show on previous occasions, and it was a standing joke that he had never yet arrived on time. This time we were determined.

We left the motel at 8 am. Most of us had managed to scramble down a breakfast and we supplemented this by taking handfuls of toast onto the bus. The arrangements were that we would meet up with my husband en route and complete the last part of the journey by car—much easier than taking the tour bus into central London, and Nigel and the band would then head straight back to the Thatched Hotel.

We made good time and met up as arranged just after 10 o'clock. My dog was there to meet me but she made more fuss over June than me. As we approached London, Tompall decided that if he had some breakfast it would probably keep his stomach quiet during the interview. We therefore started to look for a cafe that was open, and at that time on a Sunday morning the choice was somewhat limited.

We eventually found one in Shepherds Bush which, to put

it diplomatically, was some way removed from the best in London. Tompall decided on soup of the day and, on enquiring, was told by the waitress that this was Oxtail. Minutes later she was back, with a small tin of beef soup in her hand, apologising that Oxtail was off and explaining that soup of the day was now Beef! Tompall took it in good humor and had a hamburger instead.

We were soon on our way again and whilst travelling through Shepherds Bush we went past the BBG TV Centre. Tompall recalled that he had appeared there on the Val Doonican Show some years earlier, and enquired if Val Doonican was still going. As we all know, Val goes on forever.

We arrived at Radio London at 11.20 am and I made a grand entrance by falling over the step on the way in and cutting my leg. The interview with Bob Powell was spread over the whole of his 90-minute show and went smoothly. Bob played a number of tracks that Tompall had either written or recorded, and featured three tracks from his new Tour ' 87 cassette. There was also a fair amount of humor "off the air" whilst the records were being played, and it was a thoroughly entertaining session. Ian Tilbury, chief photographer for CMP [Country Music People magazine] was there at Bob's request, and he took a number of photographs of us, one of which has turned out to be my personal favourite of all those taken throughout the tour. The show finished at 1 o'clock and we took Tompall and June back to their hotel to get some rest, and I went home to do likewise.

That evening about 7.15 pm I received a phone call from Lee Williams trying to trace Tompall to see if he would stand in for Skeeta Davies, whom he also had touring, and who had gone sick with a bad throat. Tompall and June were in fact taking the band to the Plough carvery for a meal, and by the time Tompall was located it was too late. Tompall said that he would have willingly helped out, but in the end I gather that Lee got Lorne Gibson to stand in.

* * *

On Monday 9 November I spent the morning catching up on one or two outstanding jobs, and much of the day catching up on my sleep. In the morning I went into my office to give out some tickets for the North Cheam venue and of course an account of the events so far, and they were adamant that I had already picked up the American terminology and accent. "God-dammit and Gollieeeee, I haven't" I assured them! Tompall and June went shopping in nearby Sutton and generally rested, and the band went to the British Museum, which they really enjoyed.

* * *

On the following day, Tuesday 10 November, I met up with June at the Thatched in the morning, and we spent some time going over the accounts before going off to the bank. June then came back to our house and was introduced to all my cats. She was quite taken with our ginger cat who has a purr like a motorbike engine.

Then we went back to the Thatched to collect Tompall before going off for a drive and a meal in a pub, in the pretty little Surrey village of Walton On The Hill. Originally we had only intended to have a bar snack with our drinks, but we gave way to temptation and Tompall and June treated us to a very enjoyable full lunch. Afterwards we came back past Epsom racecourse, and in driving through the surrounding area, Tompall and June could see clear evidence of the devastation caused by the October hurricane.

I spent the evening packing, sorting out T-shirts and such for the next stage of the tour and making phone calls to obtain precise directions to the next batch of hotels and venues. I had an early night, but the adrenalin was back in full flow and I was awake again by 2.30 am. Will I ever sleep properly again?

BACK ON THE ROAD AGAIN

Wednesday 11 November started the longest and most intense part of the tour. Our destination that day was Nottingham and we set off reasonably early from North Cheam for what turned out to be a four hour drive. It rained for most of the journey, and everyone felt rested and cheerful. For me the time seemed to pass fairly quickly. We stopped on route for lunch, and from then on lunch on the road became a regular feature of the tour.

We were staying that night at the Waltons Hotel in Nottingham, an excellent hotel situated down a private road on a private estate. My room looked out onto a swimming pool, and the hotel also had its own sauna. The show was at the Gedling Miners Welfare Club; on phoning the organizers to confirm that we have arrived, they kindly offered to come to the hotel and show us the way to their club, a journey of about 2 miles.

This was a large club holding around 350 people, all sitting round tables. It was here that we first met up with Bob McKinley and his band "Redwing". Bob is a great Tompall fan and includes several of Tompall's songs in his act. He had first met Tompall 10 years ago in Nashville, and was highly delighted at being on the same bill as The Man, both then and on several subsequent occasions. As it turned out he possessed one of the best sound systems of the whole tour. Tompall was equally delighted to appear with Bob and it certainly made sound checks a whole lot easier.

On this occasion I had to set up the promotion stall on a table in the foyer, and June and I had to take turns at going inside to listen. It was another great show with Tompall sounding better and better. Several of the audience called out individual requests and Tompall did his best to oblige. However, one ignorant man shouted for "Mansion On The Hill" at least a dozen times and then, as soon as Tompall started to sing it, he went to get a drink. I let him off that time but if he'd done it again…! There were a number of members at this venue including Betty Bostock and her sister Sylvia, Martin Swanson and Richard Hannigan. Tompall again signed autographs afterwards and chatted to fans–this time for nearly an hour and a half.

It was gone 1 o'clock before we got back to our hotel and Tompall and June went straight to bed. The rest of us sat in the bar having a drink. Jerry and Tony persuaded the owners to get them something to eat and ended up with "Hot Pot" which they thoroughly enjoyed. Whilst this was being prepared the band went off for a sauna. I declined their very kind offer to join them, even though they promised not to look more than once!

Thursday 12 November was a free day and we originally planned to spend it at Stratford on Avon, where we were scheduled to spend the night on our way to the next venue which was in Cheltenham. However, following a brief discussion most of the party said that they would like to spend the morning looking round Nottingham. The democratic process ruled on most domestic matters throughout the tour. Tompall reserved the right to have the final say on stage and on issues related to the shows, but outside that everybody had a say, and the majority view was accepted.

It was a cold, crisp morning, and we spent most of it looking round Nottingham Castle where most of the band bought souvenirs. Tony bought his girlfriend a very expensive hand-made lace blouse, and Richie bought his son a set of old English coins. June also bought some Nottingham lace for her sister and for friends. At the castle Tompall and June spent a while looking at the paintings on the upper floor, whilst the rest of us looked round at the collection of exhibits and curios.

We left the castle about midday. Nigel stayed with the bus, because we were parked in a restricted zone, and the rest of us went to what is stated to be the oldest pub in England for a quick drink. The pub was quite close to the castle and was set in the side of a cliff type rock face. It was very small and quaint with a cobbled floor.

We left the pub in good spirits but then things started to go wrong: Friday the 13th had come a day early! Tompall needed repairs to his glasses, or "cheaters" as he calls them, and so we dropped June and him off at an optician. Most of the band jumped out at a nearby fish and chip shop, and Nigel, Bill, and I drove around the block as there was nowhere that we could park. We had only just got round the corner when the bus broke down. This solved our parking problem, even though we were stranded right on top of traffic lights at a T-Junction. It also gave the band plenty of time to eat their fish and chips.

We called out the AA and fortunately they responded to our call for help within half an hour. Unfortunately they could not fix the fault themselves, and instead had to arrange for the bus to be towed to a garage where the repairs were to be carried out. The AA assessment was that it was nothing serious, and the repairs would only take an hour.

Nigel and Tompall went with the bus, and taxis were called for the rest of us. Tompall was very good and understanding about the breakdown and remarked that it was bound to happen at least once on the tour. We all set off together only to find that our taxi driver did not have details of the garage to which we were heading. We were then subjected to a hair-raising drive as he tried to keep up with the tow truck, which in turn was driven by somebody who I can only presume was closely related to Nigel Mansell.

At the garage we were all ushered into a small waiting room where we remained all afternoon. The repairs in fact took three and a half hours, and even then the garage had not been able to get the engine's timing right. Around 4 pm Tompall thought it would be best if we abandoned our plan to stop off at Stratford, and instead headed straight for Cheltenham, and he asked me to make the necessary arrangements. I phoned the Stratford hotel to cancel our booking there, the Cheltenham hotel to book the extra night and to arrange food on arrival, and Lee Williams to let him know what was happening.

Tony just wandered off, God knows where, but fortunately he reappeared just before we were ready to leave. We set off again at 6 pm, consoling ourselves with the thought that we had at least missed the worst of the rush hour. But the next 4 hours turned out to be a nightmare for, although the bus was now running, the timing was so amiss that it would not do more than 25 mph, even on the motorway, and we still had 100 miles to go. By this time Tompall was not happy, no details, just take my word for it, Tompall was not happy.

When we finally arrived at Cheltenham we had a struggle to find our hotel, the Hatherley Manor, which was situated on the outskirts of the town, down an unlit winding road, with no obvious signs to indicate its location. It was 10.30 pm when we eventually booked into the Hotel. It was cold and wet, and as you can imagine none of us were in the best of moods. Jerry phoned Rosie, who had been trying to get him at Stratford, and I caught up on my phone call home. Once settled into the hotel we all had chicken and chips before going to our beds, well pleased to see the back of that particular day.

* * *

The next day really was Friday the 13th but it was a much better day. Nigel got up early and called the AA to look at the timing on the bus. They soon had it fixed and we had no further trouble from it for the rest of the tour. I first saw Tompall around mid-morning when he was playing the fruit machines in the bar. I reminded him that it was Friday the 13th and he jokingly replied "I thought that was yesterday". He was back in a great mood and so were the rest of the party. The venue that evening was actually at the hotel, and so we had plenty of time on our hands to relax. Tompall wanted to go horse riding but he was persuaded not to in case he had an accident. Bill went off on his own for a long walk.

We all got together for lunch in the hotel bar, and whilst the rest of us relaxed at the hotel, Ty, Jerry, and Nigel went off to spend the afternoon looking around Stratford on Avon. They were back by 5 pm when I phoned the venue organiser to arrange our sound check. She seemed completely oblivious to the importance of a sound check, complaining that she couldn't get there until she had cooked her dinner!

To make matters worse the support group Campbell's Country had problems with their bus, and they did not arrive until after 6 pm to set up their equipment. The show was due to start at 7 pm, and the early arrivals had to wait outside in the cold until the sound check was finished.

This was another large hall, holding around 300, with a dance floor in front of the stage. Our stall was sited to the side of the stage with the bar at the rear of the hall. As I was about to set up the stall, I was approached by a fan asking about a ticket. He had driven 90 miles to see Tompall in the hope of being able to buy a ticket at the door. All the tickets had been sold, so I had to make him my "assistant" for the evening. He helped me set up the stall, and also helped out during the evening, and in return he got to see the show.

It was another great show with an appreciative audience. There were a number of society members at this venue including some for the second time. My best friend Elaine Dolloway was there with her husband Haydn, along with Rose and Michael Lee, Norma Hughes, Karen Hanley, Tony Wride and Connie Higgins. Lee Williams had also travelled to this venue but I didn't see much of him as he left soon after the show. Tompall and June were presented with two cakes, one was a lardy cake [a rich, crunchy cake or bread] and the other iced, and these were eagerly devoured on the bus the next day.

A number of members and friends joined us in the bar afterwards, chatting and having a drink, and the proceedings continued until 3 am. Jerry was teasing me, from the far side of the room, by continually singing the "Jane Song", and at one stage Tompall and Tony gave an impromptu concert of gospel songs. One of the waitresses, who admitted to being on the wrong side of 50, really took a shine to the "Boys in the Band" and was persuaded without too much difficulty to raid the kitchen for an assortment of goodies for them. All in all it turned out to be an entertaining couple of hours. I slept well that night.

We awoke the following day, Saturday 14 November, to a beautiful sunny morning. Nigel was particularly looking forward to the next three days because we were now off to Stockport, his home town. The venue for that evening was the High Lane CMC, actually in Stockport, and Tompall was booked for a second appearance there on Monday. In between the venue was at the Plas Madoc Leisure Centre, only some 40 miles away, and we were therefore able to book into the one hotel for three consecutive nights, a welcome luxury.

We set off reasonably early and made our usual stop for lunch on the way. We arrived in Stockport by mid-afternoon and booked into the Belgrade Hotel, all except Nigel that is. He was staying with his wife for the next three nights so that he could snore in peace! Our hotel was comfortable although the bedrooms were relatively small. It was apparently used a lot for conferences.

Although we had started out in sunshine, the weather had gradually turned showery on route, and it had obviously been raining heavily in Stockport earlier in the day, because there were pools of water all over the place. In driving into the car park of the Belgrade Hotel, Nigel managed to park so that one such large puddle was immediately beneath the exit from the front door on Tompall's side of the bus. The rest of us were all right, getting out from the middle door, as was Nigel on his side, but poor Tompall was faced with the prospect of stepping into this enormous puddle or trying to jump to the safety of a low wall about three feet away. In the event he did neither, and with the rest of us trying not to laugh too much, he instead called out "God-dammit Nigel, move this bus up a bit". Nigel, with all the innocence of a choirboy, replied "Just a minute, Tompall", as he let us all get off first. I still laugh about that moment every time I think about it.

With Nigel on his home territory, finding the venue that evening was no problem, and venue organisers Pam and Eddie were there to meet us. The High Lane CMC was the smallest venue of the whole tour holding about 150 people, but it had a lovely atmosphere. What it lacked in size it made up for in warmth and appreciation. Being such a small club I had to set up our stall in the foyer.

The soundcheck was at 6 pm with the band going back to the hotel and returning in time for Tompall to go onstage at 9.30 pm.

Nigel had been really looking forward to Tompall appearing in front of his family and friends at his local club, and Tompall did not let him down. During his performance Tompall expressed his heartfelt thanks to Nigel for all his efforts on tour. Nigel was really chuffed.

Bob McKinley and Redwing were the support group and the whole show went really well. Members there included Harold Buffey, June Davies, Tommy Sexton and his wife Marie. Marie presented Tompall with a knitted cushion with "Tompall" on one side and "Drinkin' Them Beers" on the other, and this was made good use of on the bus before it went off to Nashville.

We arrived back at the hotel in the early hours. Nigel just dropped us off, and he and his wife Audrey then went home. The rest of us sat for a while in the lounge talking about the evening's show, with Bill and Tompall discussing possible variations on the songs they could include in future shows.

* * *

I awoke on Sunday 15 November with the start of a cold. I had dreaded this happening because a cold in my case usually ends up as a chest infection. However, I'd taken precautions by bringing a full array of medicines with me, and I dosed myself up and crossed my fingers that all would be well.

Everybody went their separate ways for most of the day and we met up again about 4 pm, ready for our departure to the venue at the Plas Madoc Leisure Centre near Wrexham. Richie, by now, was becoming impatient as Connie was due to arrive at nearby Manchester Airport the following day.

We stopped to eat on the way at a restaurant just outside Wrexham where an excited fan, on his way to the show, recognised Tompall. The Plas Madoc Leisure Centre lies on the outskirts of Wrexham on the road to Llangollen. It is set back from the road but lit up with spotlights. It was raining by this time, but our directions were good and we found the venue without difficulty.

As you would expect with a Leisure Centre, the Plas Madoc was a sports and social complex. The show was in a large hall, with a stage at one end and a bar at the side. The tables and chairs were laid out in long rows, and there was a full house of over 500 people. Our stall was at the back of the hall.

There were several supporting acts booked for this show and Tompall's section was only scheduled to last for an hour. The organiser was on a different wavelength from those we met elsewhere, and he appeared to consider his administration to be more important than the artistes. And he didn't please us with his timing either. Firstly, 10 minutes before Tompall was due on, he announced that "chicken and chips" were about to be served at the rear of the hall. You can imagine the burst of activity.

Secondly, just before Tompall's hour was up, he suddenly appeared on stage to announce that Tompall was only going to sing two more numbers! Jerry nearly choked at the man's impudence. Tompall was more charitable and suggested that he was only doing his job. I thought he'd be better suited to calling Bingo numbers. Tompall again gave a superb performance and was rewarded with a great reception.

It was at this venue that I met up with members Phil and Gwyneth Jones for the first time, although I had spoken to them both regularly on the telephone. Gwyneth told Tompall that I was "the other woman" in her husband's life, and Tompall roared with laughter and said "Jane, you rascal, you never told me". Other members there were Kathleen Davies, Winifred Jones, and Tommy and Marie Sexton, and they all got to chat with and have their photos taken with Tompall.

We left the venue just before midnight on our 40 mile journey back to Stockport. I don't remember much of the journey back as my cold was getting worse, and I was just looking forward to getting to bed. The boys in the band were really sympathetic, and as usual very helpful. Jerry volunteered to carry my cash box containing the Polio Plus collection, which was always very heavy being nearly all coins, and when we arrived back at the hotel I went straight to bed.

* * *

Monday 16 November was Richie's day with Connie flying in to join the tour. Connie is a real "Southern Belle" with one of the greatest accents you could ever wish to hear. She also has a really nice personality, got on well with everybody she met, and seemed to get pleasure out of almost everything she saw or did. She got particular pleasure out of spending Richie's money but more of that later.

She arrived at lunch time, and having settled into the hotel, Tompall, June, Connie and the band then went on to visit Lyme Park, the National Trust property where Nigel lives and works. The centre piece of this estate is a beautiful old house, set in marvelous grounds, which was full of various artifacts and treasures. They all really enjoyed the visit, which is more than can be said for the curator. There were "do not touch" signs everywhere, and Richie had already warned Connie that he would cut her fingers off if she dared to touch anything. But there were others in the party, who shall remain nameless, who were seen thumbing through ancient books, etc. One even played a tune on the harpsichord and it was now the curator's turn to be "not happy". The band then went on to Nigel's house for a roast lamb dinner, cooked by Audrey, which they said was the best meal they had had so far in England.

Meanwhile I spent much of the day in bed nursing my cold, and enjoying the luxury of having my meals brought to my room. I had in fact made a trip into Stockport shopping centre in the morning, as I had to go to the bank and do some shopping. Whilst there I bought a new jacket, mainly because the one I was wearing had got really dirty, and this amused June. She asked me if I always bought new clothes when my present ones got dirty. I told her that she ought to try that line on Tompall.

As I have already mentioned, the show that evening was back at the High Lane CMC, and it produced one of the best receptions of the tour. During his performance somebody asked Tompall to sing "The Hunger". Tompall explained that he hadn't sung it for years, in fact not since he and Waylon had had an argument over the way it ought to be sung, and he couldn't remember the words. However, Bob McKinley, who was again the supporting act, came to the rescue by singing it a line at a time, with Tompall echoing the words—an impromptu response which the audience loved.

There were one or two members there, plus Nigel's wife Audrey, but mainly people from the media and other bands. June, as usual, stayed with me on the stall, and Tommy and Marie Sexton helped out again, this the third time that they had done so. Afterwards Tompall spent some time in the bar speaking to fans and media people before we all went back to the hotel just after 1 am.

* * *

I awoke on Tuesday 17 November with my cold now starting to improve. The hotel ran an express dry cleaning and laundry service, but something went wrong with the express that day, and June had great difficulty in getting the clothes she had sent for cleaning back before we were due to leave. I had breakfast with June and Tompall in the hotel dining room and then had a lazy morning before we all set off for Doncaster around noon.

It was quite a pretty drive over the Pennines, with a number of very steep winding roads. Once or twice we came to a hill that got us all a bit worried that the bus might not make it, but thankfully it always did. We had not been underway long before Tony needed a "comfort stop". We were out in the country and clearly some way from normal facilities, and he finally settled on one of those open ended barns. To roars of laughter from the rest of us he went galloping in one end and out the other almost immediately! We couldn't believe that he'd had time to do what he went in for, and thought that he must have been chased by the farmer's bull. We issued the familiar threats of restricting his liquid intake, but to no avail. Pints of coke still arrived on the bus at the start of each trip.

We arrived at the Punch's Hotel, just outside Doncaster, around 3 o'clock. The hotel, situated near the football ground and the racecourse, was easily the most luxurious of the tour. It had a marble reception area with striped pine furniture and brass lamps in each of the rooms. The rooms were superb and each had matching curtains and bedspreads in pastel colours, and definitely had the most comfortable beds that we slept in on tour.

The venue that evening was the Tumbling Shack CMC which was about 3 miles from our hotel. The venue organiser kindly met us at the hotel and guided us to the club. It was a smallish but friendly club holding a capacity crowd of about 250. I remember this show particularly for the way in which the audience joined in with the songs—by my reckoning they sang along with 13 of the numbers.

Our stall was set up at the side, half way down the hall, and there was nearly a disaster during Tompall's performance when I leaned back against the promotion board, and it fell back against me. I had to sit there for the rest of the show, with it leaning on me, not daring to move in case it crashed over!

After his performance Tompall was ushered into an outside room away from the stage to sign autographs, and June and I didn't see him again until it was time to leave. Meanwhile the band had a game of snooker. This was the northern most venue of the tour and members there included Ethel Green and two who had travelled all the way down from Scotland—Brian Smith and Joseph Docherty. Lee Williams had also made this lengthy trip, and he came back with us to the hotel to stay overnight. I went straight off to bed to give my cold a chance to get better.

* * *

The next day was Wednesday 18 November and we were off to Telford. Lee had stayed overnight and he and Bill went for an early morning walk to look at possible venues, which Lee knew locally, for the next tour. Nigel had heard on the radio that there were traffic problems on the route we were intending to take, but after making several phone calls and discussing it with the rest of us, we decided that we would take our chances. The problems anticipated never materialised and we arrived at our hotel around half past two.

Our hotel, the Falcon, was a 400 year old listed building situated just off the M54. It had small rooms with Tudor beams and was very quaint. It was reputed to have a ghost although thankfully, and much to Tony's relief, we never saw it. Apparently Queen Elizabeth the 1st stayed there on occasions, and Bill and Jerry actually slept in what was once her parlour. The hotel owner was very knowledgeable on the history of the place and the band found it all rather fascinating. Tompall is keen to stay there again on his next visit if it is at all possible.

We were met at our hotel by one of the venue organisers who had come to guide us to the venue at Oakengates Town Hall, about 3 miles away. This was the only venue of the tour that was not sold out, and when I explain that they didn't advertise the show until the day before, you will understand why.

The hall was of a theatre type with rows of seats in tiers gradually raised towards the back. I had to set up the stall at one end of the foyer opposite the bar. After the sound check the band went back to the hotel for something to eat, and I treated myself to fish and chips from the shop opposite the Town Hall.

The show started at 8 pm with Bob McKinley once again the supporting act. I didn't see that much of the show itself, because of the location of the stall and the difficulty getting in and out during performances, but everybody there seemed to thoroughly enjoy it. I have since read one particular critic's version of that night's performance, and his allegation that there were all types of booze laid out on a chair for Tompall to drink during the show, is absolute nonsense. There was only ever coke, water, and the occasional half of lager on stage, and that was for him to sip when his throat became dry.

Tompall and June sightseeing in England in 1987. Courtesty of June Glaser

Afterwards one fan asked me if I had ever met Tompall and was very envious when I said yes. I then explained to her that the lady sitting next to me was in fact Tompall's wife June, and at this she burst into tears clinging round June's neck. June was somewhat taken aback and said that nothing like that had ever happened to her before. Also, it was at this venue that a lady, who seemed to be much the worse for drink, and who had spent most of the time that Tompall was singing, dancing by herself in front of the stage, would not leave him alone afterwards. She kept ruffling his hair and trying to kiss him. She would not let him leave at the end of the evening and followed him out to the bus. We were beginning to wonder if she had aspirations of becoming the tenth member of the entourage.

Members there that night included Ken Hanley and his wife and, as you will read in his article, Phil Jones on what was a spur of the moment visit. Phil was invited back to the hotel afterwards for a

Tompall performing in England in November, 1987, during the '87 Tour. Courtesty of June Glaser

drink, and he sat there listening intently to every word that Tompall spoke. The band, true to form, started teasing me about Phil's presence, with comments like "Jane's got herself a date". Phil eventually left in the early hours after what he described as an evening that he would never forget.

* * *

Thursday 19th November was a rest day but we had a long drive back to London for the performance at North Cheam the following evening. We set off at 12.30 pm and June managed to sleep for most of the journey. En route Tompall changed places with Jerry, joining Bill and me at the back of the bus, and was very amusing with tales of his early days in the music business.

It turned out to be a longer journey than we had expected because Nigel, bless his heart, missed the turn off for the M25. He had asked me in advance if he should be looking out for the M25 to

Gatwick and I said yes. When we reached the relevant exit the sign said "M25-Heathrow". Gatwick is of course beyond Heathrow, but it was not on this particular sign and, as I was captivated by the conversation at the back of the bus, we missed it. As a result we headed on into London, and then had to travel round the North Circular Road amidst rush hour traffic. With hindsight it would have been more sensible to have turned round at the next exit and gone back to pick up the M25.

What should normally have taken an hour ended up taking three. And whilst Nigel drove on cursing himself for missing the turnoff, Tompall wound his window down and amused himself, and us, by conversing with the local residents. We eventually got back to North Cheam about 6.45 pm after a drive that had lasted six "interesting" hours. The band then went off to eat at the local fish restaurant in Cheam Village. Bill Holmes had persuaded them that this restaurant served the best fish and chips he had ever tasted.

Meanwhile my husband collected me from the Thatched and by the time I got home I was exhausted. On arrival I was warmly welcomed by my dog—this was the longest I had ever been away from her. The phone started ringing almost as soon as I got home, plus I had several calls to make myself, but I still managed to get an earlyish night.

* * *

Since the Tour began I had been looking forward to Friday 20 November the most. This was the day when Tompall was appearing at my local venue. Many of my friends, colleagues from both my present and previous offices, plus my husband and sons were to be there. For years my work colleagues had had to listen to my unquenchable enthusiasm for my hero, and this was the day when they were going to see for themselves. Unfortunately, things got off to a bad start because Tompall woke up with laryngitis. We got him onto antibiotics right away and crossed our fingers.

Around 4 o'clock I went off to the venue to hear the sound

check and to set up the promotion stall. The doors opened at 7 pm by which time members Paula Glaser and Kay Walsh had arrived to help with the sale of the souvenir brochures. My husband, sons, friends and work colleagues steadily arrived. Member Terry Cousins and friends had travelled up from Guildford, and Bob Powell and Ian Tilbury were also there. Even my dog had turned up for the occasion, but to be honest she was more interested in a packet of crisps than the music. The Hall was packed to its 350 capacity with many people standing.

The supporting act on this occasion was a group called "Homer". They were also great Tompall fans and were eagerly looking forward to appearing with him. The show started at 7.30 pm and Tompall came on at 9.00 pm. Unfortunately, even when Homer was on stage, the sound system was not really strong enough to reach those occupying the back third of the Hall.

So with Tompall determined not to disappoint my home crowd, but nevertheless unable to perform at full power because of his laryngitis, the show turned out to be good, but not as good as some of his other performances. Not that I am complaining; he made up for not being 100% by making me feel very special when he dedicated "It'll Be Her" to me and thanked me publically in front of all my friends. It made me feel ten feet tall—bless him. Despite the bad throat Tompall managed to complete his performance, but by the end was feeling dreadful and had to leave for the hotel and bed immediately afterwards.

Paula, my husband, and I went back to the hotel for a drink with the band but we did not stay too long. All of us were worried at that stage that the rest of the tour might have to be cancelled, and in any case an early start was needed the next day if we were to go on. To add to my worries I mislaid my ring binder containing all the data for the rest of the Tour. I couldn't sleep properly fearing I might have lost it, but I needn't have worried because it was found safe the next day in the tour bus trailer.

OFF TO EAST ANGLIA

Saturday 21 November was the first of three days where the tour was scheduled in East Anglia. The venues were Pontins at Lowestoft, the Theatre Royal at Bury St. Edmunds where Tompall was to give two performances, and the Mustang CMC at Canvay Island. We set off from North Cheam at 11 am to drive around the M25 via the Blackwall Tunnel, unsure of what traffic we would encounter on what is normally a busy route. Tompall was very "croaky" and so we banned him from talking, no easy task, but with the antibiotics beginning to work things were looking more hopeful. As I've said, we were heading initially for Lowestoft, and we made good time arriving at 3.30 pm.

Our hotel, the biggest in the area, was set right on the seafront. Tompall and June had a room on the second floor. The band and I were on the top floor with rooms overlooking the seafront. The bathrooms were huge—big enough to hold a party in! Not that we did of course—there wasn't time.

The venue at Pontins was about two miles from our hotel and was the largest of the tour. The organisers expected 980 but a full house of 1200 showed up. This was the first time that a "Country Music Weekend" had been held there, and the organizers were understandably concerned as to what the response would be. They needn't have worried; it turned out to be a great success for both of them and the two charities that were being supported that night—our Polio Plus and the local Samaritans.

The show was hosted by local DJ Roy Waller of Radio Norfolk. Despite doubts about his voice, Tompall was a resounding success and was on stage for more than 90 minutes. The sound system, which had been specially hired for the weekend, was superb. Lee said that he would try and hire the same system for the whole of Tompall's next tour. Tompall enjoyed the evening very much and signed autographs for over an hour afterwards. Several members were at the venue including Douggie and Janice Girling, Dennis Thorpe, and Cindy Waldron, plus a number of old friends of Tompall's. Cindy presented

Tompall with a Roger Whitaker album, which he had signed, as she knew that Tompall liked his voice.

Back at the hotel afterwards we were sitting in the lounge having a drink when Jerry McEwen spotted a fellow guest from Scotland wearing a T-shirt, which bore the inscription "McEwans Lager". Jerry immediately set about persuading the man to part with it. Jerry had already managed to pick up a number of similar McEwan articles on Tour, including ashtrays, beer mats, and bar towels, and it was no wonder that he had the biggest of all the luggage trunks.

This particular man was a little reluctant to part with his T-shirt, because it also portrayed his beloved football team the "Glasgow Rangers". As I've already mentioned, however, he was Scottish, and eventually "the price was right" and the shirt changed hands for an undisclosed sum of money plus one of Jerry's own T-shirts.

Both June and I went to bed shortly after this, leaving Tompall, Bill, Jerry, and Nigel talking in the bar.

* * *

On Sunday 22 November we had to be out of the hotel by midday, and before we left, Bill, Connie, Richie and Nigel went for a walk along the beach to take in the bracing sea air. Bill said that, unbeknown to her, he had taken some really "great" pictures of Connie on the beach. He refused to enlarge on this statement thus getting Connie really worried. There were times when Bill"s wicked sense of humour had us all worried!

We completed the relatively short journey to our next stop at Bury St Edmunds in about 90 minutes, arriving just before 2 pm. Bury St Edmunds is a very old market town with a myriad of one-way streets, but we located our hotel without too much difficulty. There were only four parking spaces in the hotel car park and our bus took up two of them. We were staying at the Suffolk Hotel, which was a large older type building, but again with very comfortable beds. We all went to register but Tompall, without a word to anyone, headed for the dining room. When we had unloaded and taken our luggage to our rooms, Tony, Jerry, and I joined him and June for lunch.

The Theatre Royal was only half a mile away but the sound check was early because of the two shows. The first was at 5 pm and the second at 8 pm. Tompall's voice was gradually getting back to normal but two performances in one night was really going to be a test, and we were all a bit anxious. The Theatre Royal only holds 300 but is reputed to be the prettiest theater in England. Also the sound system there was said to be second only to the London Palladium. Pretty it might have been, but June and I will remember it as being the coldest venue of the tour. I had to set up my promotion stall in an alcove in the foyer. The foyer had a stone floor and in no time my feet were frozen. I phoned the hotel and asked Jerry if he would bring me some leg warmers. He arrived soon after with a pair of thick "white with red hoops" socks. I must say I looked and felt really elegant in my high heels and those socks, but I was more than grateful for them, and it did the trick and kept my feet warm.

June watched the first show and then minded the stall whilst Connie and I watched the second. Also appearing that evening were Emerald and Sarah Jory, and Tompall borrowed Sarah's guitar for the show. He was back in great voice, and he again dedicated "It'll Be Her" to me. He was enjoying himself so much during the second show that he overran his allotted time by half an hour. The theatre manager was going frantic because his staff was only under contract to work until 11 pm, and it was past that by the time Tompall left the stage. He probably had visions of having to do the sweeping up himself! Members present were Douggie and Janice Girling, for the second consecutive night, and Colin and Eve Bassett. I had met Colin and Eve previously at the party that we held in September 1986 to celebrate Tompall's birthday.

Tony went missing after the show again and was left to make his own way back to the hotel. He arrived half an hour later, not very happy, but he did see the funny side of it after a while and wasn't late again—not for a few days anyway. Douggie and Janice were invited back to the hotel for a quick drink with Tompall, June, and the band, and were treated to some of Tompall's observations on life and other matters. However, we were all tired and it wasn't long before we decided to call it a night.

* * *

I awoke on Monday 23 November to a grey, drizzly, miserable morning. I can take a hint and so I had breakfast in bed and a lie in. When I did decide to surface Jerry escorted me to the bank to pay in the Polio Plus collection. Connie and Richie had already been out and done some early morning shopping. Connie bought a beautiful Royal Doulton tea set, which she didn't let out of her sight again until she arrived back in Nashville! She has since told me that both Richie and Jackson have been terrified of using it in case they broke anything, but she makes them use it just the same.

We were due to set off for Southend at 11.30 and the hotel restaurant did not start serving meals until 12.30. That did not deter Tony, however, and he turned on his undoubted charm and persuaded a waitress to cook him some lunch at 11 am. Not the rest of us, just him! We had to make do with eating on route at a Little Chef restaurant, whilst Tony sat and watched, drinking his usual pint of coke.

We were staying that night at a motel just outside Southend, and we arrived there about 3 pm. The rooms were again superb and beautifully furnished. We were all on the same block except for Connie and Richie who were in the next block. The promoters for the Holland venues were over, and were booking into the motel just ahead of us, although we did not realise who they were at the time.

The venue was at the Mustang CMC, Canvey Island, and I phoned the promoter Alan Woodhouse and arranged the sound check for 5 pm. Although the venue was only 5 miles from the motel, we had local rush-hour traffic, and it took us nearly an hour to get there. And trying to read roadmaps in the dark was far from easy, but Richie came to the rescue by loaning me one of his clip-on torches, which he uses to read his music on stage, and this proved invaluable.

We were made very welcome at the Mustang, and they were clearly delighted to have Tompall performing there. Everything was extremely well organised and they couldn't do enough for us. Their members were the most colorful of the tour, with ladies all in hooped dresses, and the men in "Wyatt Earp" type outfits. The band couldn't believe their eyes and said that if anyone had walked into a Texas honky-tonk dressed like that, especially wearing a gun belt, everybody would have dived for cover!

The organisers treated me to fish and chips, which had become my staple diet, whilst I set up our stall in the foyer. The hall was again a fairly large one holding over 400. There were long tables at the back of the hall and a large dance floor in front of the stage. I was joined on the stall by member Carole O'Callaghan, and she was a great help to me despite her fears that she wouldn't be. Lee Williams and the Dutch promoters were also there to see the show.

Tompall and the band came back about 9 pm ready to go on stage at 9.30 pm. Tompall sounded terrific again, and just before his encore he was presented with a genuine Essex policeman's helmet by Alan Woodhouse, himself a policeman. Tompall was highly delighted with it, and showed his appreciation by starting his encore wearing the helmet. Just as he was about to launch into his final song "T For Texas", however, disaster struck and he clutched his side in agony. June and I, and many others were thrown into a state of panic, thinking he had suffered a heart attack. In fact, it turned out to be no more than a torn muscle in his side. Nevertheless, very painful.

Fortunately there was a doctor in the audience, and he attended Tompall immediately. He quickly ruled out anything serious and suggested that we take Tompall back to the motel to get some rest. We never did find out who he was, but his quick response was very much appreciated.

We took his advice and got Tompall safely back to the motel. Being in such pain, he hardly spoke on the journey back. Meanwhile, poor Nigel was praying that he wouldn't encounter any potholes in the road, and on this occasion his prayers were answered. By the time we got back, Tompall had recovered sufficiently to discuss the Holland arrangements with Bill, Lee and the Dutch promoters, but he suffered another painful spasm whilst the talks were going on. June and I sat drinking coffee whilst she waited for Tompall to return to their room. He returned within the hour and insisted that he felt fine.

* * *

Tuesday 24 November was the first of two rest days, and we were traveling back to our North Cheam base. Everybody was up fairly early wondering how Tompall was and waiting anxiously for June and him to show themselves. I had breakfast with Bill and the Dutch promoters, and they had further discussions on the Holland leg of the tour. Breakfast came and went without any sign of Tompall and June, as did the rest of the morning. Knowing that we had to vacate our rooms by midday, the rest of us did just that and loaded up the bus in anticipation.

At 11.55 am, with the rest of us outside waiting, there was no alternative but to phone through to their room to see what was happening. June appeared surprised at being disturbed and explained tactfully that she wanted to let Tompall sleep for as long as possible. I asked her if she knew that we had to be out of our rooms by midday and she said that she did. I then told her what the time was, and there was silence for what seemed like ages before she replied "Oh, Tompall's watch has stopped at quarter past six". In fact, as you'll read later, after five years of active service the battery had run out. We had a laugh about it afterwards but, as you can imagine, they had to get themselves dressed and packed fairly quickly. And on the journey back it was their turn to be teased over such a "feeble excuse" for still being in bed at 11.55 am.

We eventually left the motel about 12.30 pm and arrived

back at North Cheam a couple of hours later. The journey back had its amusing moments with everyone trying on Tompall's policeman's helmet and posing for photographs. Once back at the hotel, Tompall and June went off to rest. Tompall was still in quite bad pain but insisted that he did not need a doctor. Much as we wanted to we dare not overrule him! Jerry and Nigel relaxed at the hotel, and Tony and Bill went up to London for the rest of the day. Connie took Richie on another shopping expedition! This time it was to Cheam Village where they have an unusual and attractive shop which specializes in brass ornaments, etc., and Connie bought, amongst other things, a brass model of Concorde for Jackson.

AND NOW THE END IS NEAR

Wednesday 25 November was the last rest day of the tour. The band went their separate ways making the most of their last chance to go shopping, sightseeing, or to just do their laundry. Tony and Bill visited the Tower of London, where Tony bought some books, and they then went on to Harrods where Bill bought some rather expensive Christmas crackers for friends back in the States. Unfortunately, Tony left the books he had bought in Harrods, and then spent virtually the whole of the next morning on the phone trying to locate them. They were eventually found about two weeks later and forwarded to me to send on to him.

I relaxed at home. In fact, I was stretched out on the sofa about 2.30 pm when the phone rang. Peter answered it, but I was up like a shot when he told me that it was Tompall on the other end of the line. Tompall wanted to get his watch looked at, but it was early closing day locally and he didn't know where else to try. Midweek early closing seems to be a peculiarity of this country, and visitors find it a strange custom. I was, of course, more than happy to meet him and find somewhere that was open.

And so Peter and I drove over to the Thatched to collect Tompall, and we set off for the nearest "non early closing" shopping centre which was at Tooting, about 4 miles away. We were presuming that all the watch required was a new battery, although we would not know for certain until one was fitted. An easy task you might think, but what a performance it turned out to be. We went to five jewelers' shops before finding one that, not only stocked batteries, but also fitted them. Whilst at the jewelers Tompall bought June a new watch as a surprise present. He gave it to her when we got back and she was delighted with it.

Along the way, Tompall wanted to look in Marks and Spencers and he really "went to town" when let loose in the delicatessen section. He bought enough food for about three days for his and June's supper, despite the fact that they were due to be taken out to dinner that evening by Lee Williams. June told me afterwards that she cannot afford to let him go shopping for her, and I can well believe that. We got back to the hotel about 5 pm and chatted for half an hour with June and Tompall before returning home.

As I've said, Tompall and June were meeting Lee Williams that evening for dinner and they were taken to the local steakhouse. Many of the "goodies" from Tompall's Marks and Spencer's spending spree ended up being donated to our larder the next day.

* * *

Thursday 26 November brought us to the last British venue of the tour. Originally the intention was to stay at a hotel near the venue at Gravesend, but because of the need for an early start to Gatwick Airport the next day, it was agreed that it would be more sensible to return to the Thatched Hotel after the show. They were able to accommodate all but two of the party, and rather than book into another hotel for just one night, Connie and Richie were content to stay the night with us.

We set off from North Cheam around 2.30 pm. By now Tompall's side was much better, although the extent of the bruising now coming through made us all aware of the pain that he must have experienced. We had arranged to call in on Bob Powell's Country Music People Shop at Orpington on route to Gravesend. We stayed there for about half an hour during which time photographs were taken of Bob with Tompall and the band, one of which you will have seen in January's issue of CMP. Afterwards Bob kindly laid on coffee and cakes for us. Bob's dog "Casey" was also present and certain members of the band made sure he had his share of the cakes—whilst Bob wasn't looking!

We arrived at the venue at the Woodville Halls, Gravesend, at 4.30 pm, but at that time there was nobody around other than the office staff. We therefore decided to go and look for something to eat and ended up once again with fish and chips. By the time we had returned to the hall it was 5.30 pm and the venue organiser, Bob Stammers, had arrived. The Johnny Young Band, the support group on this occasion, arrived shortly afterwards and the sound check was completed by 7 pm. During the sound check I had set up our stall in the foyer ready for the doors opening at 7.30 pm.

The Woodville Halls holds around 400 people. The tables were arranged around 3 sides of a large central dance floor, with extra seats on a balcony overlooking the stage. Members there included Bill and Dee Bentley and Carole O'Callaghan.

During the day Tompall had been having further problems with his throat and had been using a throat spray. And as he later realised, he had been using it too frequently and having too strong a dosage. By the evening this was having a paralysing affect on his vocal chords which prevented him from singing at his best. In consequence, this show was not the ideal ending to the British part of his tour.

Our journey back was almost all motorway, and we made good time arriving at the Thatched Hotel just over an hour later around midnight. Connie and Richie then came back to our house for the night and were formally introduced to all our cats. Richie was tired and wanted to get an earlyish night whilst Connie wanted to take some photographs of the cats. With the early scheduled start for Holland next day Richie eventually won the argument.

* * *

Friday 27 November officially brought the British leg of the tour to an end, and I recall that I was feeling a mixture of sorrow and relief. Sorrow that it was all about to end, but at the same time relief that nothing serious had befallen the party. Mind you, given the opportunity I would have carried on for another month at least.

We had to be at Gatwick Airport by 10 am which meant leaving the Thatched House Hotel by 9 am. We were up at 7 am, had a light breakfast, and Peter drove Richie, Connie, and me over to the Thatched. It was a cold and very frosty morning and the tour bus, realising that its services would shortly no longer be needed, took umbrage and wouldn't start. However, with the aid of jump leads, and the threat of what Tompall might do to it if it didn't co-operate, the bus eventually saw the error of its ways and sprang into life!

I traveled with them all to Gatwick and stayed until they boarded their flights: Tompall, June, and the band heading for Amsterdam, and Connie on her way back to Nashville. Both flights were due out at 11 am and both left on time. Now I really expected this to be the final goodbye, but as luck would have it, it wasn't. Because of the excess baggage clause in their Dutch airline tickets, Tompall and the party were unable to take all their hand luggage with them. Ever willing to please, and sensing an opportunity to meet up again on the Monday night, I offered to look after their hand luggage until then. Thus I had a smile on my face as Nigel and I drove back home.

After a quick snack Peter, Nigel, and I returned the tour bus to our Rotary Club friends. We made Nigel a couple of sandwiches to eat on his journey home and took him to Morden Underground Station. From there he caught a tube to Euston and a train back to Stockport. I have spoken to Nigel a couple of times since and he tells me that he really misses everybody. He says it was well worth all his anxieties, and was an experience he wouldn't have missed for the world. He is now looking forward to the next tour— Tompall has already asked him if he would like to be his "roadie" again. No doubt Nigel is still a bit of a hero down at his local CMC. After all, he can claim to be the only man to have literally "driven Tompall out of Stockport"—three times at that!

* * *

The tour party's flight to Holland was in an 18-seater jet. Even June, an experienced flyer, was apprehensive about going on it. Tony's "DX keyboard" was taken inside the cabin and given its own seat. My fear of flying was the main reason why I didn't seriously consider going on this part of the tour, and when I heard the size of the aeroplane I went cold at the thought of it. Which just goes to show that even my devotion has its limits. Still I'm working on it—maybe next time!

Anyway they arrived safely in Holland and were met by the Dutch promoters. It was only a 30-minute drive to their hotel, which was just outside Amsterdam. They were booked to stay at the one hotel and travel daily to each of the three venues. As you will read later, June did give me some details of the time in Holland, but it was individual incidents as they came to mind rather than a day by day account, and sadly I can't recall what was said well enough to reproduce it now in any coherent way. And although there were subsequent reports on the shows, they were all in Dutch and I couldn't understand them.

But one thing I can clearly recall related to the last venue where Tompall sang "Release Me" as an encore, and there were fans sat on the floor crying. June said I would have loved it, which has made me all the more determined to conquer my fear of flying. Overall, they enjoyed their stay in Holland, but the travelling around made it quite tiring. On stage Tompall was back at his scintillating best.

* * *

On Monday 30 November I returned to work, and whilst I was looking forward to relating the many tales and incidents to my colleagues, I was not relishing the thought of coming down off cloud nine and facing up to reality again. Still, I had the evening to look forward to.

I had checked in the afternoon that they had all arrived safely at their hotel on the outskirts of Gatwick. Then at 7 pm Peter and I set off to meet them for the final time and to pass on their hand luggage which included Bill's Christmas crackers, Tompall's policeman's helmet, and Tony's porcelain figures.

As soon as we got into the hotel, we spotted June and the band in the dining room just finishing off their evening meal. Tompall was asleep in his room. "Hi there, Jane" the band called out in unison, ever determined to make me blush! Well it was their last chance to tease me, so I let them make the most of it. We all adjourned to the bar where we had a drink and a chat. I passed on the hand luggage and June gave me the edited highlights of their Holland trip.

Just as we were about to leave Tompall finally appeared to make my evening complete. We then spent another 30 minutes talking in the foyer before saying our final goodbyes. We returned home, rather tearfully in my case, just in time to beat the blanket of fog that was falling on the area.

I have since heard from Tompall and June that they had a safe and uneventful journey home, and how much they all enjoyed themselves. So much so that both are hoping that another tour can be arranged over here in the not too distant future.

For me the tour was the experience of a lifetime, and I'll always be grateful for the pleasure and excitement that it gave me. Of course, it was Tompall and June who made the tour so special, but there were also many others who contributed in no small way. For instance I cannot praise the band too highly for their part in all this. Their friendship, good manners, and the way that they all looked after me, will always be cherished. Nigel too played his part. Then of course there was Lee Williams, the venue organisers, the Polio Plus people, not to mention many members and friends.

To you all a great big thank you.

Epilogue

As I reflected upon the information that I gathered to write this book, including interviews with Tompall and others, printed articles, songs written by Tompall and more, I noted similarities between his life and that of Dutch post-Impressionist painter Vincent Willem van Gogh. Both men were talented artists, though in different fields of the arts. Both quarreled with their fathers, both had strong friendships with other talented men in their profession with a subsequent falling out—van Gogh with painter Paul Gauguin and Tompall with Waylon Jennings, both suffered from long-term illnesses in their later years of life, and neither man was fully appreciated during his lifetime. Vincent van Gogh slowly gained notoriety after letters he had written surfaced after his death. My hope is that the same will occur for Tompall once his army letters home are read by the public and people understand the many unique characteristics Tompall possessed.

Tompall Glaser was a talented, complicated man who is considered by many to be brilliant in the way that he was involved with—and greatly impacted—nearly every aspect of country music. People who knew Tompall over the years have strong opinions about the man, and their opinions run the gamut, as you have read in this book. Some liked him, some disliked him, but one thing is certain: every single person I have talked to respects the man and what he achieved during his professional career.

Tompall's feelings about his life's work in the field of country music are captured throughout this book. However, nearly 80-years-old and reflecting on his past accomplishments, he shared some additional comments during our times together.

Concerning his failure to become a household name he said, "I wish that I would have become a huge 'superstar,' but since I didn't, I am not really proud of anything."

Relative to his lack of friends throughout the years Tompall said, "I question why it was so hard for people to like me."

Tompall still believed that not hailing originally from Tennessee impacted how far he could go in Nashville. He said, "I feel that part of the reason I didn't make it further as a country music star was because I wasn't a native Tennessean, or at least someone who was considered a Southerner, and also because of constant rumors that I was Jewish. Those rumors started soon after I arrived in Nashville and never went away."

I asked Tompall to share the one thing that he would like to be remembered for. He stated, "I feel that my legacy, what I should be best remembered for—is that I opened up country music and caused the industry to allow people to get into the music business who otherwise would never have been accepted. I opened it up by being different. Prior to me, no Westerner was allowed to make it big in country music."

When I first began interviewing Tompall and researching his life's accomplishments, my sole intent was to write a book that would document a handful of important things that I knew Tompall had done. However, as I learned more about Tompall's professional career I came to understand the tremendous and unsung role that he played in Nashville's country music awakening. I also discovered his impact on those around him during the mid-1950s to the mid-1980s, and I became more and more impressed with all that he had accomplished in his life. Here is a man that owned as many as seventeen corporations, including several publishing companies, a talent agency, a photography studio and a production company. He dabbled in areas beyond country music—such as writing poetry and book publishing, and Tompall's companies employed dozens of people.

Based on my findings, there was one important question I could not get out of my mind: Why isn't Tompall (and Tompall & The Glaser Brothers) in Nashville's *Country Music Hall of Fame?*

In 2011, Tompall & The Glaser Brothers were inducted into the Nebraska Country Music Foundation's Hall of Fame. They joined the likes of Lefty Frizzell, John Montgomery, Freddy Hart, Michael Martin Murphey and Bud Mayfield. The *Nebraska Country Music Hall of Fame* was established to meet their guiding principle of "the promotion, performance, and teaching of country music and its principles to the young and old, and to keep country music entertainment a part of our past, present, and future."

The fact that Tompall & The Glaser Brothers are in the *Nebraska Country Music Hall of Fame* is welcomed. However, it is not enough. Tompall must be recognized in a wider, more prominent venue for what he has done. I consider induction of Tompall Glaser into Nashville's *Country Music Hall of Fame* as the bare minimum of recognition he should be awarded for all that he has accomplished.

Not to diminish the accomplishments of other people who have been selected to be inducted into Nashville's *Country Music Hall of Fame*, but compare the resume of current *Country Music Hall of Fame* members to that of Tompall and his brothers. Few have had the effect on country music that Tompall has had over the span of three decades. Consider the number of successful musicians whose musical style Tompall has influenced, the musicians and engineers whose careers Tompall not only gave a leg-up to but fostered and encouraged, the long list of classic country music songs that he wrote, the accolades he received for publishing songs like "Gentle On My Mind," and so very, very much more.

The exact wording concerning qualifications necessary to be elected to the CMA *Country Music Hall of Fame* can be found on their website at http://www.cmaworld.com/info/hall-of-fame. The general *Candidate Criteria* includes these nine things:
- Basic Standard
- Individual Candidacy
- Scope of Activity
- Span of Influence
- Influence on Others

- Quantity vs. Quality
- Devotion to Others
- Professional Conduct and Image
- Personal Morals and Behavior

Tompall's life's work exceeds each of these stated criteria.

I have contacted the Country Music Association (CMA), the very organization where Tompall once held an executive Board of Directors position, the organization that ultimately chooses who is inducted into the *Country Music Hall of Fame*, and they have not had the courtesy to respond to my inquiries. I feel a sense of injustice that the CMA is ignoring the accomplishments of Tompall Glaser, and I hope that you feel the same way after reading this book.

One word frequently used by several people when talking about Tompall was "genius." One of the Webster Dictionary's definitions of genius is "a peculiar, distinctive or identifying character or spirit." This depicts someone who is unique, and someone who is difficult to understand by someone who is not themselves a genius. Human nature is such that we attempt to categorize people based upon certain criteria, such as intelligence, personality, and so on. But it is impossible to categorize someone who is unique.

Also, as someone who has been personally involved in the business world for more than three decades, I have learned the importance of separating *emotions* from *accomplishments*. I don't necessarily "like" or "get along with" everyone that I work with, yet I respect outcomes that people achieve.

Accomplishments should be the measure by which Tompall is judged. Period. As Kinky Friedman said, Tompall not only mattered, he was *significant* in the development of country music. While Tompall burned some professional bridges and never became a country music superstar, he was a primary catalyst for many of the changes in country music during his career—and he did it all "his way."

If you feel that Tompall has been shortchanged by the CMA,

please write to them or call them to express your feelings. They can be reached at:

Country Music Association, Inc.
One Music Circle South
Nashville, TN 37203
Phone: (615) 244-2840
Website: www.cmaworld.com

Appendix

TOMPALL GLASER ALBUMS

1960: This Land – Folk Songs (Tompall & The Glaser Brothers)

1961: Just Looking for a Home (Tompall & The Glaser Brothers)

1962: Country Folks (Tompall & The Glaser Brothers)

1966: Tompall & The Glaser Brothers (Tompall & The Glaser Brothers)

1967: Through the Eyes of Love (Tompall & The Glaser Brothers)

1968: The Wonderful World of the Glaser Brothers (Tompall & The Glaser Brothers)

1969: Now Country (Tompall & The Glaser Brothers)

1970: …tick…tick…tick… [Movie Soundtrack] (Tompall & The Glaser Brothers)

1971: Best of Tompall & The Glaser Brothers (Tompall & The Glaser Brothers)

1971: The Award Winners (Tompall & The Glaser Brothers)

1972: Tompall (of Tompall & The Glaser Brothers) (Tompall)

1972: Rings and Things (Tompall & The Glaser Brothers)

1972: Tompall & The Glaser Brothers Greatest Hits (Tompall & The Glaser Brothers)

1973: Greatest Hits From Two Decades (Tompall & The Glaser Brothers)

1973: Charlie (Tompall)

1973: Tompall (Tompall)

1974: Tompall & The Glaser Brothers Greatest Hits (Tompall & The Glaser Brothers)

1974: Take the Singer with the Song (Tompall)

1975: Tompall (Sings the Songs of Shel Silverstein) (Tompall)

1975: Vocal Group of the Decade (Tompall & The Glaser Brothers)

1976: Wanted! The Outlaws (Tompall, Willie, Waylon, & Jessie) Released 1-12-76; Re-released on 2-15-96

1976: Great Tompall & His Outlaw Band (Tompall)

1977: Wonder of It All (Tompall)

1977: Tompall Glaser and his Outlaw Band (Tompall)

1978: Unwanted Outlaw (Tompall)

1980: More of Tompall & The Glaser Brothers (Tompall & The Glaser Brothers)

1981: Loving Her Was Easier (Tompall & The Glaser Brothers)

1982: After All These Years (Tompall & The Glaser Brothers)

1986: Nights on the Borderline (Tompall)

1986: The Very Best of Tompall & The Glaser Brothers (Tompall & The Glaser Brothers)

1987: Love Ballads From World War II (Tompall)

1988: Country Store Collection (Tompall)

1992: The Rogue (Tompall)

1992: The Outlaw (Tompall)

2002: The Best of Tompall Glaser & The Glaser Brothers (Tompall & The Glaser Brothers)

2006: Outlaw to the Cross (Tompall)

2006: Tompall Glaser – My Notorious Youth: Hillbilly Central #1 (Tompall)

2006: Tompall Glaser – Another Log on the Fire: Hillbilly Central #2 (Tompall)

COMPILATIONS

1992: The Rogue (Tompall)

1992: The Outlaw (Tompall)

2001: The Best of Tompall Glaser & The Glaser Brothers (both Tompall and Tompall & The Glaser Brothers)

2006: My Notorious Youth: Hillbilly Central #1 (Tompall)

2006: Another Log on the Fire: Hillbilly Central #2 (Tompall)

2006: Loving Her Was Easier/After All These Years (Tompall)

MOVIE SOUNDTRACKS

1970: ...tick...tick...tick...
1976: Marlo Thomas Movie Soundtrack
1990: Another 48 Hrs.: "Drinking Them Beers"

MOVIE APPEARANCES

1997: Yesterday & Today: Outlaws (Hosted by Larry Gatlin on
     TNN)
2000: Johnny Cash: Half Mile A Day (Video Documentary)

RECORDING CONTRACTS

Starday Records
Decca Records
RCA
MGM
MGM/Curb
Arista
Nashville Talking Machine (Private Recording Label)

AWARDS RECEIVED

1968-1970: #1 Music Publishing Business in the World
1970: #1 Country Group of the Year
1970: Voted Most Popular Country Group in the World in England
1970: The First-Ever Robert J. Burton Award (Presented by BMI
     in Honor of Its Founder); Awarded to John Hartford and
     Glaser Publications, Inc
1970: CMA Vocal Group of the Year Award
1971: CMA Country International Award
1967-1970: Named Top Vocal Group by TNN for Four Straight
     Years
1965-1975: Named Top Music Group by Music City News Four
     Times

1965-1975: Named Top Music Group by Billboard Twice
1965-1975: Named Top Music Group by Cashbox Three Times
1972: Vocal Group of the Decade by Record World
1965-1975: Awarded Trophies by K-Bar-T, the National Organization of Fan Clubs, Twice
1976: Platinum Album by RCA for "Wanted! The Outlaws"
awarded "Most Awarded Country Group" of the time by *Billboard* Magazine
Twice voted Wembley Festival's #1 Country Group in the World

MEMBERSHIPS

1962-1977: *Grand Ole Opry*
1970-1972: Board of Directors of the Country Music Association (CMA)

NOTABLE PERFORMANCES

1956: October television performance on Arthur Godfrey's Talent Scouts
1957: November 19th episode of televised American Bandstand show
1959: Marty Robbins' televised Town Hall Party (back-up to Marty Robbins)
1960: Showboat Casino, Las Vegas (30 minute shows but were supposed to play for one hour so they just played their same set twice, playing 2x for one hour total).
[Note: this was Tompall's first trip to Las Vegas. Marty Landau was Marty Robbins West Coast booking agent. Mr. Landau was a well-known country music manager and booking agent, an early pioneer who worked with country music acts. He often accompanied the acts that he booked. Tompall played the craps tables and lost several hundred dollars. Marty Landau found out about this and told Tompall to give him $5.00. He then went to the craps table and won all of Tompall's money back except $300, and gave

Tompall the winnings. Marty told Tompall, "now stay away from those damn craps tables!"]

1962: Carnegie Hall, New York (as supporting act for Johnny Cash)

1962: The Mint, Las Vegas (as supporting act for patsy Cline)—six week engagement

1963: Far East Tour, including Okinawa, Japan

1963: The Mint, Las Vegas (as headliners)—six week engagement

1965: Holland and Belgium

1966: European Tour—included 10 days in Germany

1967: The Wilburn Brothers Television Show

1970; 1973; 1974; 1976; 1978; 1980; 1983; 1985: International Festival of Country Music, Wembley, England (1974, 1976, and 1978 as a solo act)

1970: The Johnny Cash Show

1971: The Porter Wagoner Show

1971: The Merv Griffin Show

16. 1980: Pop! Goes the Country

1982: Austin City Limits

1988: Inverness, Scotland

1988: Beltring, Kent, Great Britain

Songs sung on the 1982 Austin City Limits Show:

- Just One Time
- T For Texas
- The Last Thing On My Mind
- The California Girl and the Tennessee Square
- Ring, Ring
- Sweet City Woman

Band appearing with the Glasers: Doyle Gresham, steel guitar; Bill Holmes, bass guitar; Richie Simpson, drums; Paul Gauvin, lead guitar.

A COWBOY'S LAMENT

By: Tompall Glaser

Must a friend always bend
With the wind or the trend
And be lost when the gross is the most?
Well, it's happened again,
And will happen again,
But next time I just hope I'll know why.

It's too late to begin
Making new lifelong friends;
It's too soon to have none 'til the end.
You may say they're not friends
That they only pretend
That you can see through all of them.

You're a wise fool of course,
Or, you've never been forced
To live through my hour of remorse,
Of watching a friend
You have always called friend
Be the one who has just done you in.
He still looks like the friend
That you always called friend,
And you still can't see him pretend.
You can't say you've changed,
Or that he's deranged,
It appears that all should be the same.

But, the sting of the bruise
That you get when you're used
Is a slow and devouring pain
That cannot dull the brain
Till you feel it again
Then it all fades away with the shame.

A friend till the end
Is how all friends begin,
And we never do realize when
The end begins to unfriend the friend
Like the friend that just unfriended me.
But, we're all just too much alike my friend
To have never been someone's unfriend.
I never did see when that someone was me
So, I reckon that neither did he.

DISCOGRAPHY

Tompall Glaser Recordings*

SESSIONS:

Late 1957, Nashville, TN – Tompall & The Glaser Brothers:
001 MDR-1234 YOU'RE IN MY HEART AGAIN Robbins 1001
002 MDR-1235 FIVE PENNY NICKEL 1001

February 1958, Nashville, TN – Tompall & The Glaser Brothers
003 MDR-1242/J7OW-1011 I WANT YOU 1003
004 MDR-1243/J7OW-1012 BABY BE GOOD 1003

June 1958, Nashville, TN – Tompall & The Glaser Brothers
005 MDR-1252/SO-351 YAKETY-YAK 1006 Rich 1004
006 MDR-1253/SO-352 SWEET LIES 1006
007 SO-396 CRY OF THE WILD GOOSE Rich 1004

16 November 1958, Bradley Film & Recording Studio, 804 16th Ave.
South, Nashville, TN – Tompall Glaser & The Glaser Brothers
008 106135/NA 10475 OH LITTLE MARY (LET ME BE)
9-30805/VL-73807
009 106136/NA 10476 LAY DOWN THE GUN 9-30805/DL-
74041

13 April 1959 Bradley Film & Recording Studio, 804 16th Ave.
South, Nashville, TN – Tompall Glaser & The Glaser Brothers
010 107106/NA 10669 SHE LOVES THE LOVE I GIVE HER
9-30900/DL-74041
011 107107/NA 10670 OOIE-GOOIE 9-30900/Vocalion VL-
73807

16 June 1959 Bradley Film & Recording Studio, 804 16th Ave.
South, Nashville, TN – Tompall Glaser & The Glaser Brothers

012 107842/NA 10768 TWENTY-ONE MILES FROM HOME
9-31011/DL-74041
013 107843/NA 10769 I'LL NEVER TELL 9-31011/Vocalion
VL-73807

9 December 1959 Bradley Film & Recording Studio, 804 16th Ave.
South, Nashville TN – Tompall Glaser & The Glaser Brothers
014 108561/NA 10931 AIN'T LOVE LIKE A CRYIN' SHAME
unissued
015 108562/NA 10932 ALIBI 9-31051/DL-74041
016 108563/NA 10933 CARELESS LOVE, GOODBYE 9-31051/
DL-74041

23 February 1960 Bradley Film & Recording Studio, 804 16th Ave.
South, Nashville, TN – Tompall Glaser & The Glaser Brothers
(Producer: Owen Bradley)
017 108824/NA 10986 UNKNOWN TITLE: UNISSUED
018 108825/NA 10987 I NEVER WILL MARRY DL-74041
019 108826/NA 10988 THE WRECK OF THE OLD NUMBER
9 DL-74041 DL-74172
020 108827/NA 10989 DOWN THE MOUNTAIN DL-74041

23 March 1960 Bradley Film & Recording Studio, 804 16th Ave.
South, Nashville TN – Tompall Glaser & The Glaser Brothers
021 108939/NA 11027 I WONDER IF YOU CARE unissued
022 108940/NA 11028 SWEET LOVE, GOODBYE 9-31180/Vo-
calion VL-73870
023 108941/NA 11029 SAME OLD MEMORIES 9-31180/Vocal-
ization VL-73870
024 108942/NA 11030 EACH NIGHT AT NINE unissued

1 April 1960 Bradley Film & Recording Studio, 804 16th Ave.
South, Nashville, TN – Tompall Glaser & The Glaser Brothers
025 109021/NA 11074 SYLVIE DL-74041

026 109022/NA 11075 CHILLY WINDS DL-74041

027 109023/NA 11076 ERIE CANAL DL-74041 DL-74485 [va]

028 109024/NA 11077 THIS LAND IS YOUR LAND DL-74041 DL-74469 [va]

4 April 1961 Bradley Film & Recording Studio, 804 16th Ave. South, Nashville, TN – Tompall Glaser & The Glaser Brothers (unknown musicians). (Producer: Owen Bradley)

029 110435/NA 11495 WORDS COME EASY 31258/DL-74303 [va]

030 110436/NA 11496 MR. LONESOME 31551/Vocalion VL-73870

031 110437/NA 11497 AIN'T LIFE A CRYIN' SHAME unissued

032 110438/NA 11498 JUDY'S GROWN UP 31258/Vocalion VL-73870

7 September 1961 Bradley Film & Recording Studio, 804 16th Ave. South, Nashville, TN – Tompall Glaser & The Glaser Brothers (unknown musicians). (Producer: Owen Bradley)

033 111071/NA 11698 LET ME DOWN EASY 31322/Vocalion VL-73870

034 111072/NA 11699 TIRED OF CRYING FOR YOU 31322/Vocalion VL-73870

25 April 1962 Columbia Recording Studio, 804 16th Ave. South, Nashville, TN – Tompall Glaser & The Glaser Brothers (unknown musicians). (Producer: Owen Bradley)

035 112150/NA 12028 I'M LOSING AGAIN 31398

036 112151/NA 12029 I CAN'T REMEMBER 31398

9 October 1962 Columbia Recording Studio, 804 16th Ave. South, Nashville, TN – Tompall Glaser & The Glaser Brothers (unknown musicians). (Producer: Owen Bradley)

037 112702/NA 12214 ODDS AND ENDS (BITS AND PIECES) 31447

038 112703/NA 12215 THE LOVER'S FAREWELL 31447

19 March 1963 Columbia Recording Studio, 804 16th Ave. South, Nashville, TN – Tompall Glaser & The Glaser Brothers (unknown musicians. Producer: Owen Bradley)

039 113287/NA 12426 BLOW OUT THE CANDLES 31551/ VL-73807

040 113288/NA 12427 STAND BESIDE ME 31494

041 113289/NA 12428 TRACKIN' ME DOWN 31494

042 113290/NA 12429 SOUTH OF THE BORDER DL-74393 [va]

2 March 1964 Columbia Recording Studio, 804 16th Ave. South, Nashville, TN – Tompall Glaser & The Glaser Brothers (unknown musicians. Producer: Owen Bradley)

043 114604/NA 12870 BABY THEY'RE PLAYING OUR SONG 31736

044 114605/NA 12871 A GIRL LIKE YOU 31632/DL-74671 [va]

045 114606/NA 12872 I'VE GOT TROUBLES 31632/DL-74539 [va]

046 114607/NA 12873 WINNER TAKE ALL 31736

18 May 1965 Columbia Recording Studio, 804 16th Ave. South, Nashville, TN – Tompall Glaser & The Glaser Brothers

047 116033/NA 13551 TEARDROPS 'TIL DAWN 31809

048 116032/NA 13552 THE LITTLE FOLKS unissued

049 116034/NA 13553 BACK IN EACH OTHER'S ARMS AGAIN 31809

12 April 1966 Nashville, TN – Tompall Glaser & The Glaser Brothers (Producer: Jack Clement)

050 N 50000 THE LAST THING ON MY MIND MGM K 13531/SE-4465
051 N 50001 MORE OR LESS K 13531/SE-4465
052 N 50002 BIG BROTHER SE-4465

16 September 1966 Nashville, TN – Tompall Glaser & The Glaser Brothers (Producer: Jack Clement)
053 N 50157 GONE, ON THE OTHER HAND K13611/SE-4465 M3G-4946
054 N 50158 HOW ARE YOU, BROWN EYES SE-4510
055 N 50159 STREETS OF BALTIMORE K13611/SE-4465 SE-4888
056 N 50160 SHE LOVED THE WRONG MAN K13754/SE-4465

22 February 1967 Jack Clement Recording Studio, 3102 Belmont Blvd., Nashville, TN - Tompall Glaser & The Glaser Brothers (Producer: Jack Clement)
057 N 50268 GENTLE ON MY MIND SE-4465 SE-4667 SE-4888
058 N 50269 I CHOSE YOU rejected
059 N 50270 NO END OF LOVE K13880/SE-4465

27 February 1967 Jack Clement Recording Studio, 3102 Belmont Blvd., Nashville, TN - Tompall Glaser & The Glaser Brothers (Producer: Jack Clement)
060 N 50271 BOB SE-4465
061 N 50272 GONNA MISS ME K14096/SE-4465 SE-4620
062 N 50273 EL PASO SE-4465 SE-4888

18 April 1967 Jack Clement Recording Studio, 3102 Belmont Blvd., Nashville, TN – Tompall Glaser & The Glaser Brothers (Producer: Jack Clement)
063 N 50305 I CHOSE YOU SE 4510

064 N 50306 THROUGH THE EYES OF LOVE K13754/SE-4510 M3G-4946

24 October 1967 Jack Clement Recording Studio, 3102 Belmont Blvd., Nashville, TN – Tompall Glaser & Glaser Brothers (Producer: Jack Clement)
065 N 50446 THE MOODS OF MARY K13880/SE-4510 M3G-4946
066 N 50447 YOU ONLY PASS THIS WAY ONE TIME SE-4510

22 November 1967 Jack Clement Recording Studio, 3102 Belmont Blvd., Nashville, TN – Tompall Glaser & The Glaser Brothers (Producer: Jack Clement)
067 N 50453 THE GREAT EL TIGRE SE-4510
068 N 50454 WHERE HAS ALL THE LOVE GONE K13954/SE-4510 SE-4667
069 N 50455 I'M SORRY, ROSEANNA SE-4510

13 December 1967 Jack Clement Recording Studio, 3102 Belmont Blvd., Nashville, TN – Tompall Glaser & The Glaser Brothers (Producer: Jack Clement)
070 N 50473 WHAT DOES IT TAKE SE-4510 SE-4667 SE-4888
071 N 50474 WOMAN, WOMAN SE-4510 SE-4667 SE-4888
072 N 50475 THAT'S HOW A WOMAN'S S'POSE TO BE SE-4510

25 April 1968 Jack Clement Recording Studio, 3102 Belmont Blvd., Nashville, TN – Tompall Glaser & The Glaser Brothers (Producer: Jack Clement)
073 N 50633 ONE OF THESE DAYS K13954/SE-4577
074 N 50634 HOME IS WHERE THE HURT IS SE-4577 SE-4667
075 N 50635 RECIPE FOR A "ME" SE-4577

8 May 1968 Jack Clement Recording Studio, 3102 Belmont Blvd., Nashville, TN – Tompall Glaser & The Glaser Brothers (Producer: Jack Clement)
076 N 50663 GUESS THINGS HAPPEN THAT WAY SE-4577
077 N 50664 WHY DO YOU DO ME LIKE YOU DO SE-4577 SE-4667
078 N 50665 THE WAY THAT WE ARE LIVING NOW SE-4577
079 N 50666 GOT LEAVIN' ON HER MIND SE-4577
080 N 50669 IS MY LOVE COMING ON TOO STRONG SE-4577

9 May 1968 Jack Clement Recording Studio, 3102 Belmont Blvd., Nashville, TN – Tompall Glaser & Glaser Brothers (Producer: Jack Clement)
081 N 50642 INSTINCT FOR SURVIVAL SE-4577
082 N 50643 HOME COUNTRY SE-4577
083 N 50644 MONEY CAN NOT MAKE THE MAN SE-4577

13 November 1968 Jack Clement Recording Studio, 3102 Belmont Blvd., Nashville, TN – Tompall Glaser & The Glaser Brothers (Producer: Jack Clement)
084 N 50855 CALIFORNIA GIRL (AND THE TENNESSEE SQUARE)
K14036/SE-4620, SE-4667 M3G-4946

11 December 1968 Jack Clement Recording Studio, 3102 Belmont Blvd., Nashville, TN – Tompall Glaser & Glaser Brothers (Producer: Jack Clement)
085 N 50856 ALL THAT KEEPS YA GOIN' K14113/SE-4620 SE-4667 M3G-4946
086 N 50857 WALK UNASHAMED K14096/SE-4620 SE-4667

31 March 1969 Jack Clement Recording Studio, 3102 Belmont Blvd., Nashville, TN – Tompall Glaser & The Glaser Brothers (Producer: Jack Clement)
087 N 50947 CHARLOTTE, IN THE MORNING RISING unissued
088 N 50948 WICKED CALIFORNIA K14064/SE-4620 M3G-4946

1 April 1969 Jack Clement Recording Studio, 3102 Belmont Blvd., Nashville, TN – Tompall Glaser & The Glaser Brothers (Producer: Jack Clement)
089 N 50949 HOMEWARD BOUND SE-4620 SE-4888
090 N 50950 PROUD MARY SE-4620 SE-4888
091 N 50951 THE EVE OF PARTING K14064/SE-4620
092 N 50952 MOLLY DARLING unissued
093 N 50953 THOSE WERE THE DAYS SE-4620 SE-4888
094 N 50954 BUT YOU KNOW I LOVE YOU SE-4620 SE-4888
095 N 50955 MOLLY DARLING SE-4620

16 December 1969 Nashville, TN – Tompall Glaser & The Glaser Brothers
096 N 51052 THEME FROM TICK...TICK...TICK (SET YOURSELF FREE) K 14113/SE-4667

2 January 1970 Nashville, TN – Tompall Glaser & The Glaser Brothers
097 70N-51053 GENTLE ON MY MIND

21 May 1970 Nashville, TN – Tompall Glaser & The Glaser Brothers
098 70N-51142 GONE GIRL K14169/M3G-4946
099 70N-51143 I'LL SAY MY WORDS K14169
100 70N-51144 HOW SHE GOT HERE FROM MICHIGAN unissued

1 October 1970 Glaser Sound Studio, 916 9th Ave. South, Nashville, TN – Tompall Glaser & The Glaser Brothers
101 70N-50209 TODAY I STARTED LOVING YOU AGAIN unissued
102 70N-50210 A GIRL I USED TO KNOW SE-4775

4 October 1970 Glaser Sound Studio, 916 9th Ave. South, Nashville, TN – Tompall Glaser & The Glaser Brothers
103 70N-51211 SUNDAY MORNIN' COMIN' DOWN unissued
104 70N-51212 BRIDGE OVER TROUBLED WATER unissued

30 December 1970 Glaser Sound Studio, 916 9th Ave. South, Nashville, TN – Tompall Glaser & The Glaser Brothers (Tompall Glaser [vcl/gt], John Hartford [gt],
Randy Scruggs [gt]). (Producer: Chuck Glaser)
105 71N-51246 ME AND BOBBY MCGEE unissued
106 71N-51247 BLUE MOON OF KENTUCKY unissued
107 71N-51248 SNOWBIRD SE-4775 SE-4888

22 January 1971 Glaser Sound Studio, 916 9th Ave. South, Nashville, TN – Tompall Glaser & The Glaser Brothers (Producer: Chuck Glaser)
108 71N-51258 I SEE HIS LOVE ALL OVER YOU SE-4775
109 71N-51259 PRETTY EYES K14249
110 71N-51260 HELP ME MAKE IT THROUGH THE NIGHT SE-4775 SE-4888

17 February 1971 Glaser Sound Studio, 916 9th Ave. South, Nashville, TN – Tompall Glaser & The Glaser Brothers (Tompall Glaser [vcl/gt], Leon McAuliffe [steel],
Keith Coleman [fiddle] + unknown musicians. (Producer: Chuck Glaser)
111 71N-51279 FADED LOVE K14249/SE-4775 M3G-4946

112 71N-51280 SAN ANTONIO ROSE unissued

21 April 1971 Glaser Sound Studio, 916 9th Ave. South, Nashville, TN – Tompall Glaser & The Glaser Brothers (Tompall Glaser [vcl/gt], John Hartford [gt], Randy Scruggs [gt] + unknown musicians. (Producer: Chuck Glaser)
113 71N-51291 ME AND BOBBY MCGEE SE-4775
114 71N-51292 STAND BESIDE ME K14339/SE-4775
115 71N-51293 WHAT IS A WOMAN WHAT IS A MAN SE-4775
116 71N-51294 THE DAYS WHEN YOU WERE STILL IN LOVE WITH ME SE-4812
117 71N-51295 THAT'S WHEN I LOVE YOU THE MOST K14291/SE-4775

26 April 1971 Glaser Sound Studio, 916 9th Ave. South, Nashville, TN – Tompall Glaser & The Glaser Brothers (Tompall Glaser [vcl/gt], Harold Bradley [gt] + unknown musicians. (Producer: Chuck Glaser)
118 71N-51302 BYE BYE LOVE SE-4775
119 71N-51303 SIMPLE THING AS LOVE SE-4775

June 1971 Glaser Sound Studio, 916 9th Ave. South, Nashville, TN - Tompall Glaser & The Glaser Brothers (Producer: Chuck Glaser)
120 71N-51329 RINGS K14291 KGC-236/SE-4812 M3G-4946

10 June 1971 Glaser Sound Studio, 916 9th Ave. South, Nashville, TN – Tompall Glaser & The Glaser Brothers (Producer: Chuck Glaser)
121 71N-51341 ROSE OF OLD PAWNEE unissued

17 June 1971 Glaser Sound Studio, 916 9th Ave. South, Nashville, TN – Tompall Glaser & The Glaser Brothers (Producer: Chuck Glaser)

122 71N-51342 LOVING HER WAS EASIER (THAN ANY-
THING I'LL EVER DO
AGAIN) M3G-4976

25 June 1971 Glaser Sound Studio, 916 9th Ave. South, Nashville,
TN – Tompall Glaser & The Glaser Brothers (Producer: Chuck
Glaser)
123 71N-51343 BACK IN EACH OTHER'S ARMS AGAIN SE-
4812
124 71N-51344 SAME OLD MEMORIES unissued
125 71N-51345 MAIDEN'S PRAYER unissued

5 August 1971 Glaser Sound Studio, 916 9th Ave. South, Nashville,
TN – Tompall Glaser & The Glaser Brothers (Producer: Chuck
Glaser)
126 71N-51347 I'VE DONE AT LEAST ONE THING unissued
127 71N-51348 THIS TIME unissued
128 71N-51349 LOVIN YOU AGAIN SE-4812
129 71N-51350 BLUE RIDGE MOUNTAINS K14390/SE-4812

10 August 1971 Glaser Sound Studio, 916 9th Ave. South, Nashville, TN –Tompall Glaser & The Glaser Brothers (Producer:
Chuck Glaser)
130 71N-51357 FREE TO RUN FREE unissued

11 August 1971 Glaser Sound Studio, 916 9th Ave. South, Nashville, TN – Tompall Glaser & The Glaser Brothers (Producer:
Chuck Glaser)
131 71N-51358 HAMILTON JONES unissued
132 71N-51359 LEAVE THAT FOR MEMORIES SE-4812

4 October 1971 Nashville, TN - Tompall Glaser & The Glaser
Brothers

133 71N-51385 SHE'S SWEET, SHE'S KIND, AND SHE'S MINE M3G-4976

134 71N-51386 DELTA LOST K14462/SE-4812

135 71N-51387 VELVET WALLPAPER M3G-4976

136 71N-51388 YOU'RE IN CAROLINA SE-4812

25 October 1971 Glaser Sound Studio, 916 9th Ave. South, Nashville, TN – Tompall Glaser & The Glaser Brothers (Producer: Jim & Chuck Glaser)

137 71N-51412 TEAR DOWN THE GRAND OLE OPRY unissued

138 71N-51413 DON'T CALL ME YOUR ONLY SUNSHINE M3G-4976

139 71N-51414 (DIDN'T WE HAVE OURSELVES) SOME KIND OF A SUMMER M3G-4976

2 November 1971 Glaser Sound Studio, 916 9th Ave. South, Nashville, TN – Tompall Glaser & The Glaser Brothers (Producer: Jim & Chuck Glaser)

140 71N-51415 LONG ROAD BACK unissued

141 71N-51416 SHE'S NEVER BEEN THIS GONE BEFORE M3G-4976

142 71N-51417 I'M GONNA MAKE A NEW MAN unissued

143 71N-51418 VIRGINIA AND THE KIDS unissued

4 November 1971 Nashville, TN – Tompall & The Glaser Brothers

144 71N-51393 SWEET, LOVE ME GOOD WOMAN K14339/SE-4812

145 71N-51394 GEORGIA SUNSHINE unissued

146 71N-51395 PHONEY WORLD SE-4812

3 December 1971 Nashville, TN – Tompall Glaser & The Glaser Brothers (With The London Symphony Orchestra)

147 71N-51425 AIN'T IT ALL WORTH LIVING FOR K14390 KGC-236/CCM-248

14 December 1971 Glaser Sound Studio, 916 9th Ave. South, Nashville, TN – Tompall Glaser & The Glaser Brothers (Producer: Jim & Chuck Glaser)
148 71N-51430 LIFE'S LITTLE UPS AND DOWNS M3G-4976
149 71N-51431 WALK UNASHAMED M3G-4946

16 December 1971 Glaser Sound Studio, 916 9th Ave. South, Nashville, TN – Tompall Glaser & The Glaser Brothers (Producer: Jim & Chuck Glaser)
150 71N-51432 TIN CUP CHALICE M3G-4976
151 71N-51433 THE CHRISTIAN M3G-4976

10 May 1972 Nashville, TN – Tompall Glaser & The Glaser Brothers [purchased January 1974]
152 74N-6155 WORDS COME EASY unissued
153 74N 6156 LET ME DOWN EASY unissued
154 74N-6157 I'M NOT AT ALL SORRY FOR YOU unissued
155 74N-6158 SWEETER THAN THE FLOWERS unissued

28 September 1972 Nashville, TN – Tompall Glaser & The Glaser Brothers [purchased January 1974]
156 74N-6159 JUST CALL ME LONESOME unissued

5 October 1972 Nashville, TN – Tompall Glaser & The Glaser Brothers [purchased January 1974]
157 74N-6160 LAY DOWN BESIDE ME Polydor 24602 340 [UK] Bear Family BCD-16187 [GER]

15 October 1972 Nashville, TN – Tompall Glaser & The Glaser Brothers
158 74N-6161 INDIANA WOMAN unissued
159 74N-6162 FREEDOM TO STAY M3G-4976

160 72N-51574 A GIRL LIKE YOU K14462/M3G-4946 CCM-248

16 January 1973 Glaser Sound Studio, 916 9th Ave. South, Nashville, TN – Tompall Glaser (Producer: Tompall Glaser)
161 73N-51635 CHARLIE K14516/SE-4918 CCM-248

June 1973 Glaser Sound Studio, 916 9th Ave. South, Nashville, TN – Tompall Glaser (Producer: Tompall Glaser)
162 73N-51731 MR. LONESOME SE-4918
163 73N-51732 AN ODE TO MY NOTORIOUS YOUTH: BARRED FROM EVERY HONKYTONK SE-4918
164 73N-51733 LONELIEST MAN SE-4918
165 73N-51734 I'LL FLY AWAY MEDLEY. I'LL FLY AWAY/I SAW THE LIGHT SE-4918
166 73N-51735 COWBOYS AND DADDIES SE-4918
167 73N-51736 BIG JIM COLSON SE-4918
168 73N-51737 BAD, BAD, BAD COWBOY K14622/SE-4918 CCM-248
169 73N-51738 GIDEON BIBLE SE-4918
170 73N-51739 LET IT BE PRETTY unissued
171 73N-51740 SOLD AMERICAN SE-4918

2 August 1973 Glaser Sound Studio, 916 9th Ave. South, Nashville, TN – Tompall Glaser (Producer: Jim Glaser) [purchased and mastered January 1974]
172 74N-6164 BABY, BABY DON'T GET HOOKED ON ME unissued
173 74N-6165 LET IT BE PRETTY K14622/SE-4918
174 74N-6166 LOVE STONED unissued/Bear Family BCD-16187 [GER]

December 1973 Glaser Sound Studio, 916 9th Ave. South, Nashville, TN – Tompall Glaser (Producer: Tompall Glaser) [mastered 1974]
175 74N-6072 TEXAS LAW SEZ M14701/CCM-248 Polydor 24602 340 [UK]
Bear Family BCD-16187
176 74N-6073 PASS ME ON BY M14701/ Polydor 24602 340 [UK] Bear Family BCD-16187

December 1973 Glaser Sound Studio, 916 9th Ave. South, Nashville, TN – Tompall Glaser (Producer: Tompall Glaser) [mastered 1974]
177 74N-6417 BROKEN DOWN MOMMA Polydor 24602 340 [UK] Bear Family
BCD-16187 [GER]
178 74N-6418 WILLY, THE WANDERIN' GYPSY AND ME Polydor 24602 340 [UK]
Bear Family BCD-16187 [GER]
179 74N 6419 TAKE THE SINGER WITH THE SONG Polydor 24602 340 [UK] Bear Family
BCD-16187 [GER]
180 74N-6420 HONEY DON'T YOU KNOW Polydor 24602 340 [UK] Bear Family
BCD-16187 [GER]
181 74N-6421 THE GOOD LORD KNOWS I TRIED Polydor 24602 340 [UK] Bear Family
BCD-16187 [GER]
182 74N-6422 BREAKDOWN (A LONG WAY FROM HOME) Polydor 24602 340 [UK] Bear Family BCD-16187 [GER]
183 74N-6423 WILL THE CIRCLE BE UNBROKEN unissued/ Bear Family BCD-16187 [GER]

15 January 1974 Glaser Sound Studio, 916 9th Ave. South, Nashville, TN – Tompall Glaser

314

(Producer: Jim Glaser)
184 74N 6163 CHARLESTON unissued

June 1974 Glaser Sound Studio, 916 9th Ave. South, Nashville, TN
- Tompall Glaser
185 74N-6417 BROKEN DOWN MAMA unissued
186 74N-6418 WILLIE THE WANDERIN' GYPSY AND ME
187 74N-6419 TAKE THE SINGER WITH THE SONG
188 74N-6420 HONEY, DON'T YOU KNOW

circa (ca.) June 1974 Glaser Sound Studio, 916 9th Ave. South,
Nashville, TN – Tompall Glaser (musicians similar as below). (Producer: Tompall Glaser)
189 74N-6437 MUSICAL CHAIRS M 14740/M3G-4977
190 74N-6438 GRAB A HOLD M 14740/M3G-4977

August 1974 Glaser Sound Studio, 916 9th Ave. South, Nashville,
TN – Tompall Glaser (Tompall Glaser [vcl/ac gt], Fred Newell [gt/
banjo/harmonica/strings], Norman Blake [dobro/fiddle/ac gt], Pete
Drake [steel], Rick Maness [bass], Kenny Malone [drums/vibes],
Larry Londin/Moi Harris [drums], Buddy Spicher [fiddle], Chuck
Cochran [piano], Willie Rainsford [piano/organ/harpsichord], Kyle
Lehning [piano/organ/synthesizer], Russ Hicks [strings] + Pall
Beares & The Glaseroonies [bck vcl]). (Producer: Tompall Glaser
& Shel Silverstein)
191 74N-6519 ROLL ON M3G-4977
192 74N-6520 I AIN'T LOOKIN' FOR THE ANSWERS ANY-
MORE M3G-4977
193 74N-6521 EARTH COLORS unissued
194 74N-6522 WHY MAKE ME PAY NOW unissued
195 74N-6523 MENDOCINO M14800/M3G-4977
196 74N-6524 ECHOES M3G-4977
197 74N-6525 OLEANDER M3G-4977

198 74N-6526 COUNTRY GOSPEL GOOD BOOK ROCK & ROLL M3G-4977
199 74N-6527 IF I'M THERE M3G-4977
200 74N-6528 WHEN IT GOES IT'S GONE unissued
201 74N-6529 A LADY NEEDS A BASTARD unissued

August 1974 Glaser Sound Studio, 916 9th Ave. South, Nashville, TN – Tompall Glaser (musicians similar as above)
202 74N-6531 NEW ORLEANS CUSTOM M3G-4977
203 74N-6533 PUT ANOTHER LOG ON THE FIRE M14800
Polydor 540/M3G-4977 CCM-248 RCA AFL1-1321 66841-2

ca. October 1975 Glaser Sound Studio, 916 9th Ave. South, Nashville, TN - Tompall Glaser (Mel Brown/Billy Williams/Fred Newell/Norman Blake [el gt], Waylon Jennings/Troy Seals [gt], Bobby Thompson [banjo], Ralph Mooney [steel], Jim Webb [dobro], Ted Reynolds/Rick Maness/Duke Goff [bass], Charles Polk/Kenny Malone [drums], Johnny Gimble [fiddle/el.mandolin], Willie Rainsford [piano], Kyle Lehning [keyboards/clarinet] + , Casey Anderson, Mary Beth Anderson [vocal chorus]). (Producer: Tompall Glaser)
204 75N-1541 THE WILD SIDE OF LIFE M3G-5014
205 75N-1542 THE HUNGER M3G-5014

ca. December 1975 Glaser Sound Studio, 916 9th Ave. South, Nashville, TN – Tompall Glaser (Mel Brown/Billy Williams/Fred Newell/Norman Blake [el gt], Waylon Jennings/Troy Seals [gt], Bobby Thompson [banjo], Ralph Mooney [steel], Jim Webb [dobro], Ted Reynolds/Rick Maness/Duke Goff [bass], Charles Polk/Kenny Malone [drums], Johnny Gimble [fiddle/el.mandolin], Willie Rainsford [piano], Kyle Lehning [keyboards/clarinet] + , Casey Anderson, Mary Beth Anderson [vocal chorus]). (Producer: Tompall Glaser)
206 75N-1590 WE LIVE IN TWO DIFFERENT WORLDS M3G-5014

207 75N-1591 I CAN'T REMEMBER M3G-5014

208 75N-1592 WHEN IT GOES, IT'S GONE GIRL M3G-5014

209 75N-1593 TIME CHANGES EVERYTHING M3G-5014

210 75N-1594 IF I'D ONLY COME AND GONE M3G-5014

211 75N-1595 GOOD HEARTED WOMAN M3G-5014

212 75N-1596 WEST CANTERBURY SUBDIVISION BLUES M3G-5014

213 75N-1597 TOMPALL IN "D" ON THE UKULELE M3G-5014

214 75N-1598 BROKEN DOWN MAMA Polydor PD-14314/ M3G-5014

ca. February 1976 Glaser Sound Studio, 916 9th Ave. South, Nashville, TN – Tompall Glaser (Mel Brown/Billy Williams/Fred Newell/Norman Blake [el gt], Waylon Jennings/Troy Seals [gt], Bobby Thompson [banjo], Ralph Mooney [steel], Jim Webb [dobro], Ted Reynolds/Rick Maness/Duke Goff [bass], Charles Polk/Kenny Malone [drums], Johnny Gimble [fiddle/el.mandolin], Willie Rainsford [piano], Kyle Lehning [keyboards/clarinet] + , Casey Anderson, Mary Beth Anderson [vocal chorus]). (Producer: Tompall Glaser)

215 76NP 1698 T FOR TEXAS Polydor PD-14314/RCA AFL1-1321 66841-2 BCD-16520 [GER]

ca. November 1976 Glaser Sound Studio, 916 9th Ave. South, Nashville, TN – Tompall Glaser & His Outlaw Band (Tompall Glaser [vcl/gt/scat], Mel Brown [el gt/piano/organ/accordion], Fred Newell [el gt/ac rh gt/guitarfiddle], Ben Keith [dobro/steel], Ted Reynolds [bass], Charles Polk [drums/percussion], Red Young [organ/piano/horn arr./bck vcl] + Johnny Gimble [fiddle/mandolin], Buddy Spicher [cello/strings/fiddle], James Gordon [sax], Mac Johnson [trumpet], Linda Small [trombone] + Marshall Chapman, Pebble Daniel, Marcia Routh, Lea Jane Berinati, Red Young, Debora Allen [bck vcl]). (Producer: Ken Mansfield & Tompall Glaser)

216 YOU CAN HAVE HER AB-978

217 RELEASE ME (AND LET ME LOVE AGAIN) AB-978

218 TENNESSEE BLUES AB-978

219 COME BACK SHANE AB-978

220 IT'LL BE HER AB-12261/ AB-978

221 LOOK WHAT THOUGHTS WILL DO/PRETTY WORDS/IT AIN'T FAIR THAT IT AIN'T RIGHT AB-978

222 SWEETHEARTS OR STRANGERS AB-12261/ AB-978

223 LET MY FINGERS DO THE WALKING (LATE NIGHT SHOW) AB-978

224 I JUST WANT TO HEAR THE MUSIC AB-978

225 MY LIFE WOULD MAKE A DAMN GOOD COUNTRY SONG unissued/ BCD-15605 [GER]

ca. June 1977 Glaser Sound Studio, 916 9th Ave. South, Nashville, TN – Tompall Glaser & His Outlaw Band (Tompall Glaser [vcl/ gt], Mel Brown [gt], Jimmy Capps/Bill Sanford/Fred Newell [rh gt], Mac Guyden [slide gt], Ben Keith [dobro], Ted Reynolds [bass], Charlie Polk/Larrie Londin [drums], Red Young [el piano]). (Producer: Jimmy Bowen)

226 IT NEVER CROSSED MY MIND AB-12309/AB-1036

227 BAD TIMES AB-12366/ AB-1036

228 WHAT ARE WE DOIN' WITH THE REST OF OUR LIVES AB-1036

229 HOW I LOVE THEM OLD SONGS AB-1036

230 ON SECOND THOUGHT AB-1036

231 DRINKING THEM BEERS AB-12329/ AB-1036

232 EASY ON MY MIND AB-12309/ AB-1036

233 THE WONDER OF IT ALL AB-1036

234 STORMS NEVER LAST unissued/BCD-15605

ca. September 1977 Glaser Sound Studio, 916 9th Ave. South, Nashville, TN – Tompall Glaser & His Outlaw Band (Tompall Glaser [vcl/gt], John Christopher [rh gt], Jimmy Colvart [el gt], Joe Os-

born [bass], Charles Polk or Larrie Londin [drums], Hargus Robbins [piano]). (Producer: Jimmy Bowen)
235 29682 DUNCAN AND BRADY AB-12329/ AB-1036
236 MY MOTHER WAS A LADY AB-1036

ca. March 1978 Glaser Sound Studio, 916 9th Ave. South, Nashville, TN – Tompall Glaser (Producer: Tompall Glaser)
237 LIKE AN OLD COUNTRY SONG unissued/BCD-15596 [GER]
238 SAD COUNTRY SONGS unissued/BCD-15596 [GER]
239 WHAT A TOWN unissued/BCD-15596 [GER]
240 DON'T THINK YOU'RE TOO GOOD FOR COUNTRY MUSIC unissued/ BCD-15596 [GER]
241 UNWANTED OUTLAW unissued/BCD-15596 [GER]
242 MAN YOU THINK TO SEE unissued/BCD-15596 [GER]
243 WHEN I DREAM unissued/BCD-15596 [GER]
244 BURN GEORGIA BURN unissued/BCD-15596 [GER]
245 BILLY TYLER unissued/BCD-15596 [GER]
246 CARRY ME ON AB-12366/BCD-15596 [GER]

between 1976/1978 Glaser Sound Studio, 916 9th Ave. South, Nashville, TN – Tompall Glaser
(Producer: Tompall Glaser)
247 THE ROGUE unissued/BCD-15596 [GER]
248 TEARS ON MY PILLOW unissued/BCD-15596 [GER]
249 FOREVER AND EVER unissued/BCD-15596 [GER]
250 SHACKLES AND CHAINS unissued/BCD-15596 [GER]
251 MY PRETTY QUADROON unissued/BCD-15596 [GER]
252 LEAN ON ME unissued/BCD-15596 [GER]
253 I'LL HOLD YOU IN MY HEART unissued/BCD-15596 [GER]
254 TRUE LOVE, TRUE LOVE unissued/BCD-15596 [GER]
255 OPEN ARMS unissued/BCD-15596 [GER]

256 I LOVE YOU SO MUCH, IT HURTS unissued/BCD-15596 [GER]

257 CHATTANOOGA SHOE SHINE BOY unissued/BCD-15596 [GER]

258 YOU CAN'T BORROW BACK ANY TIME unissued/BCD-15596 [GER]

ca. January 1980 Glaser Sound Studio, 916 9th Ave. South, Nashville, TN – Tompall Glaser & The Glaser Brothers (musicians similar as below)

259 FEELIN' THE WEIGHT OF MY CHAINS E-46595 E-47193 E-47461/5E-542

260 THE BALLAD OF LUCY JORDAN E-46595

ca. August 1980 Glaser Sound Studio, 916 9th Ave. South, Nashville, TN – Tompall Glaser & The Glaser Brothers (musicians similar as below)

261 SWEET CITY WOMAN E-47056

262 TRYIN' THE OUTRUN THE WIND E-47056/5E-542

ca. March 1981 Glaser Sound Studio, 916 9th Ave. South, Nashville, TN – Tompall Glaser & The Glaser Brothers (musicians similar as below)

263 LOVIN' HER WAS EASIER (THAN ANYTHING I'LL EVER DO AGAIN) E-47134/5E-542

264 UNITED WE FALL E-47134/5E-542

ca. June 1981 Glaser Sound Studio, 916 9th Ave. South, Nashville, TN – Tompall Glaser & The Glaser Brothers (Tompall Glaser [vcl/gt], Jim Glaser [ac gt], Paul Gauvin [ac gt], Kenny Bell [ac gt], Bobby Thompson [ac gt], Reggie Young [el gt], Reggie Young [sitar], Doyle Gresham/Sonny Garrish/Buddy Emmons [steel] Bob Ray [bass], Roger Clark [percussion] + Shelly Kurland Strings). (Producer: Jim Bowen)

265 JUST ONE TIME E-47193/5E-542
266 IT'LL BE HER E-47405/5E-542
267 BUSTED 5E-542
268 THE LAST THING ON MY MIND 5E-542
269 DRINKING THEM BEERS 5E-542
270 A MANSION ON THE HILL E-47461/5E-542

ca. September 1981 Glaser Sound Studio, 916 9th Ave. South, Nashville, TN – Tompall Glaser & The Glaser Brothers
271 SILVER BELLS E-47230

ca. March 1982 Glaser Sound Studio, 916 9th Ave. South, Nashville, TN – Tompall Glaser & The Glaser Brothers (Tompall Glaser [vcl/rh gt], Jim Glaser [ac gt], Paul Gauvin [ac gt], Joe Wilson [gt/gut string gt/keyboards], Doyle Gresham [ld gt/steel], Bill Holmes [bass], Richie Simpson [drums], Lisa Silver [violin]). (Producer: Jim Bowen)
272 I STILL LOVE YOU (AFTER ALL THESE YEARS) E-47461/E1-60148
273 CAN'T LIVE WITH 'EM E1-60148
274 ROSALI E1-60148
275 NAKED EMOTIONS E1-60148
276 HAPPY HOUR BLUES E1-60148
277 CAN I SLEEP HERE TONIGHT E1-60148
278 STAY YOUNG E1-60148
279 I COULD NEVER LIVE ALONE AGAIN 7-69947/ E1-60148
280 OH AMERICA E1-60148

ca. March 1982 Glaser Sound Studio, 916 9th Ave. South, Nashville, TN – Tompall Glaser & The Glaser Brothers (Tompall Glaser [vcl/rh gt], Jim Glaser [ac gt],
Ralph Childs [bass], Clyde Brooks [drums]). (Producer: Joe Wilson, Jimmy Bowen)

281 MARIA CONSUELA 7-69947/ E1-60148

ca. November 1985 poss. Glaser Sound Studio, 916 9th Ave. South, Nashville, TN – Tompall Glaser & The Glaser Brothers
282 NIGHTS ON THE BORDERLINE Dot MCA-39051
283 MAMMA DON'T LET YOUR BIG BOY PLAY OUTSIDE Dot MCA-39051
284 (FOR EVERY INCH I'VE LAUGHED) I'VE CRIED A MILE Dot MCA-39051
285 PUT ANOTHER LOG ON THE FIRE Dot MCA-39051
286 UP WHERE WE BELONG Dot MCA-39051
287 I DON'T CARE ANYMORE Dot MCA-39051
288 THE AUCTION Dot MCA-39051
289 LOVELY LUCY Dot MCA-39051
290 THE STREETS OF BALTIMORE Dot MCA-39051
291 'TIL THE RIGHT ONE COMES ALONG Dot MCA-39051

Specifics unknown – Tompall Glaser & The Glaser Brothers
901 THE STREETS OF LAREDO Coronet CX-150
902 BALLAD OF BELLE STARR Coronet CX-150
903 JOHN HARDY Coronet CX-150
GUNFIGHTER BALLADS OF THE BADMEN Coronet CX-150
[tracks above may have been radio or demo recordings].

ALBUMS:

Decca DL-4041/DL-74041 This Land: This Land Is Your Land, She Loves The Love I Give Her, Sylvie, Lay Down The Gun, Twenty-One Miles From Home, Chilly Winds, Down The Mountain, I Never Will Marry, Careless Love, Goodbye, Alibi, Wreck Of The Old Number 9, Erie Canal–60

Vocalion VL-3807/VL-73807 Country Folks: Judy's Growin' Up, Sweet Love Goodbye-I'll Never Tell, Blow Out The Candles, Tired Of Crying Over You, Oh Little Mary (Let Me Be), Mr. Lonesome, Let Me Down Easy, Same Old Memories, Ooie-Gooie–67

MGM E/SE-4465 Tompall & The Glaser Brothers: Gone, On The Other Hand, No End Of Love, El Paso, Gonna Miss Me, Gentle On My Mind, The Last Thing On My Mind, She Loved The Wrong Man, More Or Less, Big Brother, Bob, Streets Of Baltimore – 04-67 (MX: MGS 878/9)

MGM E/SE-4510 Through The Eyes Of Love: You Only Pass This Way One Time, The Moods Of Mary, What Does It Take, I Chose You, The Great El Tigre, Through The Eyes Of Love, Where Has All The Love Gone, Woman Woman, How Are You Brown Eyes, That's How A Woman's S'pose To Be, I'm Sorry, Roseanna–01-68 (MX: MGS 1232/3)

MGM SE-4577 The Wonderful World Of The Glaser Brothers: One Of These Days, Home Country, Got Leavin' On Her Mind, Instinct For Surviva, Recipe For A "Me," The Way That We Are Living Now, Home Is Where The Hurt Is, Guess Things Happen That Way, Money Can Not Make The Man, Why Do You Do Me Like You Do, Is My Love Coming On Too Strong – 06-68 (MX: MN: MGS 1586/7)

MGM SE-4620 Now Country: Wicked California, Proud Mary, Gonna Miss Me, But You Know I Love You, Molly Darling, Homeward Bound, California Girl, This Eve Of Parting, All That Keeps Ya Goin,' Walk Unashamed, Those Were The Days- 07-69 (MX: MGS 1832/3)

MGM SE-4667ST ...tick...tick...tick...: Theme From ...tick... tick...tick...(Set Yourself Free), California Girl (And The Tennessee Square), Why Do You Do Me Like You Do, All That Keeps Ya' Going, Where Has All The Love Gone, Woman Woman, What Does It Take, Home's Where The Hurt Is, Walk Unashamed, Gentle On My Mind - 03-70 (original soundtrack)

MGM SE-4775 The Award Winners: What Is A Woman What Is A Man, Help Me Make It Through The Night, Girl I Used To Know, Bye Bye Love, Me And Bobby Mcgee, Snowbird, That's When I Love You The Most, Stand Beside Me, I See His Love All Over You, Simple Thing As Love, Faded Love – 71 (MX: MN: MGS 2588/9)

MGM SE-4812 Rings And Things: Rings; Lovin' You Again, Delta Lost, The Days When You Were Still In Love With Me, Leave That For Memories, Sweet, Love Me Good Woman, Blue Ridge Mountains, Back In Each Other's Arms Again, You're In Carolina, Phoney World, Pretty Eyes – 02-72 (MX: MGS 2742/3)

MGM SE-4888 Tompall And The Glaser Brothers Sing Great Hits From Two Decades: Woman Woman, But You Know I Love You, Homeward Bound, Proud Mary, Those Were The Days, Gentle On My Mind, Snowbird, El Paso, Help Me Make It Through The Night, Streets Of Baltimore, What Does It Take – 02-73 (MX: MGS 3058/9, sampler)

MGM SE-4918 Charlie: Charlie, Mr. Lonesome, An Ode To My Notorious Youth: Barred From Every Honkytonk, Loneliest Man, I'll Fly Away Medley (I'll Fly Away/I Saw The Light), Cowboys And Daddies, Big Jim Colson, Bad Bad Bad Cowboy, Gideon Bible, Let It Be Pretty, Sold American – 09-73 Tompall Glaser

MGM M3G-4946 Greatest Hits: Rings, Faded Love, Gone Girl,* Through The Eyes Of Love, All That Keeps Ya Goin,' Moods Of Mary, California Girl, Walk Unashamed, Wicked California, Gone On The Other Hand, A Girl Like You* – 74 (*previously unissued on album)

Polydor [UK] 24602 340 Take The Singer With The Song: Texas Law Sez, Broken Down Momma, Pass Me On By, Willy The Wandering Gypsy And Me, Lay Down Beside Me, Take The Singer With The Song, Honey Don't You Know, The Good Lord Knows I Tried, Breakdown (A Long Way From Home), I'll Fly Away Medley (I Saw The Light - I'll Fly Away - Love Lifted Me) - 74 Tompall Glaser

MGM M3G-4976 The Vocal Group Of The Decade: Loving Her Was Easier (Than Anything I'll Ever Do Again); The Christian; Freedom To Stay; Tin Cup Chalice; Life's Little Ups And Downs; Velvet Wallpaper; She's Sweet, She's Kind, & She's Mine; She's Never Been This Gone Before; (Didn't We Have Ourselves) Some Kind Of A Summer; Don't Call Me Your Only Sunshine – 02-75

MGM M3G-4977 Tompall Sings The Songs Of Shel Silverstein: I Ain't Lookin' For The Answers Anymore, Roll On, Mendocino, Country Gospel Good Book Rock & Roll, Put Another Log On The Fire, Musical Chairs, Grab A' Hold, Echoes, Old New Orleans Custom, If I'm There, Oleander – 02-75 Tompall Glaser

RCA Victor AFL1-1321 Wanted! The Outlaws: My Heroes Have Always Been Cowboys, Honky Tonk Heroes, I'm Looking For Blue Eyes, You Mean To Say, Suspicious Minds, Good Hearted Woman, Heaven Or Hell, Me And Paul, Yesterday's Wine, T For Texas, Put Another Log On The Fire – 12-01-76 Waylon Jennings, Jessi Colter, Willie Nelson, Tompall Glaser solo recordings

MGM M3G-5014 The Great Tompall And His Outlaw Band: The Wild Side Of Life; We Live In Two Different Worlds; I Can't Remember; When It Goes, It's Gone Girl; The Hunger; Time Changes Everything; If I'd Only Come And Gone; Good Hearted Woman; West Canterbury Subdivision Blues; Tompall In "D" On The Ukelele; Broken Down Momma – 01-76 Tompall Glaser & The Outlaw Band

ABC AB-978 Tompall And His Outlaws Band: You Can Have Her, Release Me (And Let Me Love Again), Tennessee Blues, Come Back Shane, It'll Be Her, Look What Thoughts Will Do/Pretty Words/It Ain't Fair That It Ain't Right, Sweethearts Or Strangers, Let My Fingers Do The Walking (Late Night Show), I Just Want To Hear The Music – 01-77

ABC AB-1036 The Wonder Of It All: It Never Crossed My Mind, Bad Times, What Are We Doin' With The Rest Of Our Lives, How I Love Them Old Songs, On Second Thought, Drinking Them Beers, My Mother Was A Lady, Duncan And Brady, Easy On My Mind, The Wonder Of It All – 10-77

ABC (No number) Unwanted Outlaw: Like An Old Country Song, Sad Country Songs, What A Town, Don't Think You're Too Good For Country Music, Unwanted Outlaw, Man You Think To See, When I Dream, Burn Georgia Burn, Billy Tyler, Carry Me On - unissued (1978) (issued on Bear Family BCD-15596)

Elektra 5E-542 Loving Her Was Easier: Loving Her Was Easier, It'll Be Her, Busted, Feelin' The Weight Of My Chains, Just One Time, Last Thing On My Mind, United, Drinking Them Beers, Tryin' To Outrun The Wind, Mansion On The Hill – 09-81

Elektra E1-60148 After All These Years: I Still Love You (After All These Years), Can't Live With 'Em, Rosali, Naked Emotions, Happy Hour Blues, Oh America, Can I Sleep Here Tonight, Stay Young, I Could Never Live Alone Again, Maria Consuela – 07-82

MCA-Dot MCA-39051 Nights On The Borderline: Nights On The Borderline, Mamma Don't Let Your Big Boy Play Outside, (For Every Inch I've Laughed) I've Cried A Mile, Put Another Log On The Fire, Up Where We Belong, I Don't Care Anymore, The Auction, Lovely Lucy, The Streets Of Baltimore, 'Til The Right One Comes Along – 03-83

Country Store [UK] CST-27 Country Store Collection: Gentle On My Mind, Wild Side Of Life, We Live In Two Different Worlds, Faded Love, When It Goes It's Gone Girl, Hunger, Good Hearted Woman, Take The Singer With The Song, Time Changes Everything, If I'd Only Come And Gone, Broken Down Mama, Charlie, I Can't Remember, Lay Down Beside Me – 88 (sampler)

Bear Family [GER] BCD-15596 The Rogue: The Rogue, Tears On My Pillow, Forever And Ever, Shackles And Chains, My Pretty Quadroon, Lean On Me, I'll Hold You In My Heart, True Love, Open Arms, I Love You So Much It Hurts, Chattanooga Shoeshine Boy, You Can't Borrow Back Any Time, Like An Old Country Song, Sad Country Songs, What A Town, Don't Think You're Too Good For Country Music, Unwanted Outlaw, Man You Think You See, When I Dream, Burn Georgia Burn, Billy Tyler, Carry Me On - 92 (previously unissued ABC tracks)

Bear Family [GER] BCD-15605 The Outlaw: It Never Crossed My Mind, Bad Times, What We Are Doing With The Rest Of Our Lives, How I Love Them Old Songs, On Second Thought, Drinking Them Beers, My Mother Was A Lady, Duncan And Brady, Easy On My Mind, Wonder Of It All, Storms Never Last,* You Can Have Her,* Release Me, Tennessee Blues, Come Back Shane, It'll Be Her, Look What Thoughts Will Do - Pretty Words - It Ain't Fair, Sweethearts Or Strangers, Let My Fingers Do The Walking, I Just Want To Hear The Music, My Life Would Make A Damn Good Country Song* - 92 (reissue of AB-978 + AB-1036 + *previously unissued tracks)

Collector's Choice Music CCM 248-2 Best Of Tompall Glaser & The Glaser Brothers: Streets Of Baltimore, Gone On The Other Hand, Gentle On My Mind, Through The Eyes Of Love, Moods Of Mary, One Of These Days, California Girl, All That Keeps Ya Goin,' Walk Unashamed, Wicked California, Gone Girl, Faded Love, Rings, Sweet Love Me Good Woman, Ain't It All Worth Living For,* Girl Like You, Charlie, Bad Bad Bad Cowboy, Texas Law Sez,* Musical Chairs, Put Another Log On The Fire, Wild Side Of Life, T For Texas (Blue Yodel No 1), Lovin' Her Was Easier - 09-04-02 (*previously unissued in USA)

Bear Family [GER] BCD-16187 My Notorious Youth, Hillbilly Central #1: Charlie, Mr. Lonesome, An Ode To My Notorious Youth, Loneliest Man, I'll Fly Away Medley (I'll Fly Away - I Saw The Light), Cowboys And Daddies, Big Jim Colson, Bad Bad Bad Cowboy, Gideon Bible, Let It Be Pretty, Sold American, Texas Law Sez, Broken Down Momma, Pass Me On By, Willy The Wandering Gypsy And Me, Lay Down Beside Me, Take The Singer With The Song, Honey Don't You Know, The Good Lord Knows I Tried, Breakdown (A Long Way From Home), I'll Fly Away Medley (I Saw The Light - I'll Fly Away - Love Lifted Me), Love Stoned,*

Will The Circle Be Unbroken* – 01-06 (reissued of SE-4918 + 2460 2348 + *unissued tracks)

Bear Family [GER] BCD-16520 Another Log On The Fire, Hillbilly Central #2: I Ain't Lookin' For The Answers Anymore; Roll On; Mendocino; Country Gospel Good Book Rock 'n' Roll; Put Another Log On The Fire; Musical Chairs; Grab A Hold; Echoes; Old New Orleans Custom; If I'm There; Oleander; The Wild Side Of Life; We Live In Two Different Worlds; I Can't Remember; When It Goes, It's Gone Girl; The Hunger; Time Changes Everything; If I'd Only Come And Gone; Good Hearted Woman; West Canterbury Subdivision Blues; Tompall In 'D' On The Ukulele; Broken Down Mama (Polydor); Loving You Again*; T For Texas* – 01-06 (reissue of M3G-4977 + M3G-5014 + *bonus tracks)

Miller Music, 2006, Outlaw To The Cross: Stand Beside Me, Where No One Stands Alone, What A Friend, Lean On Jesus, Great Speckled Bird, Life's Railway To Heaven, When They Ring Those Golden Bells, Just A Closer Walk With Thee, Let The Lower Lights Be Burning, Peace In The Valley, Glory Train To Heaven.

Note: *Soundtrack album Ballad Of Namu The Killer Whale (United Artists UAS-6540) does not belong to Tompall & The Glaser Brothers but to folk singer Tom Glazer (it's often listed in Tompall Glaser discographies).*

SINGLES:

Robbins (1957-58) w. The Glaser Brothers
45-1001 You're In My Heart Again / Five Penny Nickel - 57
45-1003 I Want You / Baby Be Good – 03-58
45-1006 Yakety Yak / Sweet Lies – 07-58
1004 Yakety Yak / Cry Of The Wild Goose – 02-61 (released on Rich)

Decca (1958-65) w. The Glaser Brothers as by Tompall & The Glaser Brothers

9-30805 Lay Down The Gun / Oh Little Mary (Let Me Be) – ca. 05-01-59
9-30900 She Loves The Love I Give Her / Ooie-Gooie - 05-59
9-31011 I'll Never Tell / Twenty-One Miles From Home - 11-59
9-31051 Careless Love, Goodbye / Alibi - 03-60
9-31180 Same Old Memories / Sweet Love, Goodbye - 11-60
31258 Judy's Grown Up / Words Come Easy - 05-61
31322 Let Me Down Easy / Tired Of Crying For You - 10-61
31398 I'm Losing Again / I Can't Remember - 05-62
31447 Odds And Ends (Bits And Pieces) / False Hearted Lover - 12-62
31494 Stand Beside Me / Trackin' Me Down - ca. 10-05-63
31551 Mister Lonesome / Blow Out The Candles – ca. 28-10-63
31632 A Girl Like You / I've Got Troubles - 06-64
31736 Winner, Take All / Baby They're Playing Our Song - 02-65
31809 Teardrops 'Til Down / Back In Each Other's Arms Again - 06-65

MGM (1966-75) w. The Glaser Brothers as by Tompall & The Glaser Brothers

K 13531 The Last Thing On My Mind / More Or Less - 06-66
K 13611 Gone, On The Other Hand / The Streets Of Baltimore – ca. 12-11-66
K 13754 Through The Eyes Of Love / She Loved The Wrong Man - 06-67
K 13880 No End Of Love / The Moods Of Mary – ca. 01-68
K 13954 One Of These Days / Where Has All The Love Gone - 06-68
K 14036 California Girl / All That Keeps Ya Goin' - 02-69
K 14064 Wicked California / The Eve Of Parting - 06-69

K 14096 Walk Unashamed / Gonna Miss Me - 11-69

K 14113 Theme From ...tick...tick...tick...(Set Yourself Free) / All That Keeps Ya Goin'- 03-70

K 14169 Gone Girl / I'll Say My Words - 10-70

K 14249 Faded Love / Pretty Eyes - 04-71

K 14291 Rings / That's When I Love You The Most - 07-71

K 14339 Stand Beside Me / Sweet, Love Me Good Woman - 11-71

K 14390 Ain't It All Worth Living / Blue Ridge - 05-72

KGC-236 Rings / Ain't It All Worth Living For – ca. 72 (reissue)

K 14462 A Girl Like You / Delta Lost - 11-72

K 14516 Charlie / Lovin' You Again - 03-73 Tompall Glaser

K 14622 Bad Bad Bad Cowboy / Let It Be Pretty - 08-73 Tompall Glaser

M 14701 Texas Law Sez / Pass Me On By - 01-74 Tompall Glaser

M 14740 Musical Chairs / Grab A Hold - 07-74 Tompall Glaser

M 14800 Put Another Log On Fire (Male Chauvinist National Anthem) / Mendocino - 03-75

(reissued on Polydor 540, date unknown)

PD 14314 T For Texas / Broken Down Mama - 03-76 (released on Polydor)

ABC (1976-78) w. The Outlaw Band

AB-12261 It'll Be Her / Sweethearts Or Strangers - 03-77

AB-12309 It Never Crossed My Mind / Easy On My Mind - 09-77

AB-12329 Drinking Them Beers / Duncan And Bradley - 01-78

AB-12366 Bad Times / Carry Me On – 02-05-78

Elektra (1980-82) w. The Glaser Brothers as by Tompall & The Glaser Brothers

E-46595 Feelin' The Weight Of My Chains / The Ballad Of Lucy Jordan - 03-80

E-47056 Sweet City Woman / Tryin' The Outrun The Wind - 10-80

E-47134 Lovin' Her Was Easier (Than Anything I'll Ever Do Again) / United We Fall - 04-81

E-47193 Just One Time / Feelin' The Weight Of My Chains - 09-81

E-47230 Silver Bells / (Johnny Lee:) Please Come Home For Christmas - 11-81

E-47405 It'll Be Her / A Mansion On The Hill - 01-82

E-47461 I Still Love You (After All These Years) / Feelin' The Weight Of My Chains - 05-82

7-69947 Maria Consuela / I Can Never Live Alone Again - 10-82

---

*Note: A very, very special thank you to Michel Ruppli, Prague-frank, Wolf Ruediger Sommer, Rene Pavlik, Michal Gololobov, and Mario Manciotti, who compiled this discography of Tompall's recordings. Please visit their website at http://countrydiscography. blogspot.com/ for detailed discographies of many other country music artists.

Index

Kevin L. Glaser is the nephew of Tompall Glaser. He resides in Wisconsin, which happens to be the state where his great-grandparents initially settled after leaving Austria and before heading to Nebraska.

Glaser enjoys cycling, walking, writing, guitar playing, and singing. He appreciates and is thankful for family and friends, and is grateful to Tompall and June for letting him tell Tompall's unique story.

Kevin has also authored *Inside the Insurance Industry*, as well as two revisions: *Inside the Insurance Industry–Second Edition*, and recently, *Inside the Insurance Industry–Third Edition*, all of which provide valuable insights into the property and casualty insurance industry from a knowledgeable expert in the field.

As President of Risk & Insurance Services Consulting, LLC, he provides fee-only business insurance solutions to some of the most complex businesses across America. Also, Glaser is one of a select few who provide fee-only insurance and risk management advice to high net worth individuals, their families, and to their trusts.

BOOK ORDER FORM

Are you a "classic country" fan? Here's a biography you won't want to miss!

The Great Tompall:
Forgotten Country Music Outlaw
by Kevin L. Glaser
with more than two dozen images
Available in hardcover or paperback
6" x 9", 364 pages

Order your copy from
Right Side Creations, LLC by
calling 262-354-2986, visiting our
online store at **www.rtsidecreations.com** or by completing this
form and sending your check or money order by mail.

PLEASE PRINT Today's Date _____

Your Name _____

Address _____

City/State/ZIP _____

E-mail _____

Quantity: _____ ***Hardcover*** @ $29.95 = _____

Quantity: _____ ***Paperback*** @ $19.95 = _____

Ship to: ☐ Same as above Shipping: _____

5% Sales Tax if WI resident: _____

Total Amt. Enclosed: _____

If shipping to a different address:

Recipient's Name _____

Address _____

City/State/ZIP _____

SHIPPING: $6.50 first book. $2.25 each
additional book. We ship by Priority
Mail within contiguous USA only.
Contact us for international shipping
rates or other options.

Mail payment with order form to:
Right Side Creations, LLC
158 E. Wisconsin Ave.
Oconomowoc, WI 53066.

CPSIA information can be obtained at www.ICGtesting.com
Printed in the USA
BVOW03s1809191014

371441BV00011B/94/P